LLING THE WHOLE STORY

Assessing Achievement in English

ROBERT McGREGOR
MARION MEIERS

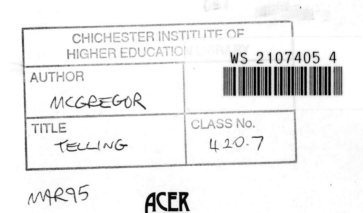

ACER

First published 1991
by The Australian Council for Educational Research Ltd
Radford House, Frederick Street, Hawthorn, Victoria 3122, Australia

Cover by Sandra Nobes
Edited by Deidre Missingham
Designed by Sandra Nobes

Typeset by Bookset Pty Ltd, Melbourne
Printed by Brown Prior Anderson Pty Ltd

National Library of Australia
Cataloguing-in-Publication data:

McGregor, Robert, 1937– .
    Telling the whole story.

    Bibliography.
    Includes index.
    ISBN 0 86431 082 X.

    1. Grading and marking (Students). 2. School reports.
    3. English language — Study and teaching. I. Meiers,
    Marion. II. Australian Council for Educational Research.
    III. Title.

373.12721

CONTENTS

PREFACE

This book has two main purposes:
1 to present a responsive approach to assessment which recognises and describes students' development, learning and achievement in English; and
2 to describe a model for English teaching built on the kinds of contexts, activities and experiences which most effectively promote the learning of language, learning through language, and learning about language, and in which development can be observed.

The book is a resource for all teachers of English, from the earliest years of schooling right through to Years 11 and 12, and for parents and members of the wider community.

In Part 1, 'Assessing development in English', we offer a rationale for taking a responsive approach to assessment in English, and describe a range of contexts representing the kinds of classroom experiences which promote the development of language competence and where students show significant signs of becoming effective makers and users of language. Chapter 3 of this part, The whole context, describes the planning and management of an active learning context in one English classroom.

Part 2, 'Observing and describing development in English', invites readers to look specifically at learning and development in talking and listening, reading, and writing, and identifies a data base of statements which can be used to focus observation and to describe development. These statements are linked to accounts of an extensive series of episodes from the classroom, working contexts which highlight different modes of language use. The final chapter in this part, Students at work, looks closely at the work and learning of one student, in the context of his own classroom environment.

In Part 3, 'Recording and reporting development', we present practical suggestions for record keeping, developing descriptive profiles and reporting, including many sample formats to assist these processes.

This book is founded on practice, including our own classroom teaching experience, and, in various ways, the teaching experience of many others. The approaches to assessment in English which form the basis of the book have been shaped and refined through discussions with teachers in schools and at in-service education programs and conferences. The collections of descriptive statements were originally derived from a survey of a wide range of sources, including school-based assessment policies, working papers on assessment, and the professional literature in the field.

We used desktop publication facilities to circulate early versions of four chapters through the informal English Club network. The responses we received from teachers in Australia and Canada to these booklets as practical teaching resources, and encouragement from the Australian Council for Educational Research, provided the impetus to expand this initial work into a more substantial publication.

In acknowledging the ways in which this book has been shaped by the realities of teaching and learning, we wish to emphasise our gratitude for the opportunities we have had to share and develop ideas with many thoughtful teachers and educators.

Above all, we continually appreciate the insights which we gain from our own direct interactions with students in many different kinds of schools.

Robert McGregor and Marion Meiers

INTRODUCTION

LITERACY AND ENGLISH

This book focuses on the development and achievement of competence in English, across all the years of schooling. The development of literacy is a responsibility shared by all teachers, in all curriculum areas. Active, critical, constructive literacy is achieved through engagement with language in many different contexts. The curriculum as a whole provides a variety of social contexts in which language is used in different ways for different purposes, allowing learners to understand the ways in which effective language use differs according to context and purpose. In this book we have chosen to focus our attention on the area of study within the curriculum commonly known as 'English', in which language itself is the stimulus to activity.

The teaching of English, in broad terms, is built on the goal of developing learners' abilities in reading, writing, speaking and listening, in ways which recognise the interconnectedness and complexities of these modes of language. Much of the activity of English classrooms is centred on creating opportunities for students to make and use language. In English, literature provides a specific focus for learning, allowing teachers and students to explore human behaviour and values, and to shape their understandings of the world. The teaching of English, then, is centrally related to one of the main purposes of schooling — that is, to enable all students to achieve literacy — but there are also particular aspects of learning and development which characterise this area of study. One of the purposes of this book is to present a working description of achievement in English.

ACHIEVEMENT IN ENGLISH

Achievement in English can be described in similar terms at all levels of schooling, but across the years K–12 it is possible to recognise a continual expansion of different aspects of achievement; that is, students will be learning to do the same things for new purposes, in increasingly complex and sophisticated ways. Achievement in English for the individual student encompasses the following broad abilities:

- the capacity to enjoy being a confident and competent user of spoken and written language for an expanding range of purposes in both expressive and receptive modes;

- the ability to use spoken and written language appropriately to meet many purposes in a wide range of contexts;
- the ability to respond thoughtfully, sensitively and with discrimination and enjoyment to an increasingly wide range of print texts and non-print texts (such as film);
- the ability to make critical and constructive choices and responses; and
- an expanding ability to use the conventions of spoken and written language effectively and appropriately to allow effective communication with a wide range of audiences.

The signs of development which are presented throughout this book focus on the detail within these broad descriptions, and are intended to help in recognising the ways in which achievement in these descriptions is occurring.

What signs of students' development can be observed in English classrooms? How can these signs of development be recognised and described clearly and accurately? How can teachers respond to students' achievements in English, nudging them forward to new learning and development?

LEARNING LANGUAGE AND EFFECTIVE ENGLISH CLASSROOMS

Language is learnt interactively and in many different contexts. The development of language, and of the kind of literacy which enables people to participate constructively and critically in society, is fostered when learners are able to become involved in activities and situations which create opportunities for authentic communication. When looking for signs of development and achievement in English, it is necessary to consider not only the evidence of a range of completed oral and written work, but also to look at learners when they are engaged in a wide range of authentic communication situations and activities.

Competence in English is complex and multi-faceted, therefore no single measure can adequately describe the richness and diversity of development which can be seen amongst any group of students. Because the aim of English teaching is to encourage the development of this versatility, the English curriculum incorporates a wide range of content, activities and processes.

Effective English classrooms are places which maximise opportunities for learning interactively. In these classrooms, students can:

- be active makers and users of language to shape meaning;
- use language for many authentic purposes and audiences;
- take advantage of having access to connected learning experiences;
- encounter a wide range of different kinds of texts;
- learn through talking as well as writing;
- work independently as well as cooperatively;
- play a variety of roles;
- set significant and achievable learning goals;
- be confident in finding individual learning pathways;
- develop initiative and resourcefulness; and
- value processes as well as products.

RESPONDING TO LEARNING

To assess students' developing competence in English, it is necessary to respond to the variety and complexity of language, and to the broad scope of the English curriculum, by looking for many different yet related signs of learning and development, and describing what has been observed. This suggests the nature of a valid assessment system, which integrates curriculum and assessment. Such an approach to assessment will draw its validity from the way it recognises the authenticity and purposefulness of the work students are asked to do, and the range of roles they are given opportunities to play. It will involve:

- considering a wide range of possible signs of learning demonstrated in both processes and outcomes;
- observing and describing students at work, and the outcomes of their work; and
- the sharing of learning goals between teachers and students.

Viewed in this way, assessment becomes a means of accomplishing many purposes in teaching and learning:

- responding to learning;
- celebrating achievement;
- answering questions;
- providing useful and valid information; and
- motivating further learning.

How can teachers respond to the variety of learning that might occur in the varying contexts of English classrooms? Professional knowledge of many ways in which developing competence can be recognised provides the basis for such responsiveness. Sensitive observation is informed by this broad professional knowledge, enabling teachers to do full justice to the complete range of the student's development as a maker and user of language. Teachers can be alert to both the expected and the unexpected signs of development; they are able to offer real evidence to students and their parents, and to form effective working relationships with them.

Teachers' professional knowledge includes:

- understanding of the nature and acquisition of language;
- knowledge about ways of learning; and
- a wide repertoire of classroom management techniques and possibilities for classroom activity.

This professional knowledge expands with classroom experience, as teachers observe a variety of learning and development, and as different groups of students create different classroom dynamics, to which teachers must be continually responsive. Teachers' recognition of the signs of developing competence in English is progressively enhanced as students display new learnings, and as their observations of these learnings are built into a working knowledge.

Often this working knowledge is intuitive, and is implicit in both the decisions made about individual development and the plans and goals for the classroom program. There are times, however, when this knowledge must be explicitly stated, and one of the purposes of this book is to show how to describe, explicitly and accurately, many aspects of development and achievement in English.

Teachers' insights about language development provide the basis for an approach to assessment that responds to what is observed by describing it precisely: being responsive to signs of students' learning and development by knowing what to look for. It becomes possible for teachers to respond to a wide range of learning and development, and to recognise signs of development even when they are not anticipated.

WHAT IS REAL EVIDENCE OF LEARNING?

The real evidence of development in English comes not from specially manufactured tests but from the students at work: from observation of their ways of working and of dealing with work in progress, as well as from the achievements of finished work. This book is concerned with evidence of development that is derived from observations and descriptions of students working on a wide range of activities in the classroom, and from a wide variety of finished work.

Valid evidence of learning is generated by observing action in various classroom contexts, and by recognising what students can and cannot do in those contexts. With this range of evidence, teachers are able to make valid overall statements about an individual student's development and achievement, and to communicate with students and their parents in precise terms about specific strengths and weaknesses.

WHAT HAPPENS IN ENGLISH CLASSROOMS?

Successful English programs generate development and achievement by providing many contexts, within the limits of time and classroom management, for authentic use of language for many different purposes. In this book we have described many examples of classroom activities that generate language learning, and we discuss the kinds of development that might be observed and described in such contexts. One of our main purposes, therefore, is to help teachers, and parents, to recognise signs of development and achievement.

In describing these classroom episodes, we have noted signs of development — observable behaviours, attitudes and achievements that suggest learning is taking place or has occurred. These episodes are accounts of actual classroom experience, and the signs of development which have been identified in each episode illustrate the variety of individual learning which can take place within any class or group.

We have emphasised observation of students' development in the context of the classroom for several reasons, one of which is that if assessment is to be valid and fair students must have the time and opportunity to learn. A wide-ranging and balanced curriculum, such as that implied by the varied range of classroom episodes described, provides this opportunity. Such a curriculum, and such opportunities for students, are prerequisites for responsive assessment based on real evidence of learning.

KEEPING TRACK OF DEVELOPMENT

The richness and diversity of experience that will flow from this approach to assessment and the variability of individual student response to classroom activities means that a comprehensive and flexible means of keeping track of the variety of individual development is needed. How can the signs of development teachers observe be recorded? Systematic, simple and practical methods of keeping records of individual development are needed to support a responsive approach to assessment that draws on a wide range of evidence from classrooms.

Throughout this book, and especially in later chapters, we discuss and illustrate the kinds of formats for record keeping that can assist teachers in observing, recording and reporting on their students' development. Observation, recording and reporting based on the gathering of a diverse range of evidence is time consuming. Some of the formats included are intended to suggest efficient ways for teachers to manage these important assessment processes.

INVOLVING STUDENTS IN ASSESSMENT

Students should play an active role in the assessment of their work and progress. Responsive assessment should give teachers the opportunity to encourage students to set goals and reflect on the extent to which they have achieved those goals, as well as allowing them to respond to their students' perceptions of their own development and achievements.

Involvement in assessing their own work gives students direct experience and practical understanding of the goals of the classroom program and their own goals within it. This can generate a commitment by students to the program, which creates a purposeful engagement with the program's activities, projects and tasks. Students are also empowered as they develop understandings of learning processes that are essential to study and work beyond school. To enable students to reflect on their learning, and to explain what they have learnt and how they have developed, is to provide opportunity for further learning. Students and teachers can thus share responsibility for keeping track of development.

WHAT DO PARENTS WANT?

The cycle of responsive assessment includes reporting on students' development and achievement to parents. This takes place in different ways — through informal contact, at arranged parent-teacher interview sessions, and through written reports. Parents are keenly interested in answers to these questions:
• What work has my child actually done?
• What, specifically, are my child's strengths and weaknesses?
• What can be done to promote and support further development?

Reports to parents, whether in the form of parent-teacher interviews or summative statements such as written reports, can provide answers to these questions when they are based upon the work completed and on observation in a range of contexts of what each child can and cannot do. The approaches to observation, recording and reporting we have suggested are designed to help teachers provide this information.

A RESOURCE FOR UNDER-STANDING DEVELOPMENT AND ACHIEVEMENT IN ENGLISH

The structure of this book approximates to the various phases in the process of responsive assessment. In Part 1, we look at the nature of responsive assessment and at what might constitute the real evidence of language development: what are teachers looking for, and why? Part 2 is concerned both with observing students at work and with responding to the achievements of finished work. We examine how signs of development can be noted when students engage with different projects and activities, and how to describe development in particular modes of language — talking and listening, reading, and writing. Finally, Part 3 offers suggestions intended to assist teachers to record flexibly, efficiently and accurately the signs of development they observe in their classrooms, and to report to others on this learning and development.

Through a commentary on learning episodes within classroom contexts, the book provides an accumulating collection of statements about effective use of language, and of signs of developing competence, which can be used to focus observation, planning and recording. These statements about development can be used in a variety of ways:

- to help teachers and students to formulate learning goals;
- to plan classroom activities;
- to describe work requirements;
- as an agenda for students to monitor their own progress;
- as reminders of aspects of language development which can be observed;
- as criteria to measure the extent to which goals have been achieved;
- as descriptors of the quality of finished work;
- as a basis for constructing formats which can be used to build up records of development over time; and
- as the basis for informed discussion between teachers, students and parents about individual progress and achievement.

This book, then, is a resource for all teachers of English, from the earliest years of schooling right through to Years 11 and 12. It is also a resource for parents and members of the wider community who wish to extend their understanding of children's learning in English, and of the development of literacy.

PART 1

ASSESSING DEVELOPMENT IN ENGLISH

1 RESPONSIVE ASSESSMENT

ASSESSMENT IN THE CYCLE OF LEARNING AND TEACHING

The assessment of students' learning, development and achievement can most usefully be regarded as a responsive, connected process, in which assessment is an integral part of the whole teaching and learning cycle. The diagram 'Responsive Assessment' shows the connections between classroom action and various elements in this cycle.

Assessment seen from this perspective relates directly to learning activities and to the work that has been done, and is based on a broad range of evidence, including informed observations of learners in action, and the learners' self-assessments. Part of this cycle involves recognising achievement and planning and setting goals for future activity. In this way assessment becomes a valid and fair process, responsive to what actually happens by valuing students' involvement in the whole gamut of learning activities, and the achievements of finished work. Within teaching programs, areas of study are defined, work requirements are described and, when appropriate, specific assessment tasks grow naturally from areas of study and work requirements.

This kind of responsive assessment can meet the needs of individual learners, and at the same time it can effectively and realistically meet demands for more public accountability. By providing significant information — about how effective the teaching has been, what needs to be taught, what work has been done, individual strengths and weaknesses, and the goals of the school and the curriculum — responsive assessment supplies answers to the following questions:

- What learning has occurred?
- What work has been done?
- What individual strengths and weaknesses have been noted?
- How far has the teaching succeeded in its aims?
- What new learning goals can be set?

Responsive assessment: Observing and describing students at work

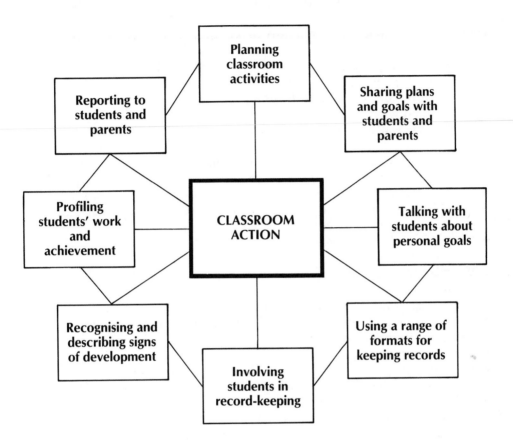

Planning classroom activities

Reporting to students and parents

Sharing plans and goals with students and parents

Profiling students' work and achievement

CLASSROOM ACTION

Talking with students about personal goals

Recognising and describing signs of development

Involving students in record-keeping

Using a range of formats for keeping records

ASKING THE RIGHT QUESTIONS

If we adopt this view of assessment as a responsive, connected process, then to assess developing competence and achievement in English in ways which will both recognise achievement and support further learning we need to find practical answers to a number of further key questions:

- How can schools effectively describe the ways in which students come to use an expanding repertoire of language skills?
- How can teachers articulate and explain their professional recognition of development and achievement?
- What are the connections between students' opportunities to use language in school and the natural interaction of language in use in everyday contexts?
- What are the most valid kinds of evidence of development and achievement in language and learning?

- How can teachers best use the evidence of students' use of language for a wide range of authentic purposes in assessing achievement and development?
- How can students be enabled to make informed decisions about how effectively they have achieved their goals?
- What signs of development and competence can be recognised and described through observing:
  — the processes of talking, listening, reading and writing
  — finished work
  — the ways in which students work?

Classrooms where learners are at work on a wide range of connected activities are contexts where teachers can most effectively respond to learning and development. What exactly can be seen in such contexts?

To enhance and focus observation, to learn by seeing what students can and cannot do, teachers need to ask:
- What can be looked for?
  and
- What might be observed?

In the classroom, teachers can often ask:
- What can be observed about students' language development as they work on these activities?
- What might be observed about their ways of working?
- What might be learnt about students as individual people?
- What signs of development might be recognised from these observations?

These are professional questions that inform observation of students at work in classroom contexts. They stem from prior experience and knowledge of what is likely to happen, of what students are likely to do and what goals they are likely to achieve. The answers to such questions might also indicate how ready students are for more challenging experiences. In other words, they guide teachers' own knowledge as they plan, manage and observe classroom activities.

Questions about what teachers expect to see also provide part of the agenda for making and recording observations, whilst observing students at work helps to suggest answers which complete this description. Sometimes the questions asked are superseded by others that stem from what students actually show they can do: that is, some signs of development might be unanticipated. Sometimes, as classroom work proceeds, it becomes clear that inappropriate questions have been asked: that the program of work has produced outcomes and signs of development that are different from what was originally planned.

A responsive approach to assessment involves gathering evidence which answer as many professional questions as possible, and leaves scope also to describe unintended or unanticipated developments. Evidence about what students actually do should be gathered from many classroom contexts. In this way, the work of students answers both teachers' and students' questions about their learning.

RESPONDING TO THE NATURE OF THE ENGLISH CURRICULUM

This responsive and broadly-based approach to assessment reflects a comprehensive view of English teaching in which central aims are to help all students to become increasingly competent makers and users of language for a wide range of purposes, and to communicate effectively in many different situations. It reflects, too, the ways in which English programs are built on the knowledge that language learning is an interactive, social process, and that therefore English classrooms must create learning environments in which it is natural for language to be used for real purposes and for real audiences. Because of the breadth of these aims, and of the essentially interactive nature of language development, assessment which responds to the complexities of the English program will take account of a wide range of evidence, including much that happens in the classroom as well as finished work of many different kinds.

A further consideration is that assessment involves communication to students, parents and other interested people, and should therefore provide feedback on learning and celebrate what has been achieved. This therefore implies a responsive approach to assessment which charts growth and achievement in personal terms.

Such assessment will reflect the responsive, two-way nature of classrooms. Students will continually have access to sensitive and constructive feedback about their work, both from their peers and from the teacher. In practice, this means that those who talk with student writers in the classroom will respond both to the *meanings* the writing is intended to convey, and also to *how* the meaning is communicated. When students read together they can work on unravelling the meanings of a text, and as they cooperatively construct these meanings they will gain confidence in their ability to express even tentative ideas as they talk, and in their ability to build on others' ideas and suggestions as they listen. Whether it is writing or reading which is in the foreground, other language skills are constantly in the background, generating interactions which are a significant part of the context of a responsive classroom.

Assessment is a process which can occur naturally and spontaneously within the teaching and learning situation, when teachers are able to observe students engaged in using language purposefully in a variety of different contexts. Feedback will encourage the learner to experiment

('Why not write a completely different beginning to your story?'), or identify resources which might promote and support further development ('Have you tried editing your work on the word-processor?') or acknowledge particular achievements ('It's good to see how well you've organised all that information on the issues raised in that novel.').

RESPONSIVE ASSESSMENT

Responsive assessment includes the sharing of goals within the classroom: perhaps the goal of mastering a new form of writing, such as a newspaper report, or a poem; of using a journal; or of gaining experience in speaking confidently to a group. These kinds of goals can be shared by teachers and students, shaping teaching and learning.

When the goals for activities and projects are shared between teachers and students, students are able to evaluate the extent to which they have achieved particular goals. Developing awareness of the significance of setting learning goals, and of reviewing the ways in which goals have or have not been achieved, is an important aspect of student self-assessment.

A responsive approach to assessment will mean, too, that teachers will recognise the significance of learning processes. Writing will be seen as a goal-setting and problem-solving process, in which writers grow as they set goals, recognise problems and work out ways of achieving their goals and overcoming problems. Reading will be viewed as a process in which readers actively engage with the text, making predictions and formulating questions. Approximations and mistakes will therefore be accepted as signs of growth, rather than as errors, and what might appear to be a recursion or a block may be seen as a stage in overcoming a particular problem — for example, how to use punctuation more effectively, or how to recognise the connections between different pieces of information in a text.

When teachers need to make decisions about the effectiveness of students' performance on specific tasks, or to judge individual levels of performance amongst a group of students on a particular task, a responsive view of assessment means that the criteria on which such decisions and judgements are to be made should be clear from the start. These criteria should relate directly to the goals of the task, and inform students' activity in planning, preparing and presenting the work required.

Responsive assessment will take account of:
• the natural variability of language development amongst individuals, according to the diversity of their background and experience;
• the contexts in which language is generated; and
• the connectedness of the wide range of language skills which come into play in any learning situation.

In short, assessment which is responsive to the complexities of individual development will:
- describe, validly and reliably, the work that has actually been done;
- be based on known criteria and goals;
- support students' work and development;
- be participative and contractual (i.e. based on agreed goals, criteria and records);
- be informed by observation of the interactive processes within the classroom; and
- be based on systematic and comprehensive record keeping.

MAKING PROFESSIONAL KNOWLEDGE EXPLICIT

Assessment methods should help teachers to focus on what developing speakers, readers, listeners or writers can do, and on what their next steps might be. When it is possible to make professional understanding and intuitions explicit, it is possible to foster individual development.

One way of being explicit about what is being achieved by students is to describe the criteria on which judgements are based. Not only does this help teachers to remember what to look for, but when teachers are accustomed to sharing these criteria with students, the students, too, will have a clearer view of their goals.

If teacher and students are working within a context which makes it relevant to set a particular goal, for example, the goal of learning to write to express a point of view on an issue of personal concern, then the students do not need to ask: 'Why are we doing this?' The purpose of the writing activity is clear to all concerned, and the effectiveness of the writing will be obvious — to the extent that others are able to understand the point of view which has been presented. If the shared task were to involve the production of a newspaper for the school community, then the criteria for effectively meeting the goal — reader-interest, accurate and clear presentation, careful proofreading — would be understood by all.

This kind of responsive assessment implies the need to articulate the kinds of criteria which inform observations of learning and development, and decisions about whether goals have been achieved. To do this, to make the basis of such judgements clear, teachers and students alike need to know what they are looking for.

If this basis is clear, what is recognised in students' learning can be described. Teachers can also:
- plan purposeful learning contexts

- explain and negotiate goals
- describe achievement.

DESCRIPTIVE STATEMENTS ABOUT LANGUAGE AND DEVELOPMENT

The descriptive statements about language which appear throughout this book can be used flexibly. They can be used to establish planned and expected patterns of development, and as reminders of those unexpected, idiosyncratic developments which sometimes characterise language growth. The statements can also be used to help in the formulation of precise descriptions of learning, and reference to a collection of descriptions can extend the range of what is recognised as learning.

Teachers can use statements describing learning as criteria for assessing development and achievement in particular contexts, or in relation to specific projects. More broadly, these statements can reflect the choices teachers make and negotiate with students in the planning and organisation of classroom programs. A collection of these statements provides teachers with a working vocabulary for planning, observing, negotiating, recording and reporting. The aspects of students' activity and performance which they are alerted to become the basis for teachers' assessments of growth and achievement in particular classroom contexts.

We use such statements in these flexible ways in this book: to describe observed learnings in particular learning situations, to provide a framework for recognising expected and unexpected patterns of development, to highlight competence in some of the processes involved in the different language modes, and to describe the achievements of finished work.

There can be, of course, no discrete body of statements to describe every aspect of language development. Growth in individual competence as a user of language to shape meaning is too subtle a process for that to be possible. When a group of students is engaged in a common activity, careful observation will reveal that different students demonstrate different kinds of development, and this, too, means that a very flexible manner of describing development and achievement in English is needed. The statements used in this book offer starting points for looking at the ways in which learners respond to the great variety of activities which make up stimulating language learning environments. They provide a lens through which we can view the interconnected processes of reading, writing, talking and listening, focusing our sights on the observation of many aspects of growth rather than a narrow range.

RESPONDING TO WAYS OF WORKING AND LEARNING

Students learn new skills and abilities in the context of the work they do across the curriculum. Language is both a means and an end in this process. It is a means of working and a means of learning; and the creation of meaning and the use of language are outcomes of the work done. Language development supports the ability to work in many different situations and on a range of tasks, and it provides ways of expressing attitudes and values. Since attitudes and values are expressed in what people say and do, language mediates attitudes and values, and the development of language is intimately associated with the growth of personal value systems and personal qualities.

When students work together in an English classroom, they contribute to class and group projects and solve problems by thinking creatively and critically. These ways of thinking are not separate from reading, writing, listening and talking, since these language processes implicitly engage and develop creative and critical mental abilities. The process of composition is a creative and critical thinking activity, involving all the language modes, though writing is the dominant mode; working with a novel requires prediction, inference, analysis, decision-making, imagination, evaluation and much more.

Language is inextricably linked with processes of thought. Activities and tasks designed to develop language also develop thinking abilities, and language activities can be structured so that significant thinking is encouraged. If we list the kinds of abilities that might be included under a broad heading of creative and critical thinking, the links with English classroom activities are apparent:

- inferring
- sequencing
- relating
- classifying
- organising
- predicting
- confirming
- questioning
- analysing
- synthesising
- deciding
- imagining
- problem solving
- evaluating.

When students use language in different contexts and situations, they learn new ways of thinking and acting. For example, tolerance and cooperation might most effectively be learnt through tasks which depend on those qualities for successful completion. Students learn responsibility and commitment through opportunities to influence the nature and direction of participation in classroom and school activities. By working in contexts where this is possible, young people also learn the uses of language that will enable them to operate successfully in the real world.

These ways of working help to generate personal qualities that will contribute to further learning.

The extended classroom contexts we describe in Chapter 3, The whole context, and Chapter 7, Students at work, and the briefer episodes included in Chapters 4, 5 and 6, suggest many ways in which children learn; for example, by:

- asking questions
- sharing personal knowledge and experience
- working with other people
- experimenting with ideas and actions
- investigating ideas and experiences
- solving problems
- organising work processes, materials and resources
- reflecting on and evaluating experience and ideas
- evaluating the effectiveness of the ways in which goals have been met
- imagining and predicting new possibilities and
- communicating ideas, information and experience to other people.

All of these ways of learning can be encompassed within the scope offered by the English curriculum for students to engage in tasks that build upon personal experience and provide authentic experience of productive ways of working. Some of the likely outcomes of a wide range of classroom activities are identified in the following chart, 'Describing signs of development'.

It is obvious that these ways of working and learning overlap and blend in many contexts and tasks: that is, many can be operating during

Describing signs of development

This chart illustrates the signs of development likely to be observed in a range of classroom episodes.

Activity	Example	Likely outcomes
Collaborative composition Year 5	Composing a story	• shows awareness of the needs of the reader • varies choice of words for different purposes and audiences • shares ideas with others • can write story using logical sequence • displays continuity and fluency in writing
Writing from experience Year 6	Listening to others' writings	• listens attentively to others' contributions • attends to sequence of detail or event • recognises the value of sharing ideas and information • asks relevant questions • understands the idea of audience in writing

Activity	Example	Likely outcomes
Reading poetry *Year 7*	Presenting group readings of poems	■ responds to writing in appreciative ways ■ develops new ideas from reading ■ recreates feeling and atmosphere of specific texts ■ collaborates with others in class activities ■ responds sensitively to literature
Imaginative recreation *Year 9*	Writing the sequel to a novel	■ recognises and recalls ideas and information ■ discerns the author's purposes ■ writes about reading in a lively way ■ revises ideas and opinions about text ■ develops new ideas from reading ■ can link ideas in writing
Exploring relationships in a text *Year 10*	Completing a relationships chart	■ makes appropriate notes from reading ■ locates relevant information from text ■ demonstrates a detailed knowledge of text ■ selects and organises appropriate evidence from reading ■ is becoming sensitive to themes in texts
Response to a novel *Year 10*	Writing about characters	■ understands characterisation in literature ■ produces purposeful and relevant writing about text ■ demonstrates a detailed knowledge of text ■ can write a piece on a given topic if required ■ uses a wide range of evidence to support views
Composing an argument *Year 10*	Revising draft of letter to the editor	■ is able to write in various forms ■ can write convincingly about an issue ■ chooses appropriate words to match ideas ■ can formulate alternative ways of expression ■ acts on advice offered by others
Finding out and reporting *Year 11*	Investigating fast foods	■ locates relevant information from various texts ■ uses information presented in a variety of ways ■ evaluates information ■ reorganises and classifies information from texts ■ writes clearly on complex issues
Report writing *Year 11*	Newspaper report of events in China 4–5 June 1989	■ locates main ideas in a text ■ selects relevant information from various texts ■ synthesises material from various texts ■ uses appropriate tense in writing reports ■ writes factual account maintaining logical sequence
Creative imitation *Year 12*	Imitating descriptive style of first page of a novel e.g. *Fly Away Peter* (Malouf)	■ creates new versions of familiar stories ■ can develop ideas in interesting ways ■ writes creatively using a wide variety of words ■ shows imagination in writing ■ creates atmosphere and mood through descriptive language

the same classroom activity. By establishing situations where children can offer their personal experience and contribute their own ideas, by establishing structures and contexts that encourage skill in working with other people, by providing an audience for students' ideas, we can create a classroom context in which knowledge, experience, ideas, abilities and skills are developed and extended.

RESPONDING TO ALL THE EVIDENCE

Responsive assessment, then, responds to many matters — to the English curriculum, to the social nature of the development of language and thought, to the questions teachers ask, to the varied ways in which students work, to the classroom context, to students' self-assessments, and to what others wish to know about the development and achievements of individual students. Above all, it is responsive to the needs of the learner, and to the extensive range of evidence students themselves offer about their development and achievement.

2 THE REAL EVIDENCE

The real evidence of the development of language abilities in school can be obtained from the careful observation of signs of learning and development, within the context of a wide range of purposeful language-based activity. These signs indicate, in various ways, the growth and expansion of language competence. Two factors influence the observation of these signs of growth:

1 a broad, stimulating language curriculum which creates a context giving students many opportunities to explore models of numerous different kinds of texts, and to actively engage with new language structures, forms and patterns of interaction; and

2 the teacher's professional knowledge of what to look for; that is, ability to recognise signs of growth and evidence of achievement, and to articulate this knowledge.

WHAT COUNTS AS EVIDENCE IN RECOGNITION OF DEVELOPMENT AND ACHIEVEMENT?

For people of all ages, learning to use language, to be literate, is intrinsically linked with everyday interactions. This kind of learning is life-long. Coping with new situations in daily life frequently requires the development of new language skills and abilities.

Becoming the secretary of a community organisation might necessitate learning how to write up the minutes of a meeting. Taking up a new sport means gradually beginning to use the specialist vocabulary of that sport. Deciding to write a history of the family farm might involve learning a series of new writing skills: how to record, synthesise and order a complex body of material, and how to present it in a readable form. The installation of new technology in the workplace or the home means that people have to read instruction manuals for computers or microwave ovens which use concepts and words which might previously have been unfamiliar. When a startling new achievement — perhaps in space exploration or genetic engineering — is reported on the news, people hear descriptions of this achievement, often in language which is new to most listeners, but which rapidly becomes part of the currency of daily life.

Literacy evolves constantly. The continuing acquisition of new language skills enables people to operate confidently, critically and independently in a wide range of social interactions, and to meet the challenges of living in an information-based society.

The evolution of language skills to cope with such changing demands represents development of the uses of literacy for individuals, and the evidence of this can be seen in the interactions in which the language skills are used. Newly acquired language skills are assessed, in real life, not through formal tests but according to the effectiveness with which people are able to use language purposefully and satisfyingly in varied and complex interactions with others.

In this book we explore some of the ways in which teachers can support students in learning to use language more effectively, and in developing the flexibility, sensitivity and confidence to cope with a wide variety of situations. Teachers need to be constantly alert to the evidence which will help to answer the following questions:

- How can the effectiveness with which students are able to use an expanding repertoire of language skills be described?
- Can understanding of the development of language in school be matched with the interaction and observation of language in use in everyday social contexts?
- What part is played in school assessment by the evidence of students' use of language for a wide range of authentic purposes?
- What signs of development and competence can be recognised and described through observing both the processes of talking, listening, reading and writing, and the achievements of students' work?

We suggest that there are three main elements in validly assessing students' achievement:
1 establishing purposeful learning contexts;
2 noting and describing how language is used for different purposes in such learning contexts; and
3 setting up a system of record keeping consistent with the aims and scope of the program.

The connections between the nature and style of the whole curriculum and the informed observation of development mean that no guide to the assessment of language development can be complete without a parallel description of classroom activities which provide an appropriate context for using language for many purposes, in many different situations.

Recognition of development can be supported and focused through access to a broad range of developmental criteria which relate to a wide-ranging language arts curriculum. It then becomes possible to observe the real evidence, because it is the quality of that context — the classroom progam — that helps to promote signs of development. The evidence is real and valid because children are assessed on what they have had the opportunity to learn. The connections between aims, goals, tasks and records are illustrated in the chart, 'Designing classroom contexts'.

In language learning, process and outcome are interrelated. The creation of a piece of writing involves considering the purposes for writing, and the need to use a variety of resources of language to meet these purposes. It also involves a series of composing processes. The student's knowledge and use of the resources of language, and involvement in the composing processes, demonstrate many things about the individual's language abilities. For example, the presentation of a student's report on the results of a series of interviews is built upon the completion of many other activities that have contributed to the findings: deciding on a focus for the investigation, talking with others about the questions to be asked in the interviews, contacting interviewees, conducting the interviews, taking notes, synthesising the information in the notes, and so on. The processes involved in the completion of a written report, or the presentation of an oral report on the interviews, indicate development and competence in all modes of language.

The outcomes of students' work also provide evidence of development and competence. Any production in either speech or written language can demonstrate a variety of signs of development and achievement.

While many classroom activities are intended to emphasise and promote particular abilities, other learning will occur spontaneously, and, sometimes, incidentally; for example:
- when a student reads a poem aloud, the reading offers insights into the student's understanding of the poem, but also something about the understanding of punctuation;
- a letter written to the newspaper indicates the extent to which the writer is aware of the potential range of readers, and of the implications for structure and language usage of writing for a distant audience;
- notes in a reading log provide evidence of the writer's capacity to capture tentative ideas in writing, as well as evidence of response to a novel or other text.

Many signs of language development and competence can be observed in the kind of work described here. Further development is fostered when assessment takes account of this range of learning. Even when a group of students engage with the same task, individuals within that group will demonstrate different kinds of learning, and this diversity of individual progress requires the teacher to be alert to a wide range of signs of development.

Designing classroom contexts

Classroom contexts where development might be observed can be designed by making explicit the focus, goals, tasks and records involved.

Focus	Goals	Tasks	Records
Project on animals Year 5	■ to identify a topic that students want to learn about ■ to establish stages in which the project could be completed ■ to ask questions about the topic ■ to find answers to the questions ■ to find information from different places ■ to tell others about what was found ■ to assess what was done	■ find books that provide information about the topic (including an encyclopedia) ■ pose a question that has to be answered ■ use the index to find information ■ choose information that answers questions ■ read daily newspapers for new information ■ decide which information best answers the question ■ think of headings for the report and various parts ■ present findings in interesting ways	■ student's reading log ■ student's project record ■ progress reports to the class ■ teacher's records based on listening to talk about topic ■ teacher's notes on drafts of writing about findings ■ teachers' records of goals achieved ■ presentation of findings ■ teacher's records of work completed ■ students' records which assess what they have done
Reading and responding to a variety of texts Year 6	■ to select an appropriate book ■ to listen to stories and poems ■ to keep a reading record	■ read a story to an audience ■ present a poem to the class ■ create a new version of a story	■ student's reading log ■ student's reading record ■ anecdotal records of student's response ■ record of work completed
Writing folio Year 8	■ to write for various purposes and audiences ■ to draft and revise writing ■ to present a folio of finished pieces	■ generate and develop a range of ideas for writing ■ identify different audiences for folio pieces ■ revise in collaboration with peers	■ student's list of ideas for writing ■ student's drafts ■ student's record of drafting and revising ■ teacher's notes and records of goals achieved ■ completed folio
Collaborative writing Year 9	■ to complete a group report on a local issue ■ to plan and conduct interviews ■ to work with other people	■ investigate a local problem or issue ■ interview a range of people ■ organise and present information in a report	■ student's record of interview questions and answers ■ student's summary of information ■ record of completed stages of work

Focus	Goals	Tasks	Records
Presentation of readings related to a theme or issue *Year 10*	• to read and understand a variety of texts • to select related texts for reading • to prepare readings for presentation • to present readings to a special audience	• locate and select suitable readings • discuss relevance to the theme or issue • decide on and arrange an audience • arrange readings in a suitable order • rehearse readings • experiment with voices	• student's record of texts read and considered • student's record of selection and ordering of readings • student's record of decisions taken about style of presentation • teacher's records of work done and goals achieved

There are occasions when it is appropriate to assess students' performance in relation to specific tasks or work requirements. Such requirements might be the preparation of a folio of several pieces of writing for a range of purposes and audiences, or the presentation of an oral report to a small group on an aspect of classroom work. The outcomes of such tasks will provide a further wide range of evidence of achievement and development, varying from individual to individual.

A rigorous, valid system of assessment therefore responds to a wide range of possible signs of learning demonstrated in processes as well as outcomes. Such a system will be based on observation and description of students at work, as well as on consideration of the achievements of their completed work. Its validity stems from the authenticity and purposefulness of the work students are asked to do and the opportunities they are given to play a variety of active roles as language users.

The classroom activities described in this book provide a context for observing and describing processes and outcomes in these purposeful contexts. They also take account of some of the problems of time, class size and classroom management which sometimes interfere with opportunities for teachers to recognise individual development in the processes of classroom work.

Time is needed for observing and describing students' abilities. One curriculum feature which helps to create this time and opportunity for valid assessment is the use of projects and workshops that provide extended contexts for language learning. The case studies in Chapters 3 and 7 provide practical examples of such projects.

Curriculum and assessment procedures in English are interwoven, and the curriculum must be designed to allow opportunities for observation and description of work in progress and classroom action, as well as of the achievement of finished work.

THE EVIDENCE OF CLASSROOM ACTION

A group of Year 5 children presents a team report to the class about their investigation of the design proposed for the building of a new school library. One child explains the features of the floor plan, which she has pinned on the display board; another talks briefly about the time-line for the project; the third member of the group tells the class of the parents' club plans to start a fund-raising drive to buy books for the new library.

The class listen attentively; after all, if the agreed time-line is followed, they will have access to the new library in their final year at the school, before they move on to secondary school. They ask questions: 'Will we be able to go into the library through that door from the courtyard?', 'When will the fair run by the parents be held?', 'Will we be able to have a say in choosing the new books?', 'Will the builders be working while we're at school?' The investigating team field the questions confidently; they prepared well for this report. They agree to do some more research to find answers to a couple of questions they were unable to answer.

For half an hour, everyone in the class takes part in this interchange. The group of four who are to prepare a report for the school newspaper have been taking notes. Another group volunteers to canvass ideas from other classes about popular books to include in the new collection.

Here we see two reports and an explanation, each given by one person to a larger group. These are relatively formal spoken presentations within the supportive context of the classroom. Yet the work that preceded these presentations spanned many other dimensions of oral language. The team began by spending some time in informal discussion planning how they would share the task that had been assigned to them: to find out what was happening about the new library. They then worked together to make lists of questions to ask the people they had decided they would need to interview — the architect, the teacher of another class who was a member of the school council and the president of the parents' club. They made phone calls to arrange times to talk to these people (they were already acquainted with all three, as two were parents of friends and one a teacher, so they were confident about ringing up). They conducted the interviews, and came back with tape recordings and notes. They replayed the tapes, made notes and prepared their reports. The task had involved them purposefully in many dimensions of language.

The interest of the whole class in the presentation and the various activities which the reports initiated clearly indicated to the team that their work had been successful. The teacher had monitored the team's work during the time they had been preparing the report and had carefully observed the actual presentation. She had noted that one member of the group who had previously been reluctant to speak to the whole class had given the clear explanation of the plans, and that the girl who spoke about the time-line had marshalled the information she had discovered in a very logical order. The boy who had interviewed the parents' club president had been extremely persuasive in his talk about the role the students would be able to play in fund raising. The group had worked well as a team, cooperating at all stages of the project. This book explores the kinds of statements it would be appropriate for the teacher to use in recording an assessment of this work.

Within the contexts of shared interchange — as formal as a spoken report or as informal as a conversation between friends, as carefully shaped as the writing of the script of a play for other students to perform or as flexible as taking notes from an interview — children learn to talk and listen, to read and write more effectively. The more varied the contexts, the more varied the incentives and purposes for talking and listening. How can we assess the quicksilver of children's language development in these widely varied contexts?

THE INTERCONNECTEDNESS OF READING, WRITING, TALKING AND LISTENING

Developments in the effective use of language for an expanding variety of situations largely depend on the range of opportunities available to children in school to use language in many different ways in authentic contexts. In such realistic situations, the four language modes are used in interconnected and integrated ways.

To talk of learning to read, or to write, or to develop abilities in talking and listening as distinct activities is, of course, to create an artificial distinction. Development in each of these modes is dependent on the other modes, and often the connectedness of the experience is so central that it is barely noticeable. People learn to read and write by talking and listening. The processes of learning to read and learning to write are intricately linked. Writers often like to talk about their work, and in doing so, clarify what they mean in their writing. Readers listen to others talking about the meanings they have constructed from the written text, then return to the text to make new meanings of their own. Listening to others talk helps children to understand how different kinds of talk are appropriate in different situations. Effective English language programs build on this natural integration of the four language modes.

The interdependence of the language modes creates difficulties for teachers in assessing growth and development in English. We often look specifically at one mode, acknowledging the complex connections with the other modes while at the same time endeavouring to identify particular strengths and weaknesses in the individual student's achievement in a single activity, or over time. This specificity does help us to build accurate and detailed profiles to describe and monitor development, but it is important not to forget the wholeness of the way students use language. Indeed, many of the criteria in the collection in this book imply a natural connection between modes of language.

In *Telling the Whole Story* we focus attention on talking and listening, on reading, and finally on writing. However, in Chapters 4, 5 and 6 we also describe contexts for observing development in these modes in which talking and listening, writing and reading are integrally linked. It is practical, and useful, to assess development in each of these modes within these contexts.

While language learning is a connected process, students working in a range of contexts for learning display competencies and needs in various aspects of language. Classroom activities also have different emphases on processes and outcomes. Focusing on the richness of this variety allows us to take account of sufficient evidence to achieve the diagnostic and evaluative precision necessary for accurate observation, recording and reporting.

The intention behind our decision in this book to consider reading, writing and oral language separately is therefore to help teachers to focus observations on individual language learners in their classrooms, and to create easy access to aspects of development in which readers are specially interested.

3 THE WHOLE CONTEXT

MANAGING EFFECTIVE ENGLISH CLASSROOMS

In practical terms, effective management of English programs stems from acknowledgement of the many aspects of development in language and learning which can be observed in interactions in the classroom, in students' attitudes and approaches to work, and in students' written and oral productions.

English programs should not only be planned and managed so that they create learning contexts in which it is possible for students to explore many kinds of language, and to use language for many purposes, but planning and management must also take account of the diversity and breadth of learning which a comprehensive approach to curriculum design will generate. In turn, the comprehensiveness of the program, combined with the diversity of learning, must be reflected in and matched by an equally comprehensive approach to assessment. Assessment must value the full range of what is happening. Responsiveness to the diversity of teaching and learning invites a greater responsiveness in teachers to the individual achievements and successes of all children. This overall view of the connections between teaching, learning and assessment raises a number of significant questions. These relate to the ways in which English teachers work from their professional knowledge and understanding of language and learning to plan and manage meaningful and workable learning contexts:

- How does professional knowledge about language and ways of learning influence practice?
- How does it foster explicit planning, and help in the articulation of the goals involved in making classrooms effective learning environments?
- To what extent does such knowledge influence the ways in which students are given access to many different kinds of texts, and to opportunities to use language for many purposes?

- How does this knowledge help teachers to focus their observations of students' work and development in informed ways?
- How does it lead to productive, systematic and encouraging response from teacher to student, and from student to student?
- How does such knowledge inform the expression of the criteria by which the effectiveness of the work and learning is described?

PUTTING KNOWLEDGE ABOUT LANGUAGE AND LEARNING INTO CONTEXT

An exploration of one extended classroom project will demonstrate how a comprehensive view of language and learning can be used:
- to articulate the purposes and goals of the project;
- to direct and manage the activity and work;
- to focus observation of students at work, and of work in progress;
- to evaluate and describe the ways in which students achieve the goals of the project in completing the work requirements; and
- to describe the quality of the finished work.

PROJECTS AS CONNECTED, PURPOSEFUL CONTEXTS FOR LEARNING

An effective way of managing English classrooms is to design the program around a series of projects, so that students' work over a specified period of time has a particular focus. This focus might be the exploration of a topical issue, a novel, the reading of a wide range of poetry, or the production of an anthology of different kinds of writing. When such a project is designed to encompass a range of experiences in the different language modes, the focus creates a connected and purposeful context for many activities. Goals can be established at the beginning of the project, deadlines agreed and set, and the scope for individual choice of activity within the project can be negotiated. Students can be responsible for planning their own use of time, and for meeting agreed deadlines. Class activity can include:

- shared, whole-class sessions — for example, the reading of a set of poems, discussion of an issue in the media, planning the presentation of an anthology, listening to a group presentation, exploring the ways in which a particular text achieves its intended purpose;
- small-group work, where groups collaborate on particular activities within a project — perhaps the preparation of a dramatised reading of an extract from a novel, or the setting up of a display of newspaper cuttings which suggest a scenario for the future, or close reading and discussion of a particular text;
- 'workshop' sessions where students are engaged in different stages of completing individual or group work requirements for the project — such as research, interviewing, drafting and revising pieces of writing, or writing an introduction to an anthology — and the teacher is freed to offer individualised advice and support.

Projects like these break away from the mould of the single 'lesson'. The organisation of the secondary school timetable into a number of 'periods' per day, often six sessions of fifty minutes, creates problems for developing the kinds of connected learning environments in which purposeful language use flourishes. Single 'lessons' set up a cycle where each lesson needs to be introduced, even when the work is continuing, and the role of planning and managing work tends to remain with the teacher. However, because work on a project is ongoing, students have a clear overview of what is required of them and how much time is available, and opportunities to share responsibility for planning and managing their work. At the beginning of each period, students can immediately start work where they left off so the need for a general introduction to the period's work is greatly reduced.

When working on a project, students are able to reflect on progress towards known goals, such as the completion of an anthology or the presentation of a group research report. The requirements of the project itself control the momentum of class activity. Variety is built into the stages of the project — there is likely to be much more whole-class and small-group work at the beginning of a project, and more individual workshop activity at the end as students put finishing touches to oral and written work. Projects offer scope for collaboration, and for using a wide range of resources including libraries, computers and newspapers.

'TAKING A TRIP'

For a mixed-ability, co-educational Year 10 class, the project 'Taking a trip' occupied five weeks of class time. The work plan given to students at the beginning of the unit outlined the overall task — to plan a trip and put together a tour folder — and provided details of specific activities. (The actual work plan given to students is presented in sections in the course of this chapter; after students received the whole plan, some time was spent at this stage in whole-class discussion of the plan.)

The work plan also specified a completion date, and made suggestions about ways of working. All students kept a copy of this plan in their workbooks or working folders. Students were also provided with a running sheet on which to keep track of their progress on the various activities involved in the project (see the Checklist on p. 43).

We have chosen this project as the basis for a case study demonstrating how a responsive approach to assessment can operate because, although it is based on a Year 10 class, this is a project which can be adapted for students from Years 4–10. It is characteristic of the design of curriculum which maximises opportunities for students to develop a wide range of skills by creating opportunities for them to participate in a diversity of purposeful activities, in a connected and sustained context. The project is also an example of the way a classroom can be managed as a workshop, giving teachers extensive opportunities to observe students at work, and to respond to the needs and interests of individuals and groups of students.

GOALS AND PLANS

The project was designed to take account of a number of understandings about learning (such as, the importance of an authentic purpose for work to be undertaken), and about the development of competence in reading and writing for different purposes. The importance of giving students access to effective models of writing for different purposes, and of establishing purposeful contexts for writing which encourage students to make appropriate choices about style, tone, and form in their writing also influenced the design of the project. A further consideration related to encouraging students to learn to make more effective use of the library as a resource. In fact, in this case it was possible for most class sessions for the duration of the project to be taken in the library, which strengthened the nature of the learning context.

LEARNING TO BE ORGANISED

The invitation to students to plan and organise a substantial research and writing project, with definite outcomes, created a significant opportunity for them to plan their work over a known period of time, to manage their time effectively, and to locate and use a variety of resources. The capacity to do these things is a component of successful learning, and students need opportunities to work in the security of a known and predictable context in order to develop this capacity.

This project was therefore expected to set up a context in which the ways different students organised and managed their time could be tracked. Those who were identified, through observation, as needing support in managing an extended project could be offered that support in the workshop situation which the design of the project created, freeing the teacher to work one-to-one with students when necessary.

At an early stage in the project, students demonstrated a range of planning and organisational skills: one student independently set up a workbook, with a different section for each task, and as she collected information and ideas she noted them in the appropriate section. This idea was copied by several other class members. Some students read widely at this stage but neglected to take notes, and then discovered that it was difficult to recover information they wanted to use. Early in the project it became obvious that some students were confident about locating resources in the library, while others needed assistance with this.

Individual preferences for working patterns could be observed, too. Some students elected to work in pairs, choosing the same 'destination' for their trip and sharing the research, but producing individual travel folders; one pair of boys planned a trip to top skate-boarding venues in three states, and worked in close cooperation throughout the project. Others worked independently on parallel projects, exchanging information and ideas as they went. Some students formed working groups of three or four while they developed their projects according to individual interests, engaging in a continuing discussion about the activities in the project, monitoring each other's work in informal ways: 'What are you doing today?', 'Where did you find . . .?', 'Have you started . . .?' Once students had begun to locate useful resources, they were willing to share their knowledge with others, and a cooperative mood developed and prevailed in the class.

During the course of the project, most students established a balance between working in class time and working at home, as it became clear to them that the project was extensive enough to warrant some commitment of home time. This highlighted another advantage of the project design — the integration of meaningful 'homestudy' tasks, which creates more effective home/school links than short-term, one-off tasks sometimes set as homework do. For some students the work done at home was a steady commitment throughout the project; for others, it involved a last-minute effort as they became aware of the imminent deadline for submitting the finished folder.

Throughout the project, notes on students' ways of working were kept on individual profile sheets like that for Taking a Trip which follows. These sheets were used progressively to record an overall assessment of each student's work and achievement for the project.

Taking a trip — assessment profile

Name:
Time management, effective use of class time, etc.:
Completion of work requirements:
Quality of finished work:

WRITING FOR DIFFERENT PURPOSES

When students are invited to write in a number of different ways, within a specified field, they can extend their understanding of how context, audience and purpose influence the nature of writing. In this project, the Year 10 students were initially given the opportunity to read a range of material about travel, with an interest focus (their chosen destination) which they had selected themselves. This reading provided models of different kinds of writing — itineraries, geographical information, reports and narrative accounts of journeys — on the general subject of travel, and a purpose for reading and exploring these models. This reading was thus an important stage in the learning sequence.

ARTICULATING THE PURPOSES OF THE PROJECT

Here is the work plan that initially introduced the overall goals for the project.

Goals

This project involves:
- planning a two-week holiday tour
- reading a variety of material
- obtaining information and making notes from sources such as magazines, tour guides, atlases, newspapers, and other people
- preparing a workable budget for a trip
- using a road atlas to plan and record travel routes
- writing informatively, descriptively and imaginatively
- writing poems and stories as well as letters to obtain information, and a summary statement for a 'tour folder'
- presenting a finished collection of different kinds of writing in a coherent way
- learning to organise an extended project and manage time effectively.

The intentions which shaped these goals were derived from an overall goal of creating opportunities for students to work and learn through a variety of connected experiences, and to read and write a variety of different kinds of texts. These experiences included:
- research;
- writing and reading for different purposes;
- working independently over an extended period of time;
- presenting an ordered, coherent collection of work; and
- reflecting on the progress of their work, and reporting this progress to others.

As students worked on the project, the set goals progressively became a focus for observing what was happening. Were all students reading a variety of material? Were they obtaining information from a variety of sources? Did some people need help with particular kinds of writing? How effectively were students organising and managing their time?

DIRECTING THE ACTIVITY AND WORK

The next section of the project plan informed students about expectations for ways of working.

The progress reports were an important feature of this project, as they involved students in the evaluation of their own work. They also created

Timing

Some of this work will be done in your own time; much will be done in the classroom and the library.

During the project, there will be some whole-class lessons on note-making, writing short stories, letters and so on.

Checkpoints

At different times you will be asked to report orally on your progress with the project. In these reports you should be able to describe what work has been completed and what you plan to do next. You should also describe any problems you have encountered, and be prepared to listen to suggestions about how to solve these.

Presentation

The final product is to be presented in a 'travel folder' of your own design.

opportunities for students to share their individual experiences of a common project, talking through problems and explaining their plans and achievements. The nature of the project meant that for much of the time students were working on their own, with a partner, or in a small group. The presentation of the progress reports established a forum for whole-class discussion.

The requirement to present the work in the form of a travel folder provided a realistic purpose for revising and finishing individual pieces of work, and then for presenting them in an ordered, coherent collection. The presentation of a collection of varied pieces of writing creates opportunities for students to review and reflect on the work they have done over a specified time, and if necessary to rework some pieces until they are satisfied that they effectively achieve the intended purpose. The folder suggests likely readers for the work, other than the teacher — interested classmates, other people interested in the trip. When students are aware of audiences for their work, they are likely to become more sensitive to making sure that their writing conveys the intended meaning, that it is written so as to interest readers, and that conventions of spelling, grammar and punctuation are satisfied.

ACTIVITIES

The work plan outlined various activities and requirements. The sequence in which these are presented represents roughly the order in which students needed to work, as some activities provided a foundation for others. The early activities involved research, note making, summarising, and keeping a record of resources. The kinds of research suggested included locating and scanning appropriate reference material in the library, talking to other people, and writing away to request information.

The first writing task — writing to a travel agency — provided students with a specific purpose and audience for writing. This task led to a series of discussions between the teacher and individuals or groups about appropriate ways of writing a letter requesting particular information, and created opportunities for teaching about letter formats, the need to phrase requests accurately and concisely, and the reasons for clear, attractive presentation.

The suggestions about sources of information were intended to introduce the notion of a range of different kinds of writing. The significance of noting appropriate details of sources signalled to students that they needed to acknowledge sources, and thus avoid plagiarism.

The sample questions given in the work plan indicated to students that they should focus research by asking relevant questions.

In these initial activities the range of skills called upon is extensive:
• locating appropriate reference material in a library;

Choosing a destination

In this project, you are able to plan, and take, an imaginary trip to a destination of your own choice in Australia.

1 Before you decide where to go, browse through some of the atlases and travel books in the library. Talk with other people about places they have travelled to.

Collecting information

2 To request information about travel in Australia, write a letter to a travel agency. Ask for information about overnight accommodation, state and national parks, museums, historical sites, and other places of interest. Remember to keep copies of any letters you write for your travel folder.

3 Take notes about places on your proposed trip from at least five sources — atlases, year books, tourist guides, newspapers and magazines.

Note the source of each piece of information you record — give titles of books, articles or chapters, publishers, dates of publication and page numbers. Questions you might ask at this stage include:

• What are the best-known towns and cities, and what makes them notable?
• What are the major and minor industries?
• What are the best-known historical sites and the most popular recreational sites?
• What is the average temperature for each season?
• What are the names and occupations of some famous people from the area?

- skimming and scanning reference books to identify areas of interest;
- talking with other people about a particular topic;
- writing a letter to an unknown audience requesting specific information;
- taking notes;
- keeping a record of sources of information;
- consulting a range of sources to locate information; and
- asking relevant questions to focus research.

As students worked on these activities, there were continuing opportunities for the teacher to observe and note the ways in which students tackled various tasks, and the skills listed above provided a focus for this observation.

These activities established a knowledge base for further work on the project. Within the whole context of the project, the purposes for writing were clear: to request information, to make notes about information and ideas to be used in later writing, to keep a record of sources of information.

By this stage, all students had gathered some information about their chosen destination, and the workshop routine was well established. All classes had been booked into the general working area of the library, and at the beginning of each session, students needed no prompting and simply continued from where they had left off at the previous session, or at home.

It become obvious that many students were coming to class sessions with clearly defined goals: to obtain further information from a particularly useful reference book, to request help in locating specific information, to ask for assistance with writing, or to have draft writing read and reviewed by other people. Progress was variable — some students were still reading; others had completed several writing tasks; some had received information in response to their letters. At this point in the project it was possible for the teacher to identify those students who were not managing time effectively, and to negotiate more effective work patterns with them.

The class reassembled at this time for the first round of 'checkpoints', progress reports. The whole class sat in a circle and took turns to give brief spoken reports, explaining their choice of destination for the trip, and describing the information they had collected so far. Some commented on ways of working — for example, using a work book with specific sections for each task. Where people had encountered problems, such as in obtaining sufficient information, or in keeping track of the information they had collected, they reported these problems.

The sharing session established common ground within the class, and suggested new possibilities to some students. One student had decided to use a folder with clear plastic display pockets as her travel folder, and showed this to the class. In the next few days, many other students obtained similar folders, showing that they recognised the value of this decision. Students whose progress to date had been slow were jolted into activity when they realised how much work others had already accomplished.

Overall, the progress reports achieved several purposes. The reporting session:
- provided an opportunity for all students to report to the whole class. For some this involved a development in confidence, as their situation provided something definite to talk about;
- suggested further possibilities for the project;
- helped students to assess their own progress towards achieving the goals of the project; and
- provided evidence of progress and problems, enabling the teacher to plan the kinds of support needed in the following sessions.

The tasks described above all required students to use factual information in various ways. Some of this information had been obtained from the research already done; further lines of enquiry and different sources of information are suggested here. This factual information provided a basis for the range of imaginative, personal writing which followed. The transition from informative, factual writing to expressive, imaginative writing was a natural one at this point — students had a good grasp of

---

Beginning to use your information

4 Write a summary statement, about half a page in length, in which you explain your reasons for travelling in Australia, and what you plan to do on your trip. Include both educational and recreational plans. This page will be the first page of your travel folder.

5 Write a one- to two-page report on the geographical features of the area. Note features such as land forms, temperature, rainfall and other factors.

6 Write a detailed itinerary for the trip, specifying dates, places and activities.

7 Decide how you will travel — car, bus, train, plane, bicycle, etc. Find out about fares, timetables. If you plan to travel by car, work out distances and cost of petrol to calculate how much the trip will cost. Also work out how long it will take to reach the different destinations.

8 Prepare an accurate budget for the trip. Allow $3000 and plan to return home with no more than $50. Transport and accommodation costs must come out of this budget.

Remember to allow for such things as meals and snacks, bus and tram rides in cities, entry charges to tourist sites, tickets for movies and other entertainment, souvenirs, postage, telephone charges and so on.

9 Make a list of what you intend to pack, keeping in mind the expected weather and the kinds of activities you have planned.

10 Draw or trace a map, indicating the points of interest that you will visit. Plot your route in red.

detailed knowledge about the route and destination for the trip. As they began to work on the personal letters, short story and diary it was interesting to observe how frequently they referred to the earlier writing.

By now the value of the checklist of work completed (see p. 43) was apparent. Students were asked to keep this checklist up to date, and to be prepared to submit it with their finished project. The progressively updated list increasingly constituted useful evidence of the ways in which students were meeting the goals of developing a series of related pieces of writing, and of organising their time effectively.

Progress reports at this stage were focused on the various writing tasks. Mostly students reported on what pieces were finished, or drafted, but sometimes questions were raised about the expectations for a particular purpose for writing: 'How long can the story be?', 'Do we have to give diary entries for every day, or can we imagine that the person only wrote in the diary occasionally?', 'Should we use sub-headings in the report?', 'Can we talk about what we should do for the book review?'

Although the project provided common goals and expectations for the whole class, individual differences in approach and interests could now clearly be observed, demonstrating how there will always be a range of achievement in a group of students. The observable differences included:

- some students' interest in learning to manage the word processor to format and present their work, and their incidental discovery that the word processor is a useful tool for revisions, which extended their own capacity to revise and edit their work;
- one student's growing enthusiasm for the project when he realised how it enabled him to use his experience of a family trip to Perth as the basis for his work;

Using your imagination

11 Write an imaginary daily diary for the duration of your trip. Include anecdotes about your adventures, descriptions of what you enjoyed most, and notes on what you would do differently next time.

12 Write a letter to a friend at home about an exciting event from your trip.

13 Write a letter to your parents, a relative or a teacher describing your trip.

14 Prepare a picture scrapbook of your trip, using pictures cut out of travel brochures and magazines. Write a caption for each picture.

15 Write a short story about someone you met on your trip. Describe the person in detail, and write about one or more memorable incidents involving this person.

16 Write a poem about the trip, focusing on sights and sounds typical of your destination.

- a strong commitment on the part of some students to the personal, imaginative writing — for example, the development of short stories with well-shaped plots, collections of short poems (one student wrote a set of haiku poems about the trip);
- continuing research by students who decided to pursue the factual aspects of the project in some detail. One boy 'discovered' the state and national Yearbooks in the library, and extracted a great deal of information from them;
- variations in ways of working: students who maintained a close cooperation with other students, even though they were developing their own material; students who preferred to work independently; one student who had a commitment to a week's work experience and needed to finish the project early, who therefore decided to do extra work at home to meet the set deadline.

MAKING CHOICES ABOUT APPROPRIATE WAYS OF USING LANGUAGE

Structure, word choice, tone and style, choice of tense — these are matters about which writers must make decisions so that any piece of writing is appropriate for the intended audience and purpose. Because this project involved students in preparing a range of kinds of writing, based on the one set of information, they became alert to differences. This alertness developed, for instance, as students wrote an itinerary (a kind of writing which is usually structured as a series of points and headings and written in the present tense, for the purpose of planning), and a diary (expressed in a more discursive manner, usually in past tense, and for the purposes of recollection and reflection).

It was interesting to observe how students approached this range of writing. The starting point was the factual information, so all students had access to relevant ideas and words, and many possibilities for writing. This created a context for their writing, and enabled them to see how personal, imaginative writing makes use of detail in different ways from factual writing. In writing both the diary and the short story, the itinerary became a useful reference for many students. In the case of the short story, the itinerary helped them with sequencing of events.

The pair of boys working on the skateboarding holiday developed an effective mode of collaborative writing at this stage: one boy referring as necessary to the itinerary, the other acting as scribe, whilst they both brainstormed the story. The task of composition was shared; other tasks, such as checking information and writing down the draft, became individual responsibilities.

By now the sessions devoted to progress reports tended to concentrate on time management; how students were planning to meet the deadline for submission of the completed project. The progress reports seemed to stimulate decisions about using time, and also allowed all students to find out how others worked, thus potentially extending their own repertoire of work strategies.

Responding to drafts of the growing collection of writing took a considerable amount of the teacher's time, but students also shared their drafts with other people in the class and, in a number of cases, with people at home. Response from peers to work in progress was interested and informed because all students were engaged in similar though not identical writing activities, all were facing related problems of handling too much or too little information, or shifting from one writing mode to another.

The final section of the work plan made connections between the research and writing, and the student's reading. Writing the review involved another kind of writing; and the opportunity to read a book about a journey, fiction or non-fiction, provided other models of writing.

Requirements for presentation were made clear, including the expectation that the work should be carefully revised and proofread. As all students had copies of the work plan right from the beginning of the project, all had access to the criteria by which it would finally be assessed. That is, the assessment criteria were contained in the work requirements, and known to all:

- the completion of all tasks by the due date (thus demonstrating the student's capacity to plan and manage an extended project);
- the presentation of the work in a finished state, in a coherent collection, with a table of contents;
- evidence of the capacity to carry out a range of research tasks, to select relevant information from a wide range of material, and to use the information appropriately;
- the demonstration of the student's capacity to present a collection of writing for different purposes and audiences;

Related reading

17 While you are working on this project, read a book about a journey or trip someone else has taken — not necessarily to the same destination as you have chosen. The librarians in the Resource Centre will help you to locate suitable books.

Write a short half-page review of this book.

Presentation

18 Collect all the completed items together in your 'travel folder' and prepare a table of contents.

ALL YOUR WORK SHOULD BE CAREFULLY PROOFREAD AND EDITED.

- the effectiveness with which the individual pieces of writing achieved the intended purpose;
- the demonstration of competence in revising and editing work so that conventions of spelling, syntax and punctuation were accurately used;
- scope for the demonstration of particular achievements (for example, ability to use the word processor to format work, or the ability to present work in an especially attractive format, or the presentation of an outstanding piece of writing amongst the collection).

The list of assessment criteria above shows how the goals of the project became workable criteria for assessment.

As well as the work plan, all students had a copy of the following Checklist of work completed, which was designed to enable them to

Checklist of work completed

Task Final	Draft completed	Draft checked	Copy
1 Letter asking for information			
2 Notes from at least five sources			
3 Summary statement			
4 Geographical features report			
5 Detailed travel itinerary			
6 Budget			
7 List of what to pack			
8 Daily diary for 2 weeks			
9 Letter to a friend			
10 Letter to parents, relatives or teacher			
11 Picture scrapbook and captions			
12 Short story			
13 Poem			
14 Map			
15 Book review			
16 Table of contents			

Your evaluation of your participation in this project:

What did you learn?

keep track of their own progress, and to contribute to the assessment of their own work. This checklist was submitted with the finished folder. It was obvious at a glance if the criteria of completing all the set tasks had been satisfied. The checklist also functioned as a useful *aide-mémoire* for students in presenting the series of oral progress reports — they did not have to make notes especially for each report, but were able to base the reports on the information noted on the checklist.

DESCRIBING THE QUALITY OF THE FINISHED WORK

Examples from three students of the short summary statements offer a sample of the range of achievement in this project. Each of these pieces can be described from three aspects — the information and tone conveyed; the responsiveness to work requirements; and the control of language and form. Each is different, although each successfully fulfills the purpose of providing a summary statement to introduce the project.

Cheryl offers a clear, informative explanation:

> For my holiday I am planning to travel to Perth and stay for a couple of nights at the Langly Plaza Hotel. Next I will travel back to Adelaide on train and stay a few nights then back to Melbourne.
>
> The reason for travelling on a train is that I have tried every other way of travelling except by train. Most of my time will be spent in the cities shopping or just sitting in the parks admiring the view because I have all ready been to most of the tourist places when I was younger.
>
> Hopefully it will be warm so I can get to see some of the beaches in two different states.

This summary can be described by the following statements:
- concise
- clearly explained
- provides summary of whole planned trip
- explains reasons for chosen mode of travel
- suggests range of activities
- attempts to establish convincing framework for project by making connections with previous travel experiences
- establishes a matter-of-fact tone
- indicates awareness of work requirements by references to modes of travel, planned activities
- logical sequence
- accurate spelling, punctuation and syntax (except 'all ready' — the use of 'hopefully' is debatable)
- explains and informs
- focus on information.

By contrast, Amber recognises and takes up some of the imaginative possibilities offered by the project, even in this short summary statement. Where Cheryl has offered only information and explanation, Amber's piece introduces a narrative element into the summary:

> My father decided to buy me a return fare ticket to Brisbane as a surprise reward for my VCE exam results. 'I'll fly you to Brisbane and back, but whatever you do up there comes entirely out of your own pocket!' my father says.
> Wow, I can hardly believe it! Queensland for two weeks!!
> But it's not just for recreational adventure — I'm sure I'll be educated greatly. Living on my own for two weeks and providing for myself will be a great adventure within itself. Touring around, admiring lots of old establishments and also the leisurely side of it, too! Water skiing, sunbathing, swimming, can't wait!!

Statements which describe this summary include:
- sets a tone of anticipation
- explains reasons for trip
- indicates possible activities
- suggests personal outcomes — educational as well as recreational
- explains destination
- shows awareness of work requirements
- sets up possibilities for the imaginative writing required in the project
- establishes the 'persona' for the project (the nature of the other pieces of writing will be influenced by this)
- concise and clear
- logical sequence of ideas
- accurate syntax and spelling
- effective use of direct speech
- mixes informal language (wow) effectively with more formal language
- overuse of '!'

Mark's summary, another example of a piece which takes an imaginative stance, also successfully meets the requirements of the task, although he has some problems with expression:

> The reason I'm traveling to Bendigo is that my boss said that I could take a holiday. And he would like me to go to Bendigo, for a two-week trip. He then told me that I had to spend up to three thousand dollars, and that I could only come home with less than fifty dollars. The holiday has all expenses payed for.
> The reason he is paying for the trip is that I done some very important work for our apple Computer company. And so he is giving me a holiday. But on the way home from my holiday I have to pick up some very important material for our company.

The list that follows suggests a number of features of the piece which can be described accurately.

- concise
- meaning clearly communicated
- logical sequence of information
- uses sufficient detail for full explanation
- establishes a persona
- provides a context for the imaginary trip
- focuses on a particular activity — the budget
- spelling not completely under control — 'traveling', 'payed'
- syntax error — 'done'
- sentence structure lacks variety, control.

The checklist which students were given included space for students' self evaluation. A range of comments was offered, but a number of students chose to focus their comments on the ways they had organised their work, and what they had learnt from this:

> I learnt that when I have things organised, I work more efficiently. At first things took a bit of effort to get going. This I realised was lack of organisation . . .

> I learnt how to prepare things more effectively, and also how to make all the different pieces of writing work in together with each other.

> I learned that I can be an organised person when I try hard. Organisation doesn't come naturally to me, and I found that I had to push myself into keeping on with the project.

This project, then, provided the context in which a wide range of the developing capacities and achievements among a group of students could be observed, recorded, and finally given an assessment in the form of a detailed description of what had been achieved. The project encompassed a wide range of learning opportunities, in all language modes:
- reading and research;
- reading a variety of texts;
- writing for different purposes and audiences; and
- engaging in a variety of oral activities — informal working talk, response to others' work and the presentation of progress reports to the rest of the class.

The project offered a connected context, 'the whole context', in which the students' purposeful use of language could be seen from different perspectives. The goals for the project, the focus for observation of students at work and the assessment criteria were closely linked, so that the assessment was based on a range of evidence, and responsive to the ways in which the goals had been achieved.

PART 2

OBSERVING AND DESCRIBING DEVELOPMENT IN ENGLISH

∎INTRODUCTION

Chapter 3, The whole context, provides an example of a planned, purposeful context in which it was possible to observe a group of Year 10 students developing and consolidating their capacity to use language in flexible ways. The purpose of the chapter was to exemplify the kind of learning context which we believe is most likely to foster learning, and to integrate key aspects of teaching, learning and assessment. Exploration of the project on which that chapter was focused raises a number of questions related to specific aspects of assessing development:

- When teachers observe students at work on classroom activities, what kinds of development in talking and listening, reading and writing are they looking for?
- How can the developments seen in students' use of these modes of language be described?
- When students present finished work in any of these modes, what signs of achievement are valued?

In this section, we offer some illustrations and examples of answers to these questions. This section of *Telling the Whole Story* is therefore divided into four chapters:

- Talking and listening
- Reading
- Writing
- Students at work.

The projects described in Chapters 3 and 7, 'Taking a trip' and 'The road not taken', provide connected contexts for many different activities which are likely to create wide-ranging opportunities for learning and development. Within such learning contexts, it is possible to look closely at specific aspects of language use: talking, listening, reading and writing. In order to identify the various signs of development and achievement that might be recognised and described in the context of the classroom, we have selected a range of classroom episodes and activities that emphasise experience in the particular mode of language use addressed in each chapter.

RECOGNISING AND DESCRIBING SIGNS OF DEVELOPMENT

To be ready to provide information to students and parents, and to discuss goals, work and assessment criteria with students so they can evaluate their own efforts, it is important to be able to say what students have shown they can and cannot do. For example, if students work towards and accomplish the goal of producing a folio of their own writings, many related yet different signs of development and achievement in each of the modes of language shown will be evident as they work to achieve that goal. Teachers need to be able to recognise and describe such signs, or the lack of them. It is important, too, to be able to describe the signs of achievement in finished work. These chapters are intended to help teachers, and others, to do these things.

Each chapter includes the following features:

- a framework within which the contexts and signs of development are described;
- descriptions of a range of typical classroom activities, presented in approximate developmental order;
- for each episode or activity, a list of signs of achievement that might be observed in such contexts — that is, examples of abilities students might have shown they have developed;
- where appropriate, a list of similar contexts related to particular activities;
- descriptions of some appropriate ways of assessing achievement, and some of the signs of achievement which can be noted; and
- four sample checklists that might be employed to describe and record signs of achievement, and as the basis of discussion with students and their parents.

These checklists reflect the signs of development observed in classroom activities and experiences at certain phases of schooling. As their design suggests, space can be provided for noting new and perhaps unanticipated signs of learning, or for important developments relating to particular contexts.

DESCRIPTIVE STATEMENTS ABOUT LEARNING AND DEVELOPMENT — A FLEXIBLE RESOURCE FOR TEACHERS

Precise descriptions of students' language development and competence require a flexible working vocabulary. The language used for assessment must communicate accurate observations of students at work, record work completed and express those observations in terms that match the intentions and the quality of the classroom program. To be fair to students, it has to use a vocabulary that is consistent with the goals and nature of the work completed, and captures the qualities of the work and achievement of individual students. This language must also be understood by students and their parents.

In Part 2 of *Telling the Whole Story*, many statements about language development are made. These statements describe concisely aspects of development in reading, writing, talking and listening. The collection of statements is designed as a flexible resource to help teachers record the wide range of information on which descriptions of students' development and competence can be based.

Most of these statements can be used flexibly to:
- describe any incidental learning;
- construct checklists and profiles;
- compose fluent prose reports to parents;
- guide school policy making; and
- provide a range of options from which to choose when negotiating goals and plans for classroom work.

A RESOURCE FOR DESCRIBING INDIVIDUAL DEVELOPMENT

Students grow towards language competence in different ways, but very few do not become competent. Many of them come from backgrounds where English is not the first language or where reading and writing are not valued activities, and this can be one of the reasons for a variability in development which requires assessment procedures sufficiently sensitive to note areas of both competence and learning needs. If teachers have access to a large body of statements about language development, upon which further statements can be built, something precise and unique can be said about every student, regardless of pace of development or of social or linguistic background, and aspects of development that need attention can be accurately described.

CLASSROOM CONTEXTS

Assessment procedures that seek to describe students' language development must take account of the complexity of classroom contexts designed and established to promote such growth. Several interrelated features characterise classroom contexts which foster the development of language competencies. One of these is the social nature of the situation itself — the opportunity to interact with others, to communicate and to respond. A second feature is the connected experience of language that this social context entails — a classroom focus that generates a pattern of related or integrated opportunities for talking, listening, reading and writing. A third key feature is the exercise of individual initiative and responsibility in that situation, where students have a stake in the process and in the outcome. Within this context, students and teachers establish achievable goals whereby tasks and activities lead to significant outcomes. The experience of individual students in this context cannot be accurately summed up in two or three lines because the students display such a diversity of abilities and needs. How can we do justice to students' achievements and their needs? How can this diversity of learning be described in ways that are valid, precise and just?

In our view, accurate descriptions of a wide range of possible language learnings can be developed from a varied collection of descriptive statements about many aspects of development and achievement. Our major focus is on signs of development and competence in making and using language that can be observed in a broad range of activities and experiences, and from which criteria for judging development or achievement can be formulated. Judgements about the quality and nature of students' language growth need to be based on observation of signs of development. Judgements based on observation of particular signs of language growth establish the status of these signs as assessment criteria.

The use of particular signs of language growth as criteria for this purpose is determined by the context of activities — the goals of the classroom program, what was intended to happen, the real nature of the program, what actually happened — and by the priorities of teachers and the schools in which they work.

Specific observable signs of language growth can be anticipated within particular activities and experiences, and it is therefore possible to decide beforehand that these characteristics are the expected criteria, the signs of learning upon which assessment will depend. However, as the signs and characteristics of language development vary from activity to activity, and between individual students, so, too, will the criteria upon which evaluations of growth rest and the description of students' development which draw on those criteria. Descriptions of competence in language use are validated when the signs of learning are demonstrated in a range of other classroom contexts.

The variability of students' development and the complexity of classroom language activities mean that no single criterion or set of criteria is necessarily accurate from one situation to another, but needs reshaping in the light of what students show they can do each time. As plans, goals and the nature of the work change, so do the criteria for assessing development and competency. The same set of criteria cannot therefore be employed from one activity to another, but will change according to the purposes and goals of particular activities and classroom contexts. The collection of statements in this book provides numerous options for formulating criteria to assess development observed in widely differing language learning contexts.

Despite the knowledge that certain activities will promote specific kinds of language learning, unanticipated signs of language development can arise, and usually do. New interests develop, only indirectly related to the goals and plans laid, and students reveal during their work hitherto unnoticed competencies. The lists of statements brought together in this book form a collection which is sufficiently comprehensive to allow sensitive and flexible responses to such learning. Whether or not these signs become criteria for assessment depends upon the extent to which it is fair and just to assess all students involved in the same activity according to these language learnings. These unexpected characteristics give rise to new criteria, new expected learnings, which might provide a basis for assessment on future occasions when such activity is planned.

A DATABASE OF DESCRIPTIVE STATEMENTS ABOUT LANGUAGE DEVELOPMENT

A collection of descriptive statements can form the beginnings of a much larger database. New signs of learning that emerge from the work done by students can be added to the database, and existing statements can be reformulated and expanded from successive learning contexts.

The defining features of any collection of statements designed to be used to describe students' language development are flexibility, precision and sensitivity. These attributes help to bring validity to statements and to assessment procedures for which criteria based on these statements are formulated. These characteristics also reflect the qualities and processes of evaluation employed in the world outside the school.

The purposes of collecting and organising the statements in this book are therefore:

- to assist teachers to bring to students' activity a framework or focus for observation and assessment;
- to provide examples of statements about language learning that can be used to shape accurate and precise records and reports;
- to establish an initial database of statements that can be refined, reshaped and expanded by teachers as their own classroom activities proceed.

These statements can, we believe, help teachers to describe growth points in children's language development in both specific and global ways.

Further, these statements also have significant potential in shaping positive classroom learning situations.

Perhaps the most pressing reason for organising the collection of descriptive statements in Part 2 according to the modes of language is to respond to the needs of the audience for school reports — students and their parents. They require an exact description of language strengths and weaknesses if they are to work with teachers to promote language growth. It is important, too, that these readers of school reports understand the professional aims of organising such activities as compiling a class newspaper or conducting interviews with people in the local community. If, for example, a student writes a story book for younger children, exactly what has she achieved by doing this? Her achievement can be described by reference to a range of learning in reading, talking, listening and thinking as well as in writing. A database of statements about each of the modes, and about ways of working, can remind us of the breadth of such an achievement, and help us to write detailed, clear and valid reports.

GOALS AND ACTIVITIES

For some activities described in Part 2, we have described goals that relate to the work to be done by students. For other activities, we have described goals incidentally in the text. Sometimes, too, working on a particular activity is a goal in itself, and so does not need to be described.

Opportunities for students' self-assessment are also described briefly within the context of activities. Approaches to and formats for self-assessment and record-keeping by students, as well as by teachers, are described more fully in Part 3.

ASKING QUESTIONS THAT FOCUS OBSERVATION

The chart 'Asking questions that focus observation' shown overleaf illustrates the kind of questions that might be asked about various classroom activities. The chart includes only a sample of such questions and clearly does not cover the very wide range of developments that might be anticipated in such contexts. However, there are occasions when teachers want to see whether or not certain things are happening — perhaps because they haven't happened yet, or because students need to consolidate their abilities in particular areas.

Asking questions that focus observation

As students work on activities and tasks, signs of development can be observed. Asking questions based on a working knowledge of what is likely to happen can provide a focus for this observation.

Activity	Examples of focusing questions
Creating wall stories *Year 2*	Does the student • respond to classroom instructions? • participate in telling a story? • recognise cause and effect? • suggest new ideas? • predict use of words?
Writing a story *Year 4*	• read his or her writing to others? • use oral language to fill in the gaps in his or her writing? • develop ideas in interesting ways? • use a logical sequence?
Listening to a reading by an expert reader *Year 5*	• listen to stories? • listen attentively with or without the text? • ask and seek answers to questions? • recall facts and information? • join in discussion?
Reading newspaper articles *Year 6*	• retell information to others? • locate main ideas in text? • expand ideas and information from text? • evaluate text from personal experience? • make appropriate notes about information in text?
Dramatised reading of short story (groups) *Year 6*	• make suggestions to the group? • help the group develop a plan of action? • respond imaginatively to text? • use lively speech? • retell stories in interesting ways?
Group writing of captions for photos of the class excursion *Year 7*	• write captions to accompany pictures? • show understanding of logical sequence? • experiment with different ways of writing information? • help and encourage others? • work well as a member of a group?
Cloze activity with a poem *Year 8*	• predict a range of suitable words? • scrutinise text for detail? • listen to the other person's ideas? • interpret figurative language? • establish effective working relationships with a partner?
Rewriting a newspaper report as a poem (pairs) *Year 9*	• write in various forms? • experiment with various ways of expressing ideas? • choose appropriate words? • express ideas concisely? • show willingness to learn from others?

Activity	Examples of focusing questions
Reviewing novels for the school newspaper *Year 11*	▪ talk and write about literature? ▪ write fluently about texts? ▪ talk and write about personal response to texts? ▪ make appropriate notes in a journal or log? ▪ understand authors' purposes?
Forum on social issue *Year 12*	▪ clearly define an issue? ▪ raise related issues? ▪ make relevant and constructive comments? ▪ show an alert and open-minded attitude?

The observations and descriptions of what might actually be recognised are explored in the following chapters. Part 3 offers a perspective on recording and reporting development and achievement. These observations and descriptions are derived from asking informed questions — the questions about likely developments in students' learning that teachers bring to classroom action — and from the classroom action itself: that is, what students show they can and cannot do.

In Chapter 3, The whole context, we provided an illustration of how much can be learnt about students' development by observing them at work in purposeful classroom contexts. What further questions about likely development can be answered from observations of students at work, and when responding to the outcomes of that work?

We begin with talking and listening, because of the ways in which experience in these modes underlies much language learning.

4 TALKING AND LISTENING

TALKING AND LISTENING IN THE CLASSROOM

Talking and listening occur in the context of social interaction, as people communicate with each other for a multiplicity of purposes. The range of everyday purposes for talking and listening is extensive:
- giving and receiving messages, instructions and directions
- telling stories
- conversing
- describing
- reporting
- demonstrating
- explaining
- speculating
- problem-solving
- planning
- interviewing
- telephoning.

In English classrooms, the same diversity of purposes can be seen in oral language interaction. In assessing students' development and achievement as talkers and listeners, it is important to take a broad view of the ways in which students are able to accomplish many different purposes through talking and listening.

When oral communication is the focus of assessment, the most effective contexts for observing and describing development and achievement will be those where students are engaged in authentic situations, and where talking and listening are essential ways of achieving the participants' purposes. These contexts will vary extensively, and will include occasions when students talk freely to share personal experiences, ask for explanations, work in groups to solve a problem, talk with a partner about an issue raised in their reading, or present a report of a project to the whole class.

It is in such working contexts that the ways in which individual students demonstrate their competence in oral language can be assessed. These contexts will encompass a broad range of activities and will provide signs of learning in reading and writing as well as in talking and listening.

Different classroom activities involve participants and spectators in a range of different roles and relationships, in varied contexts, for many different purposes, and differ widely according to the subject matter. These variations all influence the nature of language usage and all need to be taken into account, especially in the assessment of development and competence in oral language.

ASSESSING A WIDE RANGE OF ACHIEVEMENT IN TALKING AND LISTENING

The transience of speech and the invisibility of listening present special problems of assessment. If we wish to assess language use within authentic, interactive learning contexts, a decision to assess the flow of talk on the spot can create limitations, either for individuals or for participants in group discussions. Students are less likely to respond in natural, authentic ways if they are conscious that what they say will be assessed — by the teacher writing something in a record-book, or by tape-recording — every time they open their mouths. Competence in oral language is demonstrated in so many different ways that it is difficult to catch the whole picture regarding individual students. The ability to contribute ideas to a fast-moving discussion, or to put a half-formulated idea tentatively into words, is as significant as the ability to give a prepared talk to the whole class. Again, it is difficult to know whether or not a student has listened attentively, since there are few reliable outward signs of this ability, and often, unexpectedly and in a different context, students produce work that relates to attentive listening during a much earlier activity.

A very wide range of oral work can be assessed in English. The most realistic measures of achievement in the use of language are:
• the effectiveness of the ways in which the speakers' or listeners' purposes are achieved; and

• the degree of appropriateness of the language interaction to the context.

When the classroom program establishes a range of contexts where many abilities in oral language are developed and used, opportunities can be provided for all students to achieve significant purposes through talking and listening. Students' development can then be recognised and described without the need to interrupt or record snatches of informal

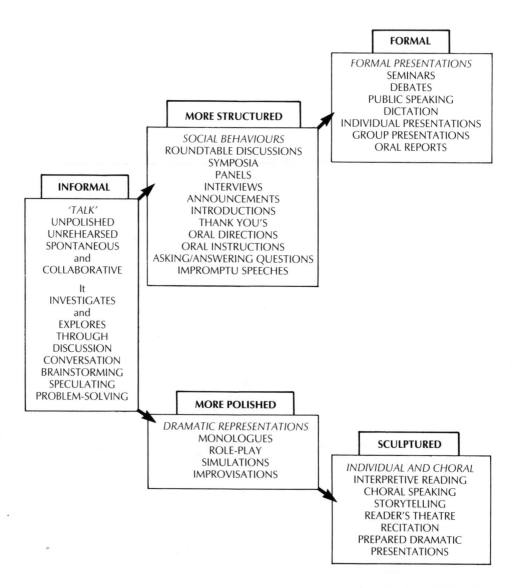

FORMAL

FORMAL PRESENTATIONS
SEMINARS
DEBATES
PUBLIC SPEAKING
DICTATION
INDIVIDUAL PRESENTATIONS
GROUP PRESENTATIONS
ORAL REPORTS

MORE STRUCTURED

SOCIAL BEHAVIOURS
ROUNDTABLE DISCUSSIONS
SYMPOSIA
PANELS
INTERVIEWS
ANNOUNCEMENTS
INTRODUCTIONS
THANK YOU'S
ORAL DIRECTIONS
ORAL INSTRUCTIONS
ASKING/ANSWERING QUESTIONS
IMPROMPTU SPEECHES

INFORMAL

'TALK'
UNPOLISHED
UNREHEARSED
SPONTANEOUS
and
COLLABORATIVE

It
INVESTIGATES
and
EXPLORES
THROUGH
DISCUSSION
CONVERSATION
BRAINSTORMING
SPECULATING
PROBLEM-SOLVING

MORE POLISHED

DRAMATIC REPRESENTATIONS
MONOLOGUES
ROLE-PLAY
SIMULATIONS
IMPROVISATIONS

SCULPTURED

INDIVIDUAL AND CHORAL
INTERPRETIVE READING
CHORAL SPEAKING
STORYTELLING
READER'S THEATRE
RECITATION
PREPARED DRAMATIC
PRESENTATIONS

(from Mowbray, 1987, p. 12)

classroom conversations. If students achieve significant outcomes, we can assume that many signs of development in oral language that are less reliably observed have also been evident.

The useful categorisation shown in the diagram on p. 58 demonstrates the range of classroom contexts that might provide such evidence.

USING SMALL GROUPS

In many classroom contexts, oral activity is clearly a powerful way of helping students develop a broader range of language competence. Small-group work is particularly significant.

Small-group discussion can be used for many purposes and is an important classroom activity. In small groups, students can actively engage with different kinds of texts; sort out, clarify and extend their understanding of issues; talk their way into solving problems; plan ways of working on set tasks; or share developing responses to what they have read or viewed. In small groups, they are able to reflect on what they have learned, in collaborative social settings that do not pose risks.

The small group offers security which can help students to feel confident about using the expressive, tentative, exploratory, thinking-aloud kind of informal language which supports learning. The small group offers a context in which other people's viewpoints can be considered, so that individual perspectives can be expanded. Reading, for example — often a private activity — becomes more active, productive and enjoyable when responses are shared, and a community of readers becomes established in the classroom.

The cooperative context of small-group activity also promotes respon-sibility and accountability among the students involved. When a group of students is working in collaboration on a project, group members rely on each other to undertake and complete tasks important to the success of the group's project. Group members need to listen to each other, to make suggestions to help the work of the group, to monitor the effectiveness of their cooperative activity — all of which can help the teacher to provide accurate descriptions of students' development in talking and listening.

In these ways, small-group activity can be a valuable means of provid-ing evidence of students' abilities, in both processes and outcomes. It can also:
- help the teacher to play a supportive and resourceful teaching role;
- through the groups' own records of work they have done, reduce the need to interrupt discussions; and
- reduce the need for the teacher to play the role of continuous assessor.

THE RANGE OF ORAL LANGUAGE ACTIVITIES

Activities which incorporate oral language into classroom programs can be broadly categorised as follows:

1 Individual student talk — informal
2 Individual student talk — formal
3 Small-group activities
4 Whole-class activities
5 Games
6 Simulations and role plays
7 Reading aloud
8 Activities focusing awareness of spoken language
9 Special presentations.

Many possible oral activities are encompassed within these categories. Some activities are 'warm-ups', useful for encouraging talk in the classroom; other activities relate to particular aspects of the English program:

■ WARM-UPS

- Students are asked to describe an everyday article without mentioning what it is, and without using their hands to demonstrate. The rest of the class write down what they think the article is and comment on the speaker's ability in describing.
- Set the scene — a park bench, a sporting match, a disco. Choose the characters — a crotchety old man and a mischievous little boy, or let the students characterise themselves. Characters start a conversation. The conversation ends when one of the characters leaves.
- Telling continuous stories requires each person to add one sentence to make a story. This can be varied — maybe more than one sentence is added, or students have to omit or include a particular topic.
- All students write a couple of paragraphs on an interesting experience. In threes, they leave the room and choose one of the stories. All then return to the classroom, pretending that the incident happened to them. Questions are asked by all other class members, who try to work out whose story it actually was.
- Two students choose a hat from a pile of different hats in the circle and start a conversation appropriate to the 'character'.
- Pairing: at odd times ask students to talk with a partner, telling each other about something, such as a chapter in a book, the previous day's lesson, a possible or probable future.

■ ACTIVITIES RELATING TO PARTICULAR ASPECTS OF ENGLISH

- Oral book reviews: ask students to talk about a book they are currently reading. This encourages class members to read and share books and authors.
- Give a demonstration with a talk, on a topic about which the speaker has some expertise — e.g. judo.
- Panel role play: discuss an issue, then set up a panel of 'experts' who are invited to give their opinion on the topic according to their role. The class ask questions which require the experts to answer in character.
- Presentation of a situation (e.g. car accident, finding of stolen money): three or four students report on the situation in role (passenger in car, belligerent truck driver, policeman, passer-by, child). The emphasis here is on language appropriate to characters and situation, and the role play can lead to experiments in writing.

These and similar activities can be used on their own, perhaps to encourage confidence, or to relate to other projects. They can sometimes form part of an overall teaching strategy, for instance in a writing workshop, or in preparation for a performance unit. Other opportunities for oral interaction often occur during extended projects, such as the production of a newspaper, the compiling of an oral history, or a theme study. The value of such extended projects lies in the ways they integrate and generate many different uses of language.

Engagement in a wide variety of oral language activities can also provide evidence of students' development of cooperative approaches to learning, as well as their abilities as talkers and listeners. For example:

- working together to develop a script or to perform a role play, or sharing anecdotes about their own experience, involves the need to listen to others, and to build on others' ideas and responses;
- making plans and taking action in a research project, or talking about what they would have done if they had been a particular character in a novel, involves the need to express ideas to share with others, and a preparedness to respond to others' ideas;
- listening to a talk by another student involves taking on the role of an attentive listener.

Oral work gives students experience in purposeful collaborative activity, as well as opportunities to express themselves, and to listen thoughtfully to others. When students:

- listen to others;
- act upon advice from others;
- talk to a group about a topic of personal interest;
- vary presentation of ideas to suit particular audiences and contexts;
- help other people to participate in discussions and activities; or
- suggest lines of inquiry in group projects,

their developing abilities in talking and listening can be observed, as well as their development as learners.

STUDENTS' SELF-ASSESSMENT

Students themselves often recognise what is happening in oral communication situations:

> . . . you have to get your ideas straight if you're going to participate in discussions. It helps develop your ability to correlate material. If you've got to research a topic and present it verbally, you're really on the spot. If it's not ordered and reasonably presentable, you look a bit of an idiot! So it has helped me to make sure that my writing is well-presented — that's a natural result of putting your ideas in order.

> . . . you have to learn to work together because you can't all talk at once. It just doesn't get you anywhere. So we've developed: you hear other people talking and, instead of just raving on, you stop and listen. In the first few lessons, we taped our discussions to see who was talking over each other and there were so many times when we tried to battle it out.

> [At our performance] we knew that we'd have an audience that would be able to understand what we were trying to put across. It was a really contoured performance, wasn't it? Even some of the lines, some of the actual lines we wrote, were written with particular members of the audience in mind.

> (Meiers, 1983, p. 5)

These students were reflecting on their participation in a group project which led to an oral presentation to an audience — a project in which the processes and outcomes were essentially in the oral mode. When students are given such opportunities to reflect on their participation in oral activity, they can recognise what has been achieved, and thus give feedback on their own learning.

HIGHLIGHTING ORAL LANGUAGE IN THE CLASSROOM PROGRAM

The status of oral language, in comparison with written language, has become more firmly established in English and language arts programs, and teachers continue to report positive developments when they give oral work a higher profile. One teacher reported what happened when she reorganised her Year 8 teaching program to include many more opportunities for talk. She had been concerned that she had not been giving students sufficient opportunity to practise talking, and to develop confidence. She describes the changes she made:

I moved my desk from the front of the room and grouped student desks in clusters of four. Groups larger than five tend to be less productive because group members have to wait so long to have a say. For the first two weeks I assigned students to particular groups. At the end of a fortnight, after there had been considerable discussion on our aims and progress, I allowed students to choose their own groups . . .

The writing program seemed to lend itself to an oral language approach. I explained to the class that the group was expected to help each other with ideas, editing and spelling, and that I was available for these tasks for the whole group rather than individuals. I also explained that successful completion of the writing assignment would also involve a demonstration of a preparedness to work and talk to the group. I asked that they keep a regular diary or log of their conversations: what they talked about, what they learnt, what role they played in the group — whether listener, leader, ideas person, etc.

The first two weeks were very noisy and little writing appeared to be happening but as the deadline approached I was interested to see more students turn to their group for help rather than to me. The writing that resulted was less trivial, showed greater depth of development in plot and character but also had more grammatical and spelling errors.

(Hogan, 1987, p. 71)

This description of classroom experience suggests that the physical arrangement of the classroom helps to establish a working climate where abilities in talking and listening can be effectively promoted. Here is a description of one such arrangement:

In the ideal classroom, furniture which can be moved quickly and easily to accommodate particular activities and modes of presentation is essential. It should be easy to facilitate:
- small group work
- plenary sessions
- a space for dramatic presentation
- opportunities to work with writing partners
- holding conferences
- clustering around an overhead projector, teacher, students or object
- reading aloud
- choral readings
- varied approaches to the publication of written products
- movement to resources within the classroom.

(Education Department of South Australia, 1987, p. 42)

Students' feedback on the importance of the learning climate in their classroom indicates how this affects their learning in both positive and negative ways. The two journal entries which follow show how these students were influenced by the general learning climate in their class:

> Mrs X's lessons are really good. You have these big discussions and really you don't think you're learning anything, but at the end of the lesson you know ever so much more than you did before.

> Teachers won't really listen to you. They've always got half an eye on what everyone else is doing. I was talking to Miss X and in the middle of it she walked off and told these other kids off. I felt really silly.

(Torbe and Medway, 1981, p. 00)

Sometimes the learning situation will go beyond the classroom, as in the case of the work done by one group of students in running a radio program. The learning potential of this work was recognised and supported by parents, who provided funds for new equipment for the school radio station, to create further possibilities for students to develop oral language abilities in real contexts.

ORAL LANGUAGE AND CURRICULUM PLANNING

Although talking and listening are the language modes most frequently used in school, they have received relatively little attention in curriculum planning. In the program described above (Hogan, 1987), oral work was well integrated with writing. It is also possible to plan whole units of work that give prominence to talking and listening in the flow of activities and work requirements. For example, in the shared reading of a novel, work requirements can be directed towards a range of oral activities such as taking part in group discussion, reporting to the whole class, reading aloud, conducting a research interview, presenting an oral book report, or preparing a dramatised reading. All these activities flow into the exploration of the book, creating many opportunities for deepening response. Reading aloud, for example, extends literary response in various ways:

> A reader reads to someone, the listener, and shapes the reading to match the needs of his listener as well as the requirements of the text. Such shaping involves strategies like varying tone, pace, pitch and rhythm. In presenting a text to an audience we are really presenting our own interpretation of that text, whether the presentation is spontaneous or rehearsed.

(Meiers and McGregor, 1988, pp. 5–6)

However, there is evidence that the ways in which talking and listening are valued do not always reflect the place of oral work in class activity. From a longitudinal study of English classrooms, Wells and Gen Ling Chan (1986) comment that, although there now appear to be many opportunities for informal talk in English classrooms:

> there are, according to our data, few classrooms in which pupils are given the opportunity to engage in sustained, task-oriented discussion with their peers or to speak at length on a topic on which, either inside or outside the school, they have acquired expertise.

> (pp. 129–30)

This finding is a reminder of the need to offer the broadest possible range of opportunities for students to use language for many different purposes, and to support them in recognising what features of language are appropriate to particular contexts.

CONSIDERATIONS IN ASSESSING TALKING AND LISTENING

When achievement and development in talking and listening are to be assessed, there are a number of considerations:
- The oral communication which is being assessed should reflect the complex range of oral activities important in adult life.
- Valid assessment should sample a broad range of oral communication purposes and contexts.
- Assessment must take into account the processes of spoken language use as well as of any products presented for the purposes of evaluation.
- The approaches to record-keeping and assessment must not be time-consuming nor too complex to operate in the normal course of teaching.
- Recording formats which can be used with a range of speech activities are useful in the assessment of oral language.
- A range of other methods of collecting evidence of the processes of language use will be useful.

Furthermore, it is important to consider tentative, exploratory talk as well as more fully-shaped talk, as Pat Jones notes in a commentary on the status of the assessment of oral communication as part of the GCSE in England:

> we should seek to encourage and develop this more tentative, exploratory

kind of talk where pupils are not so much stating understanding as moving towards it. It is vital too, that we seek to assess this kind of talk as valuable in itself, and not as a first draft, to be thrown away once the final, fully-shaped version emerges.

(Jones, 1988, p. 169)

CLASSROOM CONTEXTS FOR OBSERVING AND DESCRIBING DEVELOPMENT

In what follows, we have aimed to illustrate ways of observing and describing students' development in a variety of classroom situations. Several different classroom episodes are presented, from across the years of schooling. For each episode, we show the variety of signs of learning and development which can be observed amongst the group of students. A set of tasks in which students work towards meeting specified goals, and the criteria by which their success in achieving those goals can be judged, provides a further perspective on appropriate ways in which to assess achievement and development.

We have also included, at the end of this chapter and at the end of those on reading and writing, examples of formats on which it is possible to build up a record of students' development. These records can contribute to a profile of the student's abilities in many dimensions of language, and can also be used as the basis for discussions with students, in helping them to reflect on their own learning and progress, and to set new learning goals.

▪CLASSROOM CONTEXTS

In the next section of this chapter we describe a series of classroom episodes which involved a great deal of oral interaction, and which grew from situations where the students had real purposes for talking and listening. These episodes provide a basis for identifying statements which can be made about growth in oral competencies. In this way, we hope to highlight the interconnections between the various elements in the

establishment of effective and supportive climates for learning in English with students of any age. These elements include:
- the teacher's role in designing classroom programs, setting goals, and observing and describing development;
- the repertoire of activities which teachers encourage students to explore in English;
- the students' role in initiating and planning their own work; and
- the sharing of goals and of the criteria by which the achievements of each student can be described and evaluated.

EPISODES FROM THE CLASSROOM

One way of assessing oral English is to set up a simulation of a real-life situation, or a task which will require the participants to use oral language in particular ways. For example, two students could be seated one each side of a screen and asked to conduct a simulated telephone conversation to arrange an outing together, while the teacher 'eaves-dropped' on the conversation, supposedly assessing their competence as users of the telephone.

However, in real life there are many factors which determine one's successful use of the telephone: the availability of the person being called, the exactness with which information is expressed, replies to questions, the urgency of the matter, the length of time available to talk, and interruptions. These variables affect the context of the conversation in many ways, and it is often the skills of the speaker in responding flexibly to these variables which determines the effectiveness of the use of the telephone. The simulated conversation cannot create this real life variability, and so the test, or contrived situation, does not generate information on the subject's actual skill.

In the English classroom there are countless occasions for talking, listening, reading and writing which arise naturally as students engage in a wide range of activities. Helping another student to use the word processor requires skill in explanation as well as in writing; sharing a response to a literary text draws on the ability to read and understand and to put thoughts and feelings into words; giving a report of a small-group discussion involves careful listening and accurate recall or recording of detail. We suggest that the observation of students operating in these contexts provides the best basis for assessing development.

If we acknowledge that:

the key to effective teaching is building on what students have already learned . . . the best way to discover this is to listen and watch closely as children use language — spoken and written — in different settings and circumstances . . . careful observations over time will reveal individual styles and patterns of language use. As patterns emerge, teachers can reflect on them, comparing the information to past observations and to their knowledge of language development, to determine what their students know (competence) and can do (skill) with language.

(Jagger and Smith-Burke, 1985)

The following series of classroom episodes involved groups of students from Years K–12 in some very purposeful talking and listening. What signs of development are observed in such situations? How can they be described?

EPISODE ONE: INFORMAL TALK IN YEAR 1

The teaching goal in this situation was to encourage students to talk freely together, building and maintaining relationships through talk. Opportunities such as this help to teach children that talking and listening to each other are valued activities in the classroom.

The actual example is set in a Grade 1 classroom, but opportunities for informal talk can occur at any level of schooling.

Two 6-year-old boys, good friends, are building with Lego blocks in a corner of the classroom. This transcript represents about fifteen minutes of the time they spent on this activity:

Michael: I know, I've got a great idea.
Simon: Let's make something lovely.
Michael: Like a lighthouse, with a light flashing on and off.
Simon: Yep.
Michael: Hey, yeah, that's a great idea. I'm going to do it.
Pause

Michael: (*sings*) 'Woopity do, how are you . . .' etc
Together: 'Slide off a fence and rip your pants
And see the little fishes do the hootchy cootchy dance.'
Simon: Here's a light. I'm making . . .
Pause

Michael: (*sings*) 'see the little fishes'
Simon: This is a star. This is the flash.
Michael: (*sings*)
Simon: This is going to be the rock . . . it sits on.
It sits out here . . .
Pause

Simon: It's wrong . . .
Michael: No it doesn't . . .
Simon: It's meant to join. Oh. yeah.

Michael:	Rats . . .

Pause

Simon:	Fiona sneezes now.
Michael:	What?
Simon:	Fiona sneezes.
Michael:	Oh . . . so does Anna.
Simon:	I know. And she gets the hiccups.
Michael:	So does Anna.
Simon:	Here's the rock it sits on.
Michael:	She's growing from a baby into a big girl, isn't she?
Simon:	Yeah . . . and Fiona.
Michael:	So is my little, little big sister . . . Guess what . . . Give it to me, you're wrecking it . . . you've wrecked it.
Simon:	Hey, Mike, stick it on the rock.
Michael:	On the rock?
Simon:	Here's the rock.
Michael:	I know it is, but I've got to stick it on my . . .
Simon:	Oh, I wish . . .

Pause

Michael:	Hey, doesn't this work?
Simon:	Look, ya must . . . push it real hard and that has a flash . . . now . . . I'll push it up now . . . now . . . now where's this? . . . Oh, that's what. Have you got one of these lights?
Michael:	No.
Simon:	Costs about five dollars.
Michael:	There . . .

Pause

Simon:	Hey, let's make an ocean.
Michael:	Yep, we'll still keep this up here, won't we?
Simon:	Yeah. Don't join that on. That's a bit. This is on a ship.
Michael:	Now let me have a go switching it on and off, can I? Now . . . can I? Just let go, would you?
Simon:	Hey, the ship. I have to press this down.
Michael:	Or won't it work?
Simon:	Mmm. Just wait, Mikey, just wait, just wait. We're going to get some rocks. Stop fiddling with it, it will bust . . . and you'll have to buy some more.
Michael:	I'm going to make a big steam-roller ship.
Simon:	And I'll . . . Is it working?
Michael:	Yeah, it's working.

Pause

Michael:	(*sings*) 'Did you ever . . .
Together:	. . . go fishing on a bright summer day sitting on a fence, and the fence gave way, slide off the fence, and rip your pants, and see the little fishes do the cootchy cootchy dance.'

Simon:	Hey, Mike, I've got one now . . . In paddle steamer . . . (*clatter of Lego blocks*) . . . I'm trying to find the little thing . . . take this wire out . . . (*clatter*) . . . Oh, no . . . now I've got one of these . . . (*clatter*) . . . This is the paddle steamer, Mike.
Michael:	Is it?
Simon:	Yep. Hey, where's your other, hey Mike, stick it on this ship, 'cos this is a switch — on, this is a paddle steamer, a paddle steamer.
Michael:	Oh, like you were talking about it.

Pause

Simon:	I know where they are.
Michael:	What's this for? Si, what's this for?
Simon:	Hey, where's my Simon's motor thing? Here it is.
Michael:	Si, what's this for?
Simon:	It's a grader thing.

Pause

Michael:	Mm, mm, mm, mm,
Simon:	You make your paddle steamer, and I'll make mine.
Michael:	I'm going to make a speed boat.

Pause, clatter

Simon:	This is the . . .
Michael:	Now . . . rrrr brrr, it's going to be in short, in short, with it? A very, very short speed boat.

Pause

Michael:	(*sings under breath*) '. . . cootchy, cootchy dance . . .'
Simon:	This is going to be the ship. It's a paddle steamer . . . Oh, yeah, here's the motor.
Michael:	Motor boat, motor, motor, motor boat . . . Si? Oh, it's alright. I'm going to make a house boat . . . and a big one, now . . .
Simon:	This is the water tester — going out in the water . . . it tests the water . . .
Michael:	Brrm . . .
Simon:	One day, the house, lighthouse wasn't going, working, and the ski-boat crashed, and lost one of his skis . . . and he was skiing on one . . . and he crashed again . . . and then the light was working . . . Then he hit the rock, and he's murdered himself . . . Then they tried to find it, and they lost him.
Michael:	Chop.
Simon:	This is a sea-plane, and looks out for wrecked boats.

Pause

Michael:	Brrm, brrm.
Simon:	Here's the rock. Brrm, brrm. I've got control lighthouse landing . . . sssss . . . well, we've landed, well . . . look! . . . Say your house boat has crashed, on a rock.
Michael:	Right here.

Signs of achievement
In the course of this exchange, these boys demonstrate their competence in:

- sharing ideas
- making decisions
- agreeing on action
- describing objects
- exchanging information
- giving instructions
- explaining reasons for actions
- suggesting cooperation
- asking questions
- answering questions
- recognising and expressing problems and solutions
- using descriptive words and phrases
- expressing intentions
- telling imaginative stories
- listening to imaginative stories
- listening to others' ideas.

EPISODE TWO: SHOWING AND TELLING

Sitting in a close group on the carpet, the Grade 2 class has organised itself for a session of showing and telling each other about interesting things. This is a daily event, and the focus is always directly on talking and listening. In this situation, talk is not a prelude to writing, nor does it occur incidentally as part of reading or writing activities. It is a talking session, because it is so often through talk that learning takes place.

People take it in turns to be the leader, and everyone understands about the importance of listening attentively to what others are saying, of taking turns, of trying to speak clearly, of not interrupting, and of asking questions which show interest and encourage the speaker. The whole situation is a cooperative one. The teacher is a member of the group, and early in the year spent a lot of time working out, with the class, the ground rules for these sessions.

Today the focus is on special things. Two children have brought objects which have special value for them. To start, the first speaker describes the piece of fossilised wood she found on a camping trip with her family. The piece of rock is passed around, and people comment on the way they can see the wood grain, and how smooth and hard it feels. They ask lots of questions seeking further information, about how wood can turn into rock, and where the piece was found. The owner can answer some of the questions, and the teacher helps out with a tricky one. The group leader notices when different people have questions, and creates opportunities for them: 'It's Tony's turn now', 'Maria's been waiting to say . . .'.

A second speaker produces a new toy — a robot which can be transformed into a car. It was given to him by his grandmother, and he carefully explains how it works, demonstrating the steps in the transformation. When it's passed around, some people explore the way it works; others start describing similar toys of their own. This generates a series of personal anecdotes about special toys. Someone asks: 'What could you use it for?'

At this stage, the class divide into small groups, and each group brainstorms as many ideas as they can think of about possible uses for a 'transformer'. Nobody's ideas are rejected. After five minutes, each group chooses one idea, and a reporter is chosen to explain their idea to the rest of the class. After the reporting session, the teacher explains some of the arrangements for the games activity planned for that afternoon, and then the whole class goes outside for a short Phys. Ed. session.

Signs of achievement

Although there is considerable individual variation (not all students in the group show all the signs of development listed here), within the context of this shared activity, individuals within the group show their ability in:

- asking appropriate questions when seeking information
- retelling stories and describing experiences
- expressing opinions as part of the discussion
- recognising and expressing problems and their solutions
- referring in detail to incidents and sequences of events
- making comparisons and describing relationships
- listening to other people's stories
- maintaining the interest of the listener
- using lively, animated speech
- listening to others' ideas
- participating in discussion
- sharing ideas with others clearly and logically.

EPISODE THREE: CHOOSING BOOKS TO READ

After an introductory session introducing a set of book packs, each pack containing a number of titles, loosely linked by theme, groups of four children in a combined Grade 3/4 class were invited to explore one book pack. Individuals in the group were then to choose one book to read, with the goal of later talking about this book with the rest of the group.

As children explored the contents of the book pack, they talked about the covers, read snatches from the publisher's blurb, asked questions about the title, or referred to previous encounters with particular titles: 'Oh, I read that at home — it's funny . . .'; or with particular authors: 'I like her books . . . have you read . . .?'. In some cases, some students were very familiar with particular titles, and launched into detailed re-tellings which reflected their enjoyment of these books. They browsed through the books, sometimes becoming 'hooked' by the beginning, and starting to read on. The books in this pack varied in length, and it was interesting to note how some children in the groups initially selected the obviously shorter books, but were attracted to look at some of the longer books when others in the group expressed an interest in these books.

As the time came for choices to be finalised, some negotiation occurred when more than one student in the group wanted to read the same title: 'Well, you read it first, then give it to me . . .'; 'I'll read it quickly, so you won't have to wait long . . .'. Finally, every student recorded the title of the book selected in the checklist in the book pack, and the class began a session of sustained silent reading with the new books.

Signs of achievement
As these students made decisions about which books they were going to read, their behaviour provided much evidence of their behaviour as readers — in skimming, scanning, browsing, responding to titles, cover designs, and making predictions. They also demonstrated a wide range of oral abilities:

- listening to spoken instructions
- making decisions
- offering reasons for choices
- asking appropriate questions
- sharing knowledge of books with others
- re-telling parts of stories
- reading aloud
- negotiating action
- collaborating with others through speech
- using speech in an informal working context
- sharing experiences with others
- expressing opinions
- listening attentively to others.

EPISODE FOUR: COMPUTER TALK

This episode began when a small group of Year 6 children listened attentively to the teacher explaining the nature of a new word-processing program for the class computer. The children in this class were already practised in using the computer, familiar with basic commands, and reasonably experienced in keyboard skills. Children in the group asked questions, and commented on similarities with the program they had previously been using.

The teacher demonstrated aspects of the new program: delete and insert functions, how to scroll back and forth through the text, how to change font styles and sizes, how to make paragraph breaks, how to save files and how to search through a document for key words.

She then invited the group to take turns to work in pairs with the new program, jointly composing a short report for the school newspaper about the visit to the class of a guest speaker earlier in the day. The pairs worked comfortably together, sharing the tasks of using the keyboard to enter the text, experimenting, asking questions and explaining, reminding each other of things the teacher had explained. It was interesting to see how they were confident in expressing tentative understandings of the new program: 'I think you can . . .', 'Maybe . . .' They recalled details from the speaker's talk, and discussed the most appropriate way they could order the information in the report, then as a result of this exchange moved pieces of text within the document. They re-read the growing text continuously, revising, deleting and adding as they went.

Signs of achievement

As the group of students listened to the explanation, and then worked in collaboration on the writing task, they demonstrated a range of oral capacities:

- attending to teacher explanation
- using speech to explain
- using speech to provide and share information in different situations
- repeating ideas in different words
- asking questions
- expressing tentative understanding of new knowledge
- making connections with previous experience
- listening to and carrying out spoken instructions
- recalling information from a talk
- listening to and acting on others' ideas
- collaborating through speech and listening
- discussing different possibilities
- using talk for collaborative composition.

EPISODE FIVE: TALKING ABOUT POETRY

In Year 6, the teacher asked students to read 'Back Steps Lookout' by Rhyll McMaster, a mysterious descriptive poem with no regular pattern of rhyme. First, she read the poem to students and then asked them to read to each other in a small group. This meant that they had each heard several readings of the poem. Students were asked to write a list of questions about the poem — anything that came to their minds. Questions included:

- What is a 'silhouette of my head'?
- How can a silhouette of my head 'boat' the shallows?

- What is 'the brief dark'?
- Why doesn't the poem rhyme?
- How can mangoes 'stalk with crabs' eyes'?
- What are 'footpads with no feet'?
- Is what she sees from the back steps good or bad?
- How can night have 'a wet temper'?

They then shared with other students in their groups the questions that they felt unable to answer. Other students were asked to try to answer as many of these questions as possible. In the group talk, it was clear that one or two questions caused much debate, with students returning to the poem to justify their views.

Students were asked to write a short piece in their reading logs describing any changes to their ideas about the poem which had occurred as a result of the group discussion.

Signs of achievement
Throughout this activity, students used and developed their competence in oral language in order to:

- ask and answer questions
- collaborate with others
- share ideas with others
- express understanding of the thoughts and feelings of others
- answer questions by justifying a point of view
- explain personal feelings
- comment on personal experiences
- listen to others' ideas and views
- read poetry
- listen to poems
- listen with or without the text
- use speech to develop and extend others' contributions
- use speech to explore texts
- use speech to comment on text
- revise ideas and opinions through interaction.

EPISODE SIX: INTERVIEWS

To prepare for a program of interviews as part of a project, Year 7 students were asked to write down five questions that they would like to be asked. They were asked to think of questions in areas such as personal experiences, interests, hobbies, likes and dislikes. Students chose partners and exchanged question sheets.

Using these sheets, students interviewed one another. They were asked to think of further questions to ask when they received brief answers or when they thought there might be more interesting information to be gained.

The students formed groups of four and prepared a report to the whole class about what sorts of questions were asked and why. From this discussion, they also indicated the questions that they thought produced the best answers.

Important goals of this activity were to help students become accustomed to asking and answering questions, to learn the kinds of questions to ask, and to learn about other people's ideas and opinions.

Signs of achievement
- talking about personal experience
- talking about their own ideas and thoughts to others
- interviewing other people to gain information
- formulating questions
- asking relevant questions
- asking for and giving information
- answering questions by providing information and opinions
- listening to and recalling facts
- listening to others' experiences and ideas
- making suggestions
- asking for and giving reasons
- directing a conversation
- expressing interest
- expressing uncertainty
- expressing preferences
- using speech to think out loud
- expressing support
- expressing personal insights and conjectures
- giving and receiving information in different situations
- talking about a topic of personal interest with others
- using speech to explore ideas and opinions
- using speech to explain and defend a personal view
- participating in discussions.

EPISODE SEVEN: WRITING WITH THE WORD-PROCESSOR

Three Apple Macintosh computers and a printer were available for two or three periods a week to a Year 9 English class. It was agreed, after discussion, that pairs of students would take it in turns to use the computers to collaborate on the writing of a story. Two copies of the completed story would be printed out to include in the students' writing folders. Another literature-based project occupied the students before or after their turn on the computer.

A brief explanation of the main features of the operation of the word-processing program for each pair led straight into a writing session. In some cases, students who had recently become familiar with the computer were able to explain its operation to another pair of students, and took responsibility for coming back to check that the students they had helped were managing. Initially, there was a lot of interest in the variety of print fonts and effects which could be obtained, and considerable experimentation with the design of striking headings — bold, shadowed, outlined, and in a range of fonts. However, this period of experimentation seemed to provide a context for making decisions about the topic of their story.

Each pair worked out ways of sharing the task — taking it in turns to key in the growing text, to keep notes of ideas, to suggest the way an idea could be expressed, to review what had been written so far, to note where extra information was needed. They shared their growing knowledge of how to use the computer: 'No, I think you do this . . .', 'When I did it, this is how it worked . . .'

There was as much talking as writing whilst these stories took shape. Some pairs discovered how to move text from one place to another, and rearranged the sequence of paragraphs. One pair had trouble organising their work in paragraphs, but were delighted to find that when they read it aloud, they could hear the natural breaks and were simply able to insert paragraph breaks at appropriate points, and see the newly-formatted piece appear instantly.

Much care was given to proofreading — especially of spelling. Some groups went hunting for their dictionaries. Some students talked for a long time about the exact word they wanted to use in a particular place, and took a printout of the draft to someone else to read when asking for advice.

The computer created a context for a great variety of collaboration — on mastering a new tool, and on working closely together to compose a story.

Of course, in this context, there were many signs of learning which related directly to writing, but again it is the talk which generates ideas for action, shape and sequence.

Signs of achievement
- making group decisions about managing access to resources
- listening to explanations
- following instructions
- asking questions to clarify given information
- explaining
- instructing
- using speech to arrange ideas in sequence

- making suggestions about action to improve a piece of writing
- reading aloud as a reviewing process
- contributing ideas to a shared project
- responding to ideas suggested by others
- using oral language for planning
- maintaining working relationships with other people.

EPISODE EIGHT: INTERVIEW AND PUBLICATION

A group of Year 10 students had had the opportunity to talk with the editor of a student magazine with a wide circulation in secondary schools. They were familiar with the magazine, had enjoyed reading it for several years, and were interested to hear about some of the work editors do in producing such a magazine.

During their meeting, the discussion turned to the kinds of articles which might be included in future editions of the magazine, and which would be of high interest to teenage readers. As the ideas flowed, someone suggested that this group of students could themselves interview a well-known entertainer, and write up an article based on the interview. Everybody agreed that as teenagers themselves, they would be able to write in a way that would interest other teenagers. And so the seeds of a group project were sown.

Over the next few weeks contact had to be maintained with the editor as he explored with theatrical agents the feasibility of the idea, and obtained permission for the interview. The students therefore set themselves a number of tasks.

- discussion with their classmates about reasons why they, as a group of country students, should have the opportunity to meet a popular star;
- preparation of a letter from the group to confirm their interest in the suggestion. This letter began as a series of very rough notes, and was then transferred to the word processor as the group revised and shaped it to meet the needs of the situation. Because they were very anxious to carry out the interview, they wanted to maintain a good relationship with the editor, and so were very conscious of the readers for whom they were writing. The students' collaborative use of the word processor, as they tried to include ideas from different people, write the letter in an appropriate format, and create a coherent product, generated a great deal of purposeful talk;
- making several long distance phone calls to discuss the negotiations with the editor.

When the exciting news that two members of the group would be able to attend the press conference with an international pop group, a lot of work had to be done on deciding which members of the team would go, finalising arrangements for an overnight stay in the city, reading up on

Molly Meldrum, eat your heart out! Danielle Bunting (left), 15, and Leonie Van Donk, 16, interview Bon Jovi.

Bon Jovi, slippery when questions get personal

By DANIELLE BUNTING
and LEONIE VAN DONK,
of Leongatha Technical School

"City kids get it all," we complained to the editors of the Education Ministry's student magazine 'Pursuit'. "What about letting us interview someone famous for the magazine?"

That was the start of the adventure that brought us all the way from Fish Creek to Bon Jovi's plush suite in the Regency Hotel, Melbourne.

Yesterday, we arrived, complete in school uniforms, only to be asked politely to leave by a worried official. When we explained that we were there officially for the Bon Jovi news conference, we got the royal treatment.

We were ushered into the news conference room. After being jostled between pushing journalists and television cameras, Leonie finally stood on a chair to be seen and heard and was embarrassed when Jon Bon Jovi (the lead singer) asked if she was really that tall.

We didn't ask any more questions, but the organisers asked us back to do a quick personal interview. We couldn't believe it.

An hour or two later, we were sitting in front of the 'Terry Wil-lesee Tonight' cameras waiting for BJ to come into the room. We were so nervous, trying to find good questions to ask. But once the conversation started, we relaxed and just enjoyed their company.

We presented them with a Vegemite sandwich, a boomerang brooch and a little koala. They laughed at all that, but Jon put on the brooch and said he was going to wear it. They answered our questions and were very friendly.

They seemed to prefer the questions about their music to the personal ones, such as "Is being gorgeous necessary to your success?", which they sort of laughed off. It was all over so quickly. We got autographs, pictures and a couple of souvenir lollies from the coffee table as we left.

We headed back to the lifts and were still so excited that we wondered if we'd really done it.

Wait till the kids back at school hear about this!

● *Bon Jovi has produced the world's best-selling hard rock album of all time. 'Slippery When Wet' with sales of more than 12 million so far. The band's five Melbourne concerts, which begin tomorrow, have been sold out.*

the background of the group, and preparing likely interview questions. In the time between confirmation of the arrangements and the actual date of the interview, there was a lot of negotiation, further letter writing, research, and hard thinking about interviews.

The news clipping above indicates the success of the venture.

Unexpectedly, the opportunity arose to write this story for professional journalists, and a more detailed story was also written for publication in the student magazine. Reporting back on the experience to the whole class marked the apparent end of the venture, though the students recognised the possibilities for further work, and looked forward to the publication of their article.

This context illustrates how signs of development closely relate to the kind of work done. The activity generates situations in which certain kinds of oral abilities are developed and used.

Signs of achievement

- talking with others to find information
- negotiating with other group members to allocate tasks and responsibilities
- managing a series of long-distance phone calls
- using speech to explore ideas and justify actions
- using speech to make detailed plans
- interviewing adults to gain information, advice and opinion
- listening to advice on interviewing and report writing
- making decisions about relevant material, sequence and detail
- participating in a professional press conference
- expressing a point of view in a convincing way
- reporting outcomes to an audience
- recognising the relevance of appropriate dress and behaviour in particular contexts
- contributing to the shared production of a news story
- listening to presentation of outcomes
- talking with others about appropriate courses of action
- recognising and defining problems
- suggesting solutions to problems
- following instructions
- reporting on action to various audiences
- learning how to respond appropriately in various social contexts.

EPISODE NINE: PREPARATION OF A BIBLIOGRAPHY OF AUSTRALIAN LITERATURE

The focus of this project was the preparation of a bibliography of Australian literature held in the school library. The following account of the project comes from a series of reports included in a bicentennial publication on literature in education. As it has been described, the wide range of contexts for talking and listening becomes obvious.

A teacher comes from the USA on an exchange program to teach Year 11 English in a Victorian rural technical school. She has little knowledge of this country's literature, and would like to know more. It is likely, she thinks, that her Australian students — even if they know a bit more about it than she does — also have plenty to learn.

She negotiates a project with them: the class will work together to prepare an annotated bibliography of Australian writings available at that school's Resource Centre. Selections will be made by individuals according to their own interests, and information supplied to the teacher about the chosen texts will be stored by her on a word processor so that it can be augmented at any future stage. Meanwhile each contribution will be informative for the one who makes it as well as for fellow-students and the teacher.

How does the project turn out? Admirably. Much more than a biblio-graphical exercise, it becomes a process of literary discovery. A lot of books are being read purposefully, writing is being done as part of the shared responsibility, and some thinking and consciousness-raising about the field itself is inevitable. Without any formal fuss about defining 'Australian Litera-ture', the students must work out criteria for Australianness and for literature by making their own practical choices.

Does something marketed as 'for children' belong in a list of literary works? ('Although this won the Australian Children's Book of the Year award, it is by no means just for children. I think a mature reader would enjoy this book more', says the student reviewing Ruth Park's *Playing Beatie Bow*; while Randolph Stow's *Midnite* and Mem Fox's *Possum Magic* are also among those chosen.) Does biography count? (Alec Chisholm's *C. J. Dennis: His Remarkable Career*, and Frank Clune's *Ben Hall* are selected.) How long do authors have to live in this country if their writings are to qualify for inclusion? (Neville Shute gets a guernsey.) These are far from being academic quibbles when they arise out of something produced for a real audience.

The students are also gaining direct knowledge about some of the factors that intervene between the writing and the reading of literature: about the holdings of a particular resource centre, for instance, and about skills and information used by librarians or reviewers. (Who decides what gets chosen for comment, or purchase, in the book trade?) Decisions have to be made about the appropriate scope and quality of comments on the books. (When does neutral information become personal impression? Is that distinction valid? Does it matter?) And about the best format for presenting the findings. (What publication details should be provided with each listing?) The place of personal data about authors needs working out. (Are their habitats and hobbies relevant to an understanding of their writings?)

(Reid, 1987, p. 4)

Signs of achievement

- recognising and exploring questions related to the project
- finding information from specialists (librarians)
- asking questions
- answering questions
- listening to others' ideas
- sharing ideas with others
- explaining differences between texts
- understanding and carrying out instructions

- showing initiative in raising new and related issues
- justifying judgements made and proposed action to overcome a problem
- anticipating and recognising alternative courses of action
- negotiating a collaborative project
- maintaining cooperation within both small and large groups
- making and justifying decisions
- expressing a point of view
- expressing personal responses
- participating in task-oriented discussions.

EPISODE TEN: HYPOTHETICAL

As a project in Year 11, a student conducted a Hypothetical — a simulated conversation with a number of characters involved in a series of controversial or problematic situations. The focus of the Hypothetical was nuclear technology and stemmed from viewing the films *Silkwood* and *The China Syndrome*, and from reading newspaper files on the Chernobyl and Three Mile Island nuclear accidents. The students devised a narrative which linked contributions from most of the students in the class, who were cast as people involved in some important way in decisions about the viability of nuclear technology as a source of energy. The Hypothetical ran for 15 minutes.

Members of the audience called upon to participate in various roles were encouraged to stay in their characters and to think out courses of action that would be consistent with the positions allotted to them. Often the presenter returned to these characters when new complications were injected into the narrative, raising new problems to be solved.

The Hypothetical was not rehearsed or videotaped, and so it was sometimes difficult for the presenter to maintain the narrative in the face of spontaneous comments and interjections from members of the audience not directly involved.

Signs of achievement
- using speech to describe and narrate
- giving and receiving information in different situations
- verbal reporting of events
- listening to others' ideas and views
- showing initiative in raising new and related issues
- sustaining a character in role plays
- sustaining a point of view
- analysing a situation or issue
- justifying decisions and actions
- suggesting alternative courses of action
- expressing an alternative viewpoint
- exploring ideas

- hypothesising and predicting
- using speech to improvise
- asking relevant and searching questions
- challenging ideas of others
- identifying assumptions and implications made by a speaker
- responding to the demands of a large group audience
- selecting appropriate material and style for a particular audience
- using speech to resolve disagreements
- generating and maintaining a sense of purpose while talking
- demonstrating an awareness of issues in discussions
- using speech to develop and extend others' contributions
- using speech to elicit interesting responses from other people
- participating in problem-solving
- participating in a range of oral contexts, from casual to formal
- demonstrating a flexibility of speaking style.

MANAGING ORAL ACTIVITIES

These ten episodes are offered as examples of managed, negotiated contexts for learning through talking and listening. Implied in these contexts is a management strategy for all such contexts. One strategy could be briefly described as:

Planning: work plans are formulated cooperatively with students so that the tasks and the goals of the activity are clear to all;

Focusing: the talk is always focused on the tasks that have been agreed and stated in a clear plan of action;

Monitoring: the work of the students is observed by the teacher, sometimes at close range, sometimes at a distance;

Reporting: students give progress and final reports on their activity;

Evaluating: students have the opportunity to reflect on what they have done and to offer suggestions for improved ways of working next time.

■ASSESSING ACHIEVEMENT

The ten episodes above describe broad working contexts in English classes, in which various aspects of individual development can be assessed. Sometimes it is also important to be able to assess the achievements of finished work. Assessing achievement in this way often means looking closely at what a student has accomplished with a specified task.

Such opportunities enable students to demonstrate what they can achieve, and what they have learnt. Purposeful assessment tasks create opportunities for students to set goals which match the requirements of the task, to plan how they will work on a task, to seek advice, to revise and refine the finished product before presentation. This process of working towards a finished product is an important one. The criteria according to how effectively a task has been completed is to be assessed should be negotiated between the teacher and student at the outset. When students know the basis for the assessment of the finished work, they are able to set goals and plan more effectively. The goals for the task and the assessment criteria are closely matched.

Achievement in oral language can be assessed by constant reference to the question: 'How appropriately can this student use oral language in a particular context, for a specified purpose, with a particular audience?' The appropriateness can then be evaluated in a number of dimensions — the degree of formality, the clarity of the voice, the choice of words, the order in which information is presented, the coherence of the presentation and how interesting it is, and the responsiveness of the audience.

A number of the episodes described above, such as the Hypothetical, could be occasions for assessment of oral language. There is also a range of specific tasks which can demonstrate students' competence in various aspects of oral language.

Because oral language involves interaction, the nature of the tasks which might be used to assess achievement must be considered carefully. So too must the range of contexts, from formal to informal, and the quality of the interaction with listeners. The three tasks described below offer a range of possibilities for assessing achievement in oral language. They can be used effectively at different year levels. All tasks relate purposefully to other aspects of the English program, and derive their validity from this connection.

For all of the tasks, a common set of broad criteria provide a useful basis for assessment:
- the quality of thinking and knowledge shown in the interaction;
- the structure and organisation of the presentation;
- the quality and expressiveness of the language;
- the responsiveness of the interaction; and
- the ability to vary aspects of language appropriately according to context.

There will also be a number of more specific criteria which can be used to describe the quality of performance for each task. When assessment is to be based on a specified task, it is vital to share the criteria for making the assessment with the students from the outset, so that they can take account of these criteria in their planning and preparation.

TASK 1: PROGRESS REPORT TO A SMALL GROUP

Group projects, such as the production of a play, a class newspaper, the investigation of an issue, the preparation of a report, or the compilation of an anthology provide valid contexts for oral assessment tasks. Students can be invited to present to a small group a progress report on their involvement in the project group. They will have convincing reasons for making the report, and can be confident of having plenty to talk about because of their involvement and contribution. The preparation of a progress report requires reflection on what has been done, and what remains to be done, and such reflection is useful self-assessment. The context thus allows for purposeful talk. If a number of groups in a class are working on different projects, this kind of progress reporting also shares the experience gained while working on the projects, and creates a natural audience of interested listeners. (See the account of progress reports given in Chapter 3, The whole context, pp. 40–1)

At the beginning of the project, the requirement of giving an oral progress report should be made known to students. The teacher should nominate the particular stage of the project at which this report should be made. The size of the groups and the time available for giving the reports should also be made clear. What might be included in such reports can be discussed by the whole class. It could be agreed that the report should cover:
• the group's goals for the project;
• what has been done so far;
• what else has to be done;
• how the completion of the project is to be managed;
• the speaker's own role in the project;
• problems encountered, and how these have been overcome;
• the most satisfying aspects of the project.

The speaker should also be prepared to answer questions from the group.

For assessment purposes, the teacher would need to be a member of the small group to whom the student was reporting, as either an observer or a participant in any discussion. Once this was established, the speaker would know the audience — the teacher, and fellow students who have been working on other projects — and the report can be shaped accordingly.

The setting for the presentation of the report is another element in the context for the task — is the group to sit in a circle, or around a table? Although the context for this presentation offers the security of a small group, the situation is more formal than, say, a conversation between two students in the classroom, and therefore students need to understand how the degree of formality could influence their presentation. It might mean that students would decide to use sample materials from their project, or flow charts indicating the plan of action for the project, as visual aids for the talk.

Signs of achievement

As well as assessing the presentation in terms of the five broad criteria listed above (p. 84), specific signs of achievement which could be looked for in a presentation such as has been described could include:

- maintenance of eye contact with the audience
- a clear and well-modulated voice
- well-organised and interesting content
- the coherence of the presentation
- the extent to which the report meets the task requirements
- the interest and relevance of the opening to the presentation
- the extent to which the conclusion effectively rounds off the presentation
- the ways in which visual aids are used
- the capacity to answer questions — that is, listening to others and responding to what has been said
- the appropriateness of the overall style of the presentation to the context.

The quality of the achievement on the task could be assessed according to the effectiveness with which this set of criteria was met, and a precise description of this effectiveness written for the student in terms of the known criteria.

TASK 2: TAKING PART IN A SMALL-GROUP DISCUSSION

In the normal pattern of activities in English, small–group discussion plays an important role on many occasions. Students plan activities, share their responses to a variety of texts, solve problems and develop and prepare group presentations.

The ability to take an effective part in a small group is an important one at all levels of schooling. Achievement of this ability can be described and assessed, from time to time, throughout schooling, in ways which indicate development towards competence in participation in group discussion in many contexts and for many purposes.

Signs of achievement

- contributing actively to the discussion
- listening attentively to others in the group
- participation in the discussion
- making contributions which further the discussion
- suggesting useful ways of approaching the group task
- recognising alternative approaches to a task

- responding thoughtfully to the views of others
- building on others' ideas
- modifying own views after listening to and evaluating the ideas of others
- being prepared to defend one's own point of view
- suggesting new lines of thinking to help the discussion
- inviting fresh contributions when necessary
- summarising in the course of a discussion
- referring the group back to the purposes of the discussion
- being prepared to play the role of group leader
- recording key points in the discussion
- speaking audibly and clearly so that others can understand what is being said
- making eye contact with members of the group.

TASK 3: PRESENTING A DRAMATISED READING OF A PASSAGE FROM A TEXT

The presentation of a dramatised reading of a passage from a text, as an individual or group activity, is an effective way for students to demonstrate informed, imaginative and perceptive responses to the text in question. The choice of passage reveals aspects of what the students value and consider significant about the text. The tone and pace of the presentation can reflect understanding of nuances of style and tone in the text.

When the task is undertaken in a group, students can share their readings of the text, and develop new insights as they experiment with various possibilities for the dramatisation.

Signs of achievement

When the presentation is used as an occasion for assessment, the following signs of achievement can provide the assessment criteria:

- selection of a passage which offers a sense of coherence to the listener
- relevant introduction to the passage in the context of the whole work
- varying tone and pace of the reading to match the tone and mood of the passage
- reading clearly and audibly
- making eye contact with the audience
- being responsive to the patterns and rhythms in the text
- responding to changes in the tone and rhythms in the passage
- emphasising important aspects of the passage
- using the resources of the different voices in the group effectively
- offering an expressive and informed interpretation of the text through the reading
- presenting dialogue in convincing ways
- using gestures and movements appropriately.

:RECORDING DEVELOPMENT IN TALKING AND LISTENING

Anecdotal evidence of classroom activity, like the ten episodes described above, is a rich source of information about classroom practice. An increasing interest in creating learning situations which involve 'real world' purposes has led to the development of many programs which involve students in active, purposeful talk as a natural concomitant of the learning task. The tasks for each group in all of these episodes were quite explicit, the outcomes were products which all students could enjoy and acknowledge, and much of the achievement was due to the oral interaction between the students.

The series of record-keeping formats which follows can be used to help detailed observation in classroom contexts. These formats provide a focus for observation as students participate in various activities. Using these resources, it is possible to predict what will happen, be ready for signs of learning that were not expected, and describe them efficiently.

TALKING AND LISTENING CHECKPOINTS

How might a range of observed signs of development be efficiently recorded? These formats and the descriptive statements which they contain are offered as examples which can be expanded and adapted to suit the particular contexts in which learning has been observed. They are intended to support observation of different activities in a variety of contexts.

The assessment of development in talking and listening presents difficulties because of the transience of talk and the receptive nature of listening. With respect to listening, so much of what can be said must be inferred from behaviours in reading, writing and talking. The format included here might provide a way of recognising and recording signs of development in these modes.

This format should enable teachers to record a progressive summary of development in talking and listening for individual students. It includes a range of sample signs of development that might provide a focus for observation and description. These statements describe a wide range of talking and listening behaviours, and there is also space for adding new items that reflect the goals of particular classroom activities. The openness of the format also accommodates the recording of unanticipated signs of development in these modes, as well as development in many different situations.

A record of talking and listening such as this can provide a bridge between progressive classroom observations and the writing of reports. It can also indicate the range and variety of classroom experience and suggest future directions in planning such experience.

This open format is intended for use with a wide variety of situations where active talking and listening have been encouraged. In this way, this format can be used flexibly to record development in many different situations.

Completed sheets can be filed with other records of work and therefore be used to build up a well-documented profile of the student's abilities in oral language.

:CONCLUSION

Many other statements can be formulated from specific classroom contexts where development in talking and listening is observed. The descriptive statements listed in this chapter illustrate some ways of describing such development and the collection can be enlarged and adapted as new observations are made from classroom activity. In this way, the description flows naturally from the work by students and can be reformulated and expanded for successive learning contexts.

Talking and listening 1

Name: _____ **Year:** _____ **Date:** _____

Signs of development

Examples:

- expresses needs and wants
- listens to stories, songs and nursery rhymes
- follows a sequence of spoken instructions
- talks about personal experiences with others
- tells stories
- retells the main facts of stories read aloud
- uses new words in simple oral statements
- uses approximate syntax in speech
- joins in talk and action with others
- explains a process with recognition of cause and effect
- makes simple classifications in speech

- expresses an opinion in discussion
- justifies opinions in speech
- predicts consequences of a proposed action or event
- uses speech to direct the actions of others
- recognises problems and suggests solutions
- makes a simple analysis of a situation with supporting reasons
- describes and reflects on own feelings
- uses different types of oral language for different situations
-
-
-
-

Date	Comments

Talking and listening 2

Name: _____ **Year:** _____ **Date:** _____

Signs of development

Examples:

- asks questions when seeking information
- refers in detail to incidents and sequences of events
- explains cause and effect
- uses descriptive words and phrases
- shares ideas with others clearly and logically
- describes personal experiences to a group of children
- reflects on experiences and observation in speech
- recognises problems and suggests solutions
- alters the meaning of spoken statements by changing emphasis
- predicts likely outcomes of situations and actions
- anticipates a sequence of events

- reflects on events and draws conclusions
- understands and carries out instructions
- recognises the same idea in different words
- understands information given in different situations
- understands conversation in different situations
- shows respect for other people's experiences and ideas
- revises opinions and ideas through interaction with others
- uses speech to improvise character and situation
-
-
-

Date	Comments

Talking and listening 3

Name: _____ **Year:** _____ **Date:** _____

Signs of development

Examples:

- uses oral language in casual and formal situations
- collaborates with others in class activities
- expresses empathy with the feelings of others
- asks relevant questions in small and large groups
- expresses likely future trends and consequences
- answers questions by providing information
- attends to detail of sequence or event
- recognises emotive language and propaganda
- listens, retains and recalls facts
- revises ideas and opinions through interaction with others
- projects into situations never experienced
- interprets implied meaning in conversation

- uses speech as a means of imaginative expression
- adopts a convincing alternative viewpoint
- participates constructively in a variety of problem-solving situations
- shows leadership and initiative in classroom discussions
- encourages through talk the contributions of others
- attends closely to the views of others
- selects appropriate material and style for particular groups of listeners
-
-
-
-
-
-
-

Date	Comments

Talking and listening 4

Name: _____ Year: _____ Date: _____

Signs of development

Examples:

- shows willingness to accept and encourage the tentative contributions of others
- suggests lines of inquiry in small group situations
- responds to the audience demands of groups of varying size
- can challenge with justification ideas and views of others in a group situation
- can select material and style for a range of audiences
- asks relevant and searching questions
- shows willingness to acknowledge and express feelings
- demonstrates awareness of issues in contributions to discussions
- shows initiative in raising new and related issues
- is able to develop, sustain and defend a point of view

- listens with or without the text
- expresses appreciation of the actions and ideas of others
- identifies assumptions and implications made by a speaker
- can listen to and analyse spoken language used in a variety of ways
- assesses language of media and other sources of information and opinion
- talks persuasively and convincingly
- expresses likely future trends and consequences
- participates in a range of oral contexts, from casual to formal
- uses more formal registers appropriately
-
-
-
-
-

Date	Comments

5 READING

Children begin to learn to read long before they enter school. They readily learn that the printed word — on the pages of a book, a TV or computer screen, on road signs, or on supermarket shelves — contains information and can give pleasure. Some children can read before they arrive at school; others become readers as they are involved in a diverse range of language activities in school. One of the special tasks of the school, therefore, is to build on the prior experience of all students. Observation of students in different learning situations is a necessary means of recognising individual abilities.

Teachers' knowledge of signs of growth and development in reading will guide observation of students, and enable them to enrich and expand students' reading abilities. The following diagram illustrates how observation links theory (knowledge) and teaching practice:

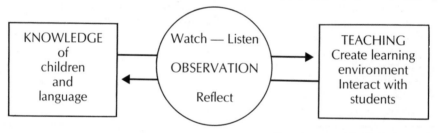

(from Jagger and Smith-Burke, p. 5)

Reading is a process which involves the location, extraction, assessment and organisation of meaning in print, and of making contact, through imagination, with new experience and ideas.

In an information-based society, competence in reading is crucial in giving people access to effective participation. Reading is a key to the development of an awareness of the variety of human experience: through understanding and appreciating the record of others' experience, individuals clarify and sustain their own beliefs and attitudes.

Are there useful ways to describe the journey the individual makes as he or she gains increasing control over this process, and takes up the role of constructive reader and thinker? What are the points of development? How can teachers view individual achievements as signs of progress? What features concerning what happens when new demands are placed on a reader are recognised?

Other dimensions of reading development include the ways that active experience of narrative helps to identify significant patterns defining ourselves and our place in the world. Readers' responses to text indicate characteristic stages of growth. For example, the growth of literary appreciation (an essential aspect of reading development) can be described as passing through an early stage of unconscious enjoyment (the reader knows what he or she likes but doesn't know why), through a stage of self-conscious appreciation (the reader asks why) to a stage where — as Margaret Early (1960) puts it — the reader 'responds with delight, knows why, chooses discriminatingly, and relies on his own judgement'.

The ability to reflect on reading which this pattern suggests is a valuable process to be encouraged in all readers.

An example of another perspective on the development of response to literature is provided by D. W. Harding (1968), who notes that 'since children learn literature from hearing it, classroom discussion of their responses should start from those activities that arise from listening . . .' He suggests four levels of response: responses to the quality and pattern of (1) sounds, (2) events, (3) roles, and (4) worlds.

Further aspects of reading development are suggested by A. Morris and N. Stewart-Dore's list of language-thinking activities:

- exploring vocabulary and concepts;
- drawing on knowledge of language structure to uncover meanings;
- locating specific information;
- making inferences;
- identifying relationships between ideas;
- clarifying understanding;
- amplifying explanations;
- justifying points of views;
- relating the known to the unknown;
- testing hypotheses;
- predicting outcomes;
- investigating possibilities, both linguistic and knowledge-based.

(Morris and Stewart-Dore, 1984, pp. 32–3)

This list is an emphatic reminder of the broad range of processes in which readers become engaged, and of the need for teachers to be alert to signs of growth in students across a range of dimensions which overlap but do not necessarily depend upon each other.

From a study of teenagers' reponse to literature, Jack Thomson (in *Understanding Teenagers Reading: Reading Process and the Teaching of Literature*, Methuen, 1987) developed the concept of 'reflexive' reading in which the reader moves from close emotional involvement with text to a more distanced, reflective detachment: 'from me to outside me, from egocentrism to reflective and reflexive understanding'.

Thomson links the growth of identity and personal values with reading. As the chart opposite shows, his developmental model of teenage response to literature includes several process stages, all of which require satisfaction through enjoyment and understanding.

Response to literature: a developmental model

Process stages: kinds of satisfaction (Requirements for satisfaction at all stages: enjoyment and elementary understanding)	Degree of intensity of interest Weak Strong Passive Active	Degree of sophistication of response Simple Developed and and Rudimentary Subtle	Process strategies
1 Unreflective interest in action			(a) Rudimentary mental images (stereotypes from film and television) (b) Predicting what might happen next in the short term
2 Empathising			(c) Mental images of affect (d) Expectations about characters
3 Analogising			(e) Drawing on the repertoire of personal experiences, making connections between characters and one's own life
4 Reflecting on the significance of events (theme) and behaviour (distanced evaluation of characters)			(f) Generating expectations about alternative possible long-term outcomes (g) Interrogating the text, filling in gaps (h) Formulating puzzles, enigmas, accepting hermeneutic challenges
5 Reviewing the whole work as the author's creation			(i) Drawing on literary and cultural repertoires (j) Interrogating the text to match the author's representation with one's own (k) Recognition of implied author
6 Consciously considered relationship with the author, recognition of textual ideology, and understanding of self (identity theme) and of one's own reading processes			(l) Recognition of implied reader in the text, and the relationship between implied reader (m) Reflexiveness, leading to understanding of textual ideology, personal identity and one's own reading processes

(Thomson, 1987, pp. 360–1)

Identifying progress in reading is clearly not just a matter of describing a simple linear sequence. A developing reader may simultaneously demonstrate competence and independence in dealing with print serving a specific function, or drawn from a particular context (e.g. instructions for building model aeroplanes, or the sporting pages of a newspaper) and operate as one whose ability to deal with other forms of text (e.g. newspaper editorials) is both tentative and emergent.

Reading development is inherently variable, depending on the personal, social and cultural experiences of the learner, regardless of age. Hence, a flexible model for describing growth seems most appropriate for our purposes, so in the chart below we have tried to identify clusters of significant statements in four broad phases which suggest growth points that readers may be moving towards, through or beyond.

These clusters of concerns suggest directions at different points of schooling. Understanding of long-range development can help teachers to decide which activities can most appropriately be offered to groups of students. Awareness of a broad sequence of development can help to focus our observations of the developing reader. Teachers can be sensitive to the emergence of positive achievements, new understandings and new learning.

Developing control over language forms not previously encountered can often be signalled by the demonstration of inadequacies and difficul-

Phases of development in reading

PHASE 1: Foundations: early primary school
- Understanding concepts of print.
- Understanding that print conveys meaning.
- Learning ways of making meaning from print: recognising, telling, retelling, predicting, imagining, self-correcting.
- Moving towards being able to read a simple published book.

PHASE 2: Development: expansion and consolidation — later primary–lower secondary school
- Developing a range of skills, e.g. prediction, scanning, skimming, close reading; silent and oral reading, longer texts.
- Imagining and empathising.
- Selecting, using, evaluating, appreciating and revising meanings from text.

PHASE 3: Towards independence: further development & consolidation — middle–upper secondary school
- Transactions with an increasing range of print material, developing and expanding skills of justifying; inferring; investigating; explaining; predicting; analysing; reorganising; evaluating.
- Developing personal choice and discrimination; developing personal response to a wide variety of text; increasing the range of text; generalising and speculating from various texts.

PHASE 4: Consolidation — upper secondary and beyond
- Familiarity with, and effective use of, a very wide range of printed text.
- Ability to discriminate, appreciate, respond in various ways: these are readers who read widely and critically; who read accurately for various purposes and at various speeds; and who read with curiosity, actively interrogating, and reflecting on, the printed text.
- Development of a reflexive relationship with the text.

---

ties. Errors, miscues and unexpected responses provide insights about how a learner is organising his or her world, and reflect development.

The sequence we would wish to describe is one of a cumulative repertoire where 'growth means being able to do more things and to do old things better, not merely hopping from one stepping stone to another' (Moffett, 1981, p. 10).

The contexts in which learners practise enlarging repertoires will become increasingly diversified, and competence in coping with the increasing range of demands represents growth. Teachers can assist this development in many ways. For instance, when success has been achieved in one setting, teachers can help the learner extend that success in a new and different setting. A child's enthusiastic and appreciative response to the patterning of a simple, repetitive story like *Rosie's Walk* by Pat Hutchins can be extended if he or she is encouraged to write a similar story.

How can individual development in reading across the varied and complex dimensions described above be systematically mapped? Collections of descriptive statements, related to the broad phases outlined above, can help to focus observation in specific ways. We do not intend these collections to be used as universal checklists, or to be doggedly worked through for all children. If a checklist is used as the only means of gaining an overview of language development, there is a risk of missing important things: no checklist can be totally inclusive.

Even the most observant teacher does not have access to students' performance in all the contexts in which they operate. A checklist may, for example, indicate the ability to use a dictionary as a sign of development. Generalisations based only on the observation of the child in the contexts of school may be invalid: a child may express justifiable irritation if the checklist indicates that he cannot use a dictionary when he regularly does so at home. A statement that the child cannot use context cues to gather meaning from print may be accurate on some texts but not on others: it may depend on what and where the child likes reading.

The sets of descriptive statements we have gathered can help to direct our observations of what is happening as students read, remind us of the broad range of goals which can be set, in collaboration with students, and make explicit the many levels at which learning may take place. These statements help in the interpretation of the available evidence in order to plan further learning experiences.

Consultation with students, parents and colleagues can be more precisely focused when observation is guided, but not constrained, by a set of statements describing expected signs of development. For some students, the statements may indicate the directions development has taken. For others, we may be reminded of significant areas of weakness. For all students, it is necessary to allow for the unexpected, for the intuitions and growth points which surprise and delight the observant teacher.

■READING: SIGNS OF DEVELOPMENT

FOUNDATIONS: EARLY PRIMARY SCHOOL

Signs of achievement

- gathering meaning from pictures
- finding small differences in printed words and letters
- matching printed letters
- recognising and understanding words, sentences, lines, letters, spaces
- knowing what a page is and turning pages correctly
- understanding sound/symbol relationships of whole words and individual letters
- recognising and naming the letters of the alphabet
- recognising some letter clusters in familiar words
- telling a story from a sequence of pictures
- participating in oral reading of familiar stories
- naming main characters from story books
- gathering meaning from a variety of picture books without written text
- re-reading own written language
- reading a simple familiar story or nursery rhyme for him or herself
- predicting a familiar word which has been left out of a sentence
- finding a familiar word in a sentence
- recognising words with special meanings such as own name, friend's name, interest words
- recognising high interest words out of context
- anticipating rhymes
- using knowledge of print to learn other words
- using contextual cues to make reasonable guesses at unfamiliar words
- seeing sounds within words
- anticipating high interest words using initial consonant cues
- self-correcting when reading does not make sense
- re-telling a story using approximate sequence
- using context to predict what might happen next in a story
- suggesting alternative endings to a story
- suggesting what happened in the gaps left by the author
- checking predictions by referring to the text
- selecting rhyming words
- recognising a variety of word patterns
- understanding the function of simple punctuation and abbreviations

- selecting an appropriate book
- enjoying listening to stories and poems
- reading silently for a short time
- reading silently with understanding
- describing the contents of a book to somebody else
- reading a simple, published book to other people
- carrying out a variety of research tasks
- using a thesaurus and dictionaries
- reading a simple story to a familiar audience
- understanding the function of print in conveying meaning
- recognising familiar words
- reading simple books
- reading for pleasure in leisure time
- responding to stories by expressing feelings and ideas
- locating needed print information.

These statements suggest signs of growth that can be expected in the foundation years. However, many children come to school already familiar with print, responsive to the power of stories, and familiar with the function of print in conveying meaning: for example, words on the TV screen; labels on food products; instructions for assembling toys; and road signs. Where their environment is rich in print materials, children learn to value the functions of print from a very early age.

Other children may be less familiar with print material, or with material printed in the English language, and will respond to the supportive, lively environment of a classroom where they are exposed to many forms of oral and written language, broadening their competence in using and shaping text.

Observation of variable individual growth will accompany the normal range of classroom activity. This follows the principle that assessment and evaluation are part of the teacher's everyday role. The teacher may stand near a small group of students talking about a picture book they have shared together, and notice the variations in their interpretations of the story. Did Rosie know the fox was following her? Did she mean to lead him through such an awkward and risky walk? Was Max pleased to find his supper waiting for him, still hot?

Classroom possibilities

The everyday experiences of the classroom provide a rich range of possibilities for observation of the building of foundations for reading:
- developing children's awareness of, and response to, the labels on objects in the classroom;
- the preparation of reading books containing children's own writing;
- sharing books (e.g. big books); story-reading sessions; the creation of wall stories;

- asking questions which encourage children to relive the reading experience through talk — what in this story reminds you of things in other stories?
- writing letters to authors, who are often willing to write back;
- setting up 'readers' circles' in the classroom to allow time for discussion;
- encouraging students to keep their own records of their reading, and responses to this reading, in a reading logbook;
- having access to many books — picture books with or without text; books set in many places and cultures; familiar and new books; and being encouraged to handle these books freely and with respect.

DEVELOPMENT: EXPANSION & CONSOLIDATION — LATER PRIMARY–LOWER SECONDARY SCHOOL

In later primary school, children build on what they have learnt in the early primary years, developing a broader range of skills, and becoming more independent as readers.

Signs of achievement

- reading many kinds of texts — narrative, poetic, procedural, informative, factual, persuasive
- making predictions, asking questions while reading
- creating new versions of familiar stories
- re-telling a range of kinds of text
- skimming and scanning to obtain an overview of a text
- expressing a point of view about issues encountered in reading
- revising interpretations of text in the light of new evidence
- revising ideas and opinions about texts
- developing additional ideas from reading
- relating personally to situations described in fiction
- becoming sensitive to characterisation and theme in fiction
- beginning to understand the significance of imaginative language in text
- demonstrating a working knowledge of library classification systems
- finding relevant texts for reference purposes
- using several reference texts for research
- using an encyclopaedia
- borrowing books from the library for information and enjoyment
- skimming and scanning a passage for relevant and useful information
- identifying the general theme or main idea of a passage

- using context clues to make informed predictions about the outcome of stories
- locating main ideas in a passage
- identifying supporting detail in a passage
- defining personal purposes for reading
- making appropriate notes for study purposes
- talking about the explicit content of a selection of reading
- producing from memory ideas and information explicitly described in text
- reorganising and classifying explicit information from a passage or book
- developing and expanding ideas and information explicitly stated in print
- selecting relevant information from various passages
- using information presented in a variety of ways such as graphs, plans, statistics, maps
- evaluating information from text according to fact or opinion; reality or fantasy; relevance to particular tasks
- coping with a variety of print presented on a computer screen
- using and evaluating text presented by electronic information systems
- using personal experience and prior knowledge to evaluate information from text
- using the major punctuation marks and conventions of print
- pronouncing unknown words by understanding parts of their structure
- extending vocabulary with new words found in print
- recognising cohesive links in a passage
- forming opinions from reading text
- drawing conclusions and predicting outcomes
- reading regularly for pleasure
- reading silently for an extended period
- reading novels with enjoyment and discrimination
- reading many different kinds of print texts
- responding to print in critical and appreciative ways
- formulating questions, finding the information required, and communicating this to others
- generalising from the reading of various texts
- making judgements about the worth and validity of information
- demonstrating a widening vocabulary from reading interest and experience

Classroom possibilities

The items in this list indicate the extensive range of activities in which students participate in English classes. Students' grow as readers in many different situations:

- listening to an oral reading by an expert reader, such as the author or the teacher;
- reading in the library;
- talking in small groups about their encounters with books;
- keeping a log-book of responses to a particular reading experience;
- preparing a text — a poem, a piece of dialogue, or a prose passage — for oral performance by a small group;

- scrutinising a text for the detail needed to write an alternative ending to that provided by the author;
- collecting and producing an anthology of favourite reading;
- learning how to make notes from informative text by orally rehearsing the main points before writing them in their own words;
- brainstorming lists of related words and phrases before reading a text on a new topic;
- being an active member of a mixed-ability group which encourages co-operative thinking, talking and exchange of ideas;
- working out the range of appropriate words to fill gaps in a poem from which some words have been deleted;
- reading silently for an extended period of time.

TOWARD INDEPENDENCE: FURTHER DEVELOPMENT & CONSOLIDATION — MIDDLE– UPPER SECONDARY SCHOOL

Throughout the years of secondary school, students' repertoire of reading abilities will continually be expanded and fine-tuned, as they build on their experience of reading so far. A wide variety of individual interests, development and ability will continue to be characteristic of any group of students, and this variety enhances and extends the possibilities of meaning made from text in the classroom.

Signs of achievement
- contributing sensitively to discussions on literature in informal and more formal contexts
- writing fluently about literature
- showing discrimination in selecting personal reading material
- gathering information and ideas from a wide range of text
- reorganising explicit ideas or information from a text
- synthesising material from more than one passage
- predicting the outcome of an incomplete passage
- interpreting figurative language
- making comparisons between characters, times and places
- talking about personal emotional responses to the content of text
- identifying with characters or experiences
- relating prior knowledge of a topic to newly encountered information
- talking and writing about the author's use of language
- defining personal purposes for reading

- recognising and recalling ideas and information from clues in a passage
- making appropriate notes for study purposes
- discerning the authors' purposes in a variety of text
- reading between the lines
- selecting information received through computers
- using language showing evidence of wide reading
- making distinctive, personal responses to literature
- responding adventurously to reading
- displaying an honest and enthusiastic response to literature
- showing a deeper awareness of the relevance of themes and issues in reading
- contributing fresh and lively interpretations to discussions about reading
- showing a broad and flexible grasp of ideas and issues in reading
- writing about reading in a lively, personal way
- being able to develop imaginative extensions to a literary text, such as sequels, extra chapters
- writing precisely and cogently about literature
- talking and writing about text in a detailed and concrete manner
- describing the tone and texture of language in text
- recreating the feeling and atmosphere of specific texts
- selecting and organising appropriate evidence from reading
- drawing conclusions and making generalisations from text
- analysing the language used to persuade readers to accept a point of view
- discerning bias and propaganda
- sorting facts and opinions
- analysing credibility of sources
- examining different points of view
- collating information from texts into a logical presentation
- comparing points of view contained in various written texts
- comparing and contrasting the content and style of two or more passages
- eliciting assumptions and implications embedded in text
- forming and defending personal judgements about a passage or text
- accepting and appreciating the interpretations of others
- understanding and enjoying a wide range of reading, including fiction and non-fiction
- relating aspects of literature to personal experience
- responding spontaneously and imaginatively to literature
- grasping the complexity of issues in a variety of texts
- producing an overview of an issue from reading a range of texts
- making discriminating personal responses to a range of literary texts
- understanding and appreciating a wide range of text
- using research skills
- producing considered views about reading
- producing purposeful and relevant writing about a variety of texts
- demonstrating perceptions which indicate a mature response to text
- expressing a detached, critical view of literature
- reflecting critically and intelligently on text

- evaluating reading material
- reflecting intelligently on the texture and tone of literature
- demonstrating continued enjoyment of reading.

Classroom possibilities

Students can work together and individually on a wide range of activities:

- as they read a novel, students keep a journal recording events in the novel, their impressions and reactions to events and people. They describe the facts of the story: where the events happened; the names and background of the people involved and so on;
- putting themselves in the place of the main character, asking what they would have done in similar situations;
- investigating the events that occurred in the novel. Do such things happen today? Do students know of similar events from their own experience?
- making a radio or TV program from events and people in the novel; for example, interviewing the main characters;
- finding out about the author; reading more of his or her writing;
- re-writing the conclusion;
- reviewing novels for the school newspaper. What books would they recommend to other students?
- give students a plan of the school or map of your town or suburb. Students trace the route they take from one part of the school to another, from school to home, or from one part of town to another. They write directions for getting from one place to another, and other students follow the directions;
- writing a 'How to' book in which they tell about some of their own skills and interests, from skateboarding to breeding tropical fish. Books are shared with other students;
- spend some time each week clipping from magazines, newspapers and old texts. Make various collages of these for students to browse through and discuss. Students make their own anthologies of clippings or use the pieces as ideas and models for writing;
- making a collection of favourite poems and presenting readings to the class;
- in pairs or small groups, students select several poems and work out ways of presenting each in dramatic form to the class;
- collecting images from poetry anthologies. Students present them in a display — a collage of language that impressed the reader;
- preparing an all-class choral version of a text using sound effects and music;
- a poem is given to the class, untitled. In pairs, students propose titles, and then discuss the reasons for their choices, finally comparing their titles with the original;
- inventing the story behind the poem. What has happened before? What is happening 'offstage'? What might happen later?

CONSOLIDATION: UPPER SECONDARY AND BEYOND SCHOOL

All of the features described in the first three collections of statements are still relevant, particularly as readers engage with new forms of text. A composite picture of the range of reading abilities we may reasonably expect to find amongst older students in the post-compulsory years can be drawn from the following list which is based on a range of senior school English course descriptions.

Signs of achievement

A competent reader:

- compares and contrasts a range of texts
- appreciates features such as style, characterisation, relevance to a particular social environment and time
- recognises recurring themes in text
- values reading as a basis for reflection, discussion and writing
- relates specific issues in a book to wider social issues and to personal experience
- understands the relationship of literature to the development of present society
- recognises the role of literature as a medium of culture, and a source of ideas, opinions and information
- explores the field of written communication
- comprehends technical literature in an area of interest
- clarifies and defends considered and relevant points of view about many texts
- pays close attention to the details of language used by others in offering points of view
- reads a variety of texts with accuracy, discrimination and enjoyment
- values the ways in which experience can be extended, deepened and enriched through reading and discussion
- is aware of the variety of forms available to the literary artist
- appreciates that some texts are understood through performance
- appreciates complex differences in points of view expressed by different authors
- has developed a sense of the role of the author
- understands how literature influences social development
- understands how literature can comment and reflect on a society
- appreciates that literature is a term embracing a wide range of texts, including novels, plays, poems, short stories, jokes, feature articles, films and oral text.

Classroom possibilities

- Ask students to divide a sheet of paper into three columns. In the first column, they list the most important characters in the novel or play being discussed. Students could rank the characters, say from most to least important, or from most to least admirable.

In the second column, students jot down an appropriate intangible gift for each character (courage, patience, the ability to laugh at oneself) that would dramatically change an aspect of that character's behaviour.

In the third column, they record a specific gift for each character (karate, psychoanalysis, a subscription to *Mad* magazine) that would help that character achieve the behaviour or quality listed in column two.

Students work in pairs and share and justify their ideas.

- When dealing with a complex text such as George Johnston's *My Brother Jack*, or *Macbeth*, students choose one major character and keep a daily journal for that character, reporting what happens to him or her as the text is read.

  Students are encouraged to record the feelings and motivations of their chosen character as well as events in the lives of those with whom he or she is involved.

  At the conclusion of reading, there is a panel presentation where students interview other students playing their chosen characters. As a variation, they could script and present interviews with each of the major characters.

- After a novel has been read, students work in small groups to prepare a 30-minute news program based on incidents in the novel. There could be an anchor person or team, reporters or researchers; commentators; interview sessions.

  Each group takes a separate section of the 30-minute program and prepares a written script which is given to a production team for approval. This team decides the sequencing of segments and suggests revisions to scripts.

  Students videotape the program in one lesson (after rehearsals) and watch the program in the next. This could be followed by the writing of reviews of the program.

- Use diagrams to think about a novel during reading.

  The name of the central character is placed in a box in the middle of a blank page and the names of other characters around the page. As the events unfold, students jot down aspects of the relationship between the central character and each of the others.

  The diagram could be repeated several times to enable students to include changes in the relationships and to create links between various moments in the novel, thus encouraging an understanding of the development of characters and relationships.

- For an anthology project, students collect various types of printed text that interests them — jokes, riddles, advertisements, photographs, environmental print, poetry, newspaper articles, letters, stories, reviews.

Favourite pieces are shared and students brainstorm ways of organising their material to present it to others. This might involve the writing of a preface and brief text around their material.

Other projects and units of work focusing on the shared reading of novels can include activities which involve informal and more focused talk which promotes understanding, interpretation, reflection and appreciation.

EPISODES FROM THE CLASSROOM

EPISODE ONE: TALKING ABOUT BOOKS IN YEAR 5

This group of four children has just finished reading Nadia Wheatley's book, *Five Times Dizzy*. A week ago, their teacher read the opening pages to them, and they were curious about Yaya, Mareka's Greek grandmother, living with her family in inner-suburban Sydney. They started to talk about the way people feel about grandmothers. They expressed a lot of curiosity about the opening scene: 'Could she really have been so still that Mareka thought she was dead?', 'What else could Mareka have done?', 'How did Yaya feel?'.

Each member of the group took a copy of the book to read over the next week. They exchanged a few comments, informally, during the week — 'Where are you up to?', 'Have you read about where she decides to get a goat for Yaya?' — and now everybody has finished.

The discussion starts when someone says that she didn't really understand why Yaya was living with the family. There are lots of suggestions, and one of the boys tells the others about the Greek family who lived next door to him for several years. He describes the grandmother who lived with this family, and they are interested to know that she, too, always wore black. The conversation moves on to an exchange of anecdotes about their own grandmothers.

The discussion shifts to talk about the fête. Someone wondered whether the people who lived in the street would really organise an occasion like this, but someone else was able to describe a street barbecue she had once been to. They talk about special days, fairs and fêtes, and the web of shared experience is being spun, enlarging the students' understanding of the book.

There is speculation about Mareka's idea of using the goat as a hired lawnmower — 'I wouldn't have thought of that!' — and the group starts to talk about the kind of person they think Mareka was. They find that their mental images about her appearance differ slightly — 'I thought she'd be taller than that' — and then discover how much these images were influenced by the illustrations in the book. Not everyone likes having pictures in books — 'I'd rather imagine what they look like' — while others enjoy illustrations which add information and detail for readers. They turn to the picture of the Smith Street fête, and spend time commenting on the details in the drawing.

As the time available for the discussion draws to a close, the group decides to work together on a small project related to the book. The idea of making a poster to advertise the goat's availability as a lawnmower is raised, and then the suggestion that handbills to put in people's letter boxes would be more appropriate. They agree to start work on the design for a handbill in the next session.

The informal discussion has focused on some of the main themes in the book — concern for older members of families, the ways communities come to accept new members, some of the difficulties of migrants. No conclusions have been reached but the flow of talk has enabled the sharing of experiences within the group. This has helped the students to make new meanings of the text. The work on the handbill will probably lead to some close scrutiny of the text for detail, and new understandings and questions will emerge.

Signs of achievement

In such a context, many signs of learning on the part of individual students might be observed. Because the project described in this episode promoted a connected experience of language, these signs of learning will be related to talking, listening and writing as well as to reading. Here are some possibilities:

- asking questions about experiences in books
- selecting relevant, detailed information from text
- identifying main ideas in a text
- reading a published text to other people
- formulating alternative ways of conveying information in writing
- choosing appropriate words to match ideas
- developing the ability to write in different ways
- developing awareness of the need for accurate spelling and punctuation
- becoming aware of the needs of the intended readers of the writing
- demonstrating willingness and sharing feelings and opinions
- making connections between their own experience and experiences in literature
- making relevant and constructive comments
- asking clear and thoughtful questions
- using speech to extend others' contributions
- showing initiative in raising new issues

- using speech to justify, anticipate and predict
- expressing original thoughts and perceptions in speech
- being a lively and enthusiastic participant in discussion
- explaining personal experiences
- drawing conclusions from what others say
- making detailed reference in speech to a literary text
- showing enjoyment of reading
- responding to print in appreciative ways
- using information in a variety of ways
- reflecting on reading
- contributing useful ideas in discussion
- building on others' ideas in discussion.

EPISODE TWO: POETRY READINGS IN YEAR 8

As part of a project on 'Heroes and Villains', a Year 8 class was asked to present group readings of the poem 'Clancy of the Overflow' or any other Australian narrative poem of their choice. After the initial reading of the poem by the teacher, it was obvious that many students lacked a clear idea of the events and characters it described. Students were then asked to form their own groups and to prepare, in two sessions, a reading of the poem.

During the early rehearsals, when one or two groups showed some uncertainty, several students commented on how difficult it was to read the poem convincingly. Other students then suggested memorising each part and using some basic movements. These suggestions were adopted by most groups.

Several rehearsals involved group discussion about who would say what and when, and experiments were conducted using various voices. During this preparation, students were free to rehearse away from the classroom, with the teacher moving between groups, making suggestions and answering various questions. (One group was directed away from a nearby classroom when their enthusiastic reading disturbed senior students watching a biology film.) There were opportunities during this time, therefore, to observe the extent to which students stayed on the task and made contributions to the work of the groups.

The groups presented their readings during one session. Many students had memorised their parts and groups had clearly made decisions about movement and position in the performance area at the front of the room. Other groups were invited to comment and ask questions when all readings had been given. The teacher was able to observe and record a number of things about each group's reading and about the contribution of individuals.

A whole-class discussion of the readings was held and the class made suggestions for procedures next time. This enabled the drawing up of a guideline sheet for further group poetry readings, and group presentations in general.

Signs of achievement

One of the goals of this activity was to promote understanding of poetry through performance. By preparing group readings of a poem, students actively deal with the text in ways that increase their knowledge and appreciation of the poet's intentions. Informal talk about how to produce particular words and lines in their own speech involves students in discussion about meaning. Reading the poem to the class also entails a consideration of audience and of the various ways of using voice. In this activity, signs of learning by students related to talking and listening as much as to reading. The idea of audience generated within group talk — talking to other members — and by preparing and performing the reading had clear implications for writing.

Signs of achievement included:
- demonstrating a detailed knowledge of text
- showing ability to describe the tone and texture of language in text
- revising ideas about a text
- demonstrating the ability to recreate the feeling and atmosphere of specific texts
- contributing sensitively to discussions on literature
- developing appreciation of a writer's use of language
- developing ability to interpret figurative language
- developing new ideas from reading
- following spoken instructions
- attending to detailed sequence of events
- readily joining in discussion
- sharing ideas with others clearly and logically
- using intonation and expression appropriate to different situations
- using speech to describe and narrate
- using speech to improvise character and/or situation
- developing a feeling for the rhythm and movement of words
- retaining and recalling facts and messages from listening
- making comparisons and contrasts when retelling a story or describing experiences
- using speech as a means of imaginative expression
- being imaginatively involved in presentation
- developing awareness of audience
- reflecting intelligently on text
- appreciating performance of text
- valuing reading as a basis for reflection and discussion
- using animated, lively speech in classroom activity
- using speech for a variety of purposes

- making suggestions to help the work of the group/class
- participating effectively in group and class activities
- listening attentively to others
- responding imaginatively to literature
- responding sensitively and perceptively to literature
- understanding information presented in different contexts
- appreciating a wide range of literature
- expressing thoughtful views about text
- reading a variety of text.

EPISODE THREE: A 'GOOD READING GUIDE'

Working in small groups, students in a Year 8 class prepared a 'Good Reading Guide' based on the books people in their group had read over a six-month period. They planned to present the finished Guide to the school library for other Year 8 students to use. In an introduction they explained their reading workshop group's interests, and the goals they had set themselves in developing the Guide.

Their Guide was to include advice, suggestions and recommendations. Groups were reminded to be sure to give the title, author and publisher of the books included. The introduction was to explain briefly why each text listed interested the readers in the group, and note any special aspects which might interest other Year 8 readers. The Guide contained a short review — about 100 words — of each book. Where people in the group had different reactions to the same text, two different reviews of that text were included.

Some groups decided to develop a set of starred recommendations for the titles listed in the Guide: for example, five stars (★★★★★) meant 'the highest recommendation', four stars (★★★★) 'highly recommended', and so on.

Signs of achievement
- reading a wide range of books
- talking about wide reading with other people
- selecting preferred reading from a wide range
- writing a brief account of books for other readers
- creating a reading resource for other readers
- listening to other people's responses to reading
- broadening knowledge of possibilities for reading
- explaining reading choices and preferences, in discussion and in writing
- reviewing personal reading patterns
- recognising that different readers can have different responses to the same book.

EPISODE FOUR: FINDING OUT AND REPORTING

This project, with a Year 10 group, involved finding out about recycling arrangements within the school, in particular within their own class-room, and writing a report of this research as a set of guidelines for a 'green English classroom'.

The project involved a wide range of reading for a number of practical purposes. This reading included many different kinds of texts — surveys, notes, newspapers, instructions for operating technical equipment such as photocopiers and offset printers, letters, school policy documents, budget statements and guideline statements. It also involved students in the consideration of reading strategies such as notemaking. Activities, mostly carried out in groups, included:

- conducting surveys — for example, the amount of paper used by a class for a week;
- research — the costs of running photocopiers, community attitudes to recycling;
- setting goals and planning — how to use the information from surveys and other research in practical ways;
- brainstorming: 'How many ways can we think of to reduce the wastage of resources in this class?'
- reflection on ways of learning: 'Is it better to make notes of important points from reading, or to underline a photocopied text?'
- collaboration: working in a group to develop a set of guidelines;
- reading and writing for a purpose: writing letters to agencies within the community to find out about recycling plans, reading guidelines as models of writing in this way, writing the class guidelines.

Signs of achievement

- reading a wide range of kinds of text
- reading to obtain specific information
- taking notes from reading
- considering ways of reading and recording information
- locating required information from a range of sources
- selecting relevant information from reading
- analysing information
- analysing attitudes and issues presented in a range of reading material
- using models from reading to develop a piece of writing.

EPISODE FIVE: *TARONGA*

A Year 10 class began reading Victor Kelleher's novel *Taronga* by listening to their teacher read the first chapter. This reading was inter-rupted a couple of times to allow students to catch some preliminary thoughts in their reading journals. After hearing the first few pages, students wrote some notes about what they thought the main character, Ben, might have meant when he thinks: 'I'm like the dingo . . . the two of us . . . the same'. In these notes, they speculated on the kind of person they thought Ben might have been. At the end of the first chapter, Ben says: 'Because it's too much like "Last Days"'. At this stage, they wrote in the journals about what they thought 'Last Days' might mean.

Following this shared reading, they continued reading independently and writing in their reading journals, capturing and tracking their developing responses to the book. They were invited to list questions they wanted to ask about what was happening, and to write about interesting things said by the characters. Other possibilities suggested to students for writing in the reading journals included:

- Make notes of your workshop group discussions.
- Trace the connections you are making between events in your own experience and events in the novel.
- Does *Taronga* remind you of other books you have read? If so, how?
- Why were the various characters included?
- Describe the mental pictures you form of places and people in the novel.
- What impression of Kelleher do you gain from this book?
- What kind of reader do you think Kelleher had in mind for this novel?

Taronga is set in an undefined future time, and invites speculation on possible futures. In groups, students developed their own scenarios for the future. Each group was allocated one section of noticeboard space in the English classroom. In this space, the groups were to develop a display of newspaper cuttings about reported events and discoveries which suggest what life might be like in the future. Students had ready access to a large collection of back and current copies of daily newspapers from the school library.

Some groups concentrated on particular categories — medical advances, new technology, political trends, employment trends. They designed headings for each display, and labels and notes were used to make the display understandable to other people. This activity generated a great deal of talk within the groups about material encountered in looking through the newspapers, and about the kind of future suggested in *Taronga*.

The workshop groups also worked from the following list of group activities:

- Make a map of Ben's journey.
- Draw up a diagram which shows all the characters in the book, and their relationships to each other. Write Ben's name in the middle of the page, and build up a web showing all the other characters.
- Talk about the issues which are raised by this novel — man's relationship with the animals, brutality, the urge to survive. Brainstorm a list of as many issues as you can think of.

As a follow up to reading and thinking about this novel, students were invited to choose from the following list of writing topics. These were designed to extend their response to the novel in imaginative ways.

- Write a story in response to the question: 'What if . . .?'
- Write some pages from the diary which Ben or Ellie might have kept while they were together in Taronga Zoo.
- Write as if you were living in the same situation as Ben or Ellie. What would you do?
- Create an extra scene for the novel, introducing some incidents or episodes which could change the course of events.
- Write an alternative ending to the novel which is less optimistic than Victor Kelleher's own. (What does 'optimistic' mean?)
- At the end of the novel, Ben says: 'Letting the animals go wasn't just an ending. It was a beginning for me too.' (p. 198). Write a sequel to *Taronga*, taking up the story which is just beginning at this point.
- Write about the ending of the book — does it suggest a new beginning for the world, or does it suggest that the pattern of man's destruction will be repeated?

This project gave all students opportunities to develop and explore their responses to this book, and to make connections with things in the world around them. There were many opportunities for sharing and developing ideas and feelings raised by the novel.

Signs of achievement

- listening to a reading of a text
- reading independently
- making predictions while reading
- exploring questions asked while reading
- capturing thoughts and ideas in a reading journal
- describing images formed while reading
- maintaining a reading journal while reading a novel
- exploring issues raised in a novel
- collecting newspaper information related to issues in a novel
- working with a group to talk about issues in the media
- working in cooperation with others to develop and extend responses to reading
- representing aspects of structure in a novel diagrammatically
- making a diagrammatic representation of connections within a novel
- identifying a range of issues raised by a novel
- making connections between different novels
- blending ideas gathered from reading newspapers and a novel to write imaginatively about the future
- thinking about the past, present and future
- writing creatively in response to a novel
- reflecting on their own reading.

EPISODE SIX: YEAR 12 SYMPOSIUM

Two Year 12 classes studied the theme of identity as part of their course. Several texts were read and discussed, including Jessica Anderson's *Tirra Lirra by the River*. After a series of sessions in which extracts from the text were read aloud and discussed, students were asked to develop a list of questions on the novel relating it to the theme of identity, and about which they wished to hear other's views. Each student jotted a list of questions which were then listed for the whole group. These included:

- Why did Nora Porteous return to Brisbane?
- Why did she have a face-lift?
- Do we ever see her real self?
- Does her identity change?
- How important was independence to Nora?
- What were Nora's feelings about her past life?
- Who influenced her most during her life?

The process of formulating and sharing questions gave students an opportunity to explore their tentative reactions to the novel and the theme study. It was also intended to provide an opportunity for students to show the extent to which they could synthesise their understandings sufficiently to pose stimulating and challenging issues. As the questions came, there was a clear progression: at first, questions referred to concrete, specific incidents, but gradually others were asked that focused more generally on identity and general aspects of the theme as illustrated in the novel.

Students were then invited to select a question — not their own — and, with a partner, to prepare a short statement addressing the question. They were asked to talk about the question with the whole class, drawing upon specific details in the text to support their position. A scribe was appointed to take notes of what was said. In a session which we called 'symposium', the talks ranged over seven or eight questions from the list. The following are examples of general positions taken:

> Nora was too dependent on what other people did, how they acted toward her. She tried to find a perfect world wherever she went, but no person and no place could live up to the perfect world she concocted.

> Nora's life was a succession of substitutes for her ideals . . .

> She became more assertive and positive after her marriage ended, and found that she could enjoy relationships without suppressing her own identity.

Students heard each other out and asked some challenging questions of the speakers. Copies of the notes taken by the scribe were made available for all students. This activity was followed by a plenary session where students discussed general aspects of the theme as developed by the novel, and summarised five or six key issues into arguable propositions.

These included the search for identity, influence of other people, and the roles people play.

Signs of achievement

The activity was primarily designed to synthesise aspects and issues on the theme study drawing upon students' knowledge of a text. However, the structure of the activity provided moments when these understandings could be shown and further developed in interaction with others, and through more formal oral presentation. Signs of achievement included:

- recognising and defining a problem or issue
- generalising from a number of related ideas
- adopting a convincing alternative viewpoint
- reflecting on events, drawing conclusions and recognising issues involved
- adopting more formal registers
- attending to the views of others
- enjoying the challenge of small-group work
- identifying assumptions and implications in speech
- contributing useful ideas in classroom discussions
- asking clear and thoughtful questions
- eliciting responses from other people
- suggesting lines of inquiry to a small group
- talking to a variety of audiences
- using speech for exploratory and speculative thinking
- making and justifying reasoned judgements
- maintaining an open-minded, alert attitude to issues
- being able to take a leadership role in class and group discussions
- selecting appropriate material and style for a particular audience
- demonstrating confidence in personal speech.

■ ASSESSING ACHIEVEMENT

TASK 1: KEEPING A READING JOURNAL

When students keep a reading journal over a significant period of time it can provide a rich source of evidence of their development as readers.

The journal should contain a growing collection of thoughts and reactions to their reading and viewing over time. Another way of describing a reading journal is as a 'think book', which helps readers to make sense of their responses to a text. It is not meant to be a collection of finished, polished writing, but a collection of the random thoughts, responses and ideas through which readers' developing thinking is often expressed. A reading journal offers an open invitation for readers to think about their reading by writing about it.

Here is a list of some of the things which could be included in the journal:

- an accumulating record of all the texts encountered by the reader/writer over a certain period of time, such as a term, semester or year. This record could be kept in a special section of the journal;
- personal jottings about reading and viewing;
- attempts to describe the effects of a book or a film;
- questions the reader wants to ask about books and films, and the people and events in those books and films;
- predictions made while reading a long text, like a novel — after the opening chapter, before or after a gap in the narrative, just after a significant section, or just before the ending. How might the story develop? Does what has just happened affect the reader's attitude?
- sketches and drawings, which can free readers to express their ideas about the characters and places in the texts;
- responses to reading. These can be explored by completing unfinished sentences: 'I wonder . . .'; 'I can't really understand . . .'; 'I suppose . . .'; 'I can tell . . .'; 'There's something bothering me about . . .';
- thoughts and feelings when re-reading a book, or seeing a film for the second time: 'When I read it again . . .'; 'The second or third time I read it . . .';
- comments about first readings (which are like first drafts in writing), and about the rewarding and complex readings which come after discussion, reflection, and further reading;
- quoted lines or phrases that catch attention, or which puzzle the readers.

Using a double-column format is one way of capturing the personal memories and feelings which often accompany response to texts:

What happens in the text	*What happens to the reader*
Events, characters, situations	'I remember when . . .'
	'What if . . .?'
	'That's like . . .'
	'I wonder . . .'

Signs of achievement

- recognising the diversity of responses to reading
- showing willingness to express tentative and exploratory responses
- using writing to think about reading
- keeping track of personal responses to reading
- expressing responses to characters and ideas in literature
- questioning texts
- making predictions from reading
- reflecting on many aspects of reading

- evaluating responses to reading
- developing thoughtful, sensitive responses to literature
- sustaining an ongoing record of reading.

TASK 2: WRITING A REVIEW

When students have thought and talked about a text they have read or viewed, they are in a position to write a review. The reviewing task should require students to:
- give some idea of the content, without re-telling the story;
- describe the reviewer's responses;
- make an overall judgement about the work; and
- help other people to decide whether or not they wish to see the film, or read the book.

For this assessment task, students could also be asked to:
- comment on special features of the work;
- provide interesting background on the text being reviewed;
- make comparisons with other works by the same writer or director;
- make comparisons with other works on the same subject;
- stimulate further thinking and discussion about the text.

Before undertaking this assessment task, students should be given access to a wide range of sample reviews, to be read and explored in group activities, as they develop an understanding of writing for the purposes of 'reviewing'.

The following activities will assist in the process of developing this understanding:

1 Invite students to join a reading group to collect and discuss a sample range of reviews. Apart from length, are there ways in which the writer's consideration of the audience for the review affects what is written?

   Students should talk together about the points covered in each review in the sample.

2 When students have read and talked about examples of written reviews, they could also find reviews of books and films presented on radio and television. Over a couple of weeks, all members of the reading group could carry out some research on this aspect of reviewing.

   Students should scan radio and television program guides for information about programs which include reviews, and then:
   - watch and listen to these programs; and
   - make notes about the programs they have heard and viewed, and compile a group log of 'non-print' reviews. The group log could then be used as a basis for talking about the extent to which non-print reviews cover the points listed under the heading: 'What are reviews about?'.

Finally, each student should choose a book he or she has read more than once, which has been discussed with other people, and write two different reviews of this book — one for student readers, the other for teachers interested in the books students read.

Signs of achievement
- giving an overview of important aspects of a book
- writing reviews for different audiences
- choosing a book from personal reading to review
- using a collection of reviews from various sources as models for writing own reviews
- clarifying responses to a text
- describing personal responses in a review
- presenting opinions about texts
- expressing detailed knowledge and understanding of texts in writing
- making an overall judgement about a text
- helping other people to decide whether or not they wish to see a film, or read a book
- writing concisely and coherently.

TASK 3: SIMULATING AN INTERVIEW WITH A CHARACTER IN LITERATURE

There are a number of possibilities for this oral assessment task, which involves students taking on the role of a character from literature so that they can meet other people in different situations and act in role throughout the meeting.

Preparation for the role play will involve:
- discussion of the characters in the text;
- selection of the character to be portrayed in the simulated interview;
- thorough re-reading and research of the texts for details which will enable the actor to take on the role with knowledge and confidence; and
- working with a small group, who coach the interviewee, with reference to events and conversations in the text which reveal important aspects of the character's personality.

The simulation could take the form of a press interview, held in the school library at an advertised time. Other students, knowledgeable about the text, could question the 'character'. Another possibility could be a panel session, in which several 'characters' answer questions from the audience on a variety of subjects. The simulation of the interview involves an interaction, and a close knowledge and understanding of the text.

Signs of achievement
- exploring the role a character plays in a literary text
- investigating the relationships between characters in the same text
- showing understanding of the changes and development in a character evident in a whole text
- recognising significant experiences in a character's experience
- showing insight into the effects of setting on a character's actions
- showing understanding of a character by adopting appropriate movements, gestures, and tone of voice
- incorporating dialogue from a text into role play
- demonstrating insight into the actions and thoughts of a character in literature
- developing a close and detailed knowledge of a text
- expressing responses to literature in an interactive oral situation
- presenting a coherent and thoughtful perspective of a character in literature.

▪CONCLUSION

The evidence derived from knowledgeable observation, across the spectrum of reading processes, attitudes and activities suggested in our lists of statements, will add up to a descriptive profile of the developing reader. This profile — efficiently and concisely recorded — together with systematic observation of the learner's experience in the other language modes of reading, talking and listening, can then be incorporated into a balanced summary profiling the growth that has taken place over time, in a particular program and learning context. Consideration of the broadest possible range of criteria, formulated from the stated evidence, will make it possible to recognise and celebrate the real strengths and achievements of each individual.

Each individual achieves particular abilities by a different pathway, and we hope that the global nature and range of this bank of criteria are appropriate to this variability of growth. Our descriptions of learning and development are offered as growth points, signs, signals and trends by which to chart individual development, and as a data base upon which teachers might build their own 'kidwatching' signs and signals appropriate to their particular classrooms:

> No two snowflakes, popcorn kernels, or children are exactly alike. Therefore, to watch, enjoy, and describe snowflakes, popcorn kernels, and kids, a variety of devices is needed that can be used flexibly and, in the case of snowflakes and kids, fast.

> (Watson, 1985, p. 127)

Reading 1

Name: _____ **Year:** _____ **Date:** _____

Signs of development

Examples:
- holds book the right way up
- turns one page at a time from the start
- recognises directionality of print
- recognises and names letters of the alphabet
- recognises own name and familiar words
- recognises common signs and labels
- find familiar words in known print
- requests reading of familiar stories
- freely chooses books to read
- expresses attitude to certain books
- points to each word as it is read aloud
- retells approximate sequence of stories
- tells stories from pictures
- distinguishes between upper- and lower-case letters
- reads silently for short periods
- writes or draws about stories
- recognises familiar words and phrases
-
-
-
-
-
-
-

Date	Comments

Reading 2

Name: _____ Year: _____ Date: _____

Signs of development

Examples:
- points to each word as it is read aloud
- uses pictures as cues to meaning
- recognises words within other words
- predicts a word omitted from a known sentence
- tells the meaning of lines of print
- recognises environmental print in stories
- often reads familiar words
- can tell where sentences start and finish
- retells stories read aloud in approximate sequence
- retells a story using same or similar words

- can explain simple cause and effect in stories
- chooses books to read
- reads aloud with pauses at punctuation marks
- predicts words and meanings from context
- relates details of characters and events from stories
- shows understanding of print through illustration and own writing
- self-corrects when reading aloud
- reads different kinds of print
-
-
-
-

Date	Comments

Reading 3

Name: _____ **Year:** _____ **Date:** _____

Signs of development

Examples:

- reads aloud with meaning
- recognises familiar words
- predicts from book cover, opening line, opening paragraph
- shows interest in newspapers and other print
- retells stories in writing
- revises reading aloud of print
- asks questions about print
- predicts from context of stories
- acts out events and people in print
- gives opinions on stories
- locates key words in lines of print
- reads aloud with understanding of sentences

- follows printed instructions
- expresses feelings about characters
- reads books for a given purpose
- looks through print materials for important information
- locates main ideas in various printed materials
- selects and uses information from different texts.
-
-
-
-
-

Date	Comments

Reading 4

Name: _____ Year: _____ Date: _____

Signs of development

Examples:

- locates, selects and organises material from a variety of texts
- compares and contrasts a range of texts
- recognises recurring themes in texts
- discerns bias and propaganda
- analyses credibility of sources of information in texts
- produces purposeful and relevant writing about text
- draws conclusions and makes generalisations from texts
- produces an overview of an issue from reading a range of texts
- appreciates the role of performance in understanding texts
- writes about reading in creative and analytical ways

- evaluates a variety of texts
- develops and justifies personal response to literature
- appreciates complex differences in points of view expressed by different authors
- understands how literature influences social development
- contributes personal interpretations to discussions about texts
- reflects critically on text
- relates issues from texts to social concerns and personal values
- produces thoughtful, considered views about reading
-
-
-

Date	Comments

6 WRITING

THE LEARNING AND TEACHING OF WRITING

Learning to write, from the very beginning, means learning how to make sense through writing, how to shape meaning, and how to communicate effectively with readers. In order to describe the ways in which students become more able to communicate meaning in writing, for many purposes and many audiences, it is useful to have some understanding of the signs of growth as students develop and what these signs imply for individual writers. In this chapter, we provide a working guide to the task of observing and describing individual development in writing, across all the years of schooling.

Professional insights into the teaching and learning of writing have been strengthened in the past decade by research on many aspects of writing. Hillocks (1986) reviewed research on the composing process, concluding that there is now a knowledge base from which to ask more and more penetrating questions. Studies of the role of response to writing, such as those by Freedman (1987), Spear (1988), and Anson (1989) have highlighted the importance of leaving ownership of the writing in the hands of the student writer, of communicating high expectations for all students, and of providing students with sufficient help during the writing process. Halliday's (1985) work on functional grammar has been explored by Christie (1990) and others, for example Martin (1985), and this work has offered fresh insights into the importance of structure, context and purpose in writing. The recursive nature of composing has been examined systematically, for example in the work of Hayes and Flower (1980). The role of word processing in writing has been explored by a growing number of researchers, such as Rodrigues and Rodrigues (1986), Snyder (1987) and Kamler and Woods (1987).

As a result of all this work, theorists now appear to agree on a number of points:

1 Writing can be taught — it is not something that develops instinctively.
2 We can identify and share effective teaching strategies.
3 Effective teaching strategies tend to be based upon a fluid notion of writing processes.

4 Central to that notion is the idea that writing is a gradual movement toward form — that if one concentrates upon the final product too soon, one is less able to improve the writing.

5 Teachers can best influence student writing by commenting on drafts in process rather than by marking finished products. Teachers' comments on early drafts should be limited to content and organization. Comments on surface features (spelling, usage, punctuation, sentence structure) should be reserved for almost-completed student drafts.

6 Discovering what the student intends to say and developing those ideas is primary. Only after students develop fluency will they have written enough to make revising effective and meaningful.

7 Writing processes are recursive. Prewriting and invention — the discovery of ideas and form — need to continue throughout the process of writing toward an end product. Even while creating a first draft, writers will edit. Even while editing, writers may discover new insights and need to revise again.

8 Teachers cannot tell students about writing processes and expect them to write accordingly. They must demonstrate those processes through a variety of ways — writing workshops, peer review sessions, brainstorming — and always with students writing.

9 Teaching writing well may require much classroom time and, as a result, limit the number of final drafts a student submits. Yet the number of writing acts a student experiences — prewriting, writing drafts, responding to writing, revising, editing — will increase.

10 There is no one right way to teach the processes of writing. There are, however, desirable and undesirable ways.

(Rodrigues and Rodrigues, 1986, pp. 5–6)

Classrooms with an active, workshop environment are seen as the most appropriate context for writing, and the importance of allowing students adequate time to work on drafts, and perhaps being pressed to complete fewer final drafts, is acknowledged.

Clearly, then, the recognition of development in writing is a complex business. Many processes are involved in writing, all of which need to be considered when we report on progress. The insights generated by the research of the past decade have a number of implications for assessment and for teaching, including the way in which assessment processes are inseparable from teaching and learning processes.

TEACHING THE CRAFT OF WRITING

The variable, fluid and idiosyncratic nature of the craft of writing can readily be observed in any classroom, regardless of the ages of the students. Appropriate environments which allow for this natural variability can be found where classrooms operate as active, well-managed workshops, which create a supportive environment in which students are encouraged to work cooperatively to practise the craft of writing for real purposes and audiences.

In such classrooms students are learning language in operation and not from 'dummy runs'. There will be a wide range of differences within any group, across a number of different dimensions. For example, observations of children who are using word processors for writing often reveals that some children make greater use of the features of the word processor which assist planning, while others focus more on features which aid revision. This variability can be observed as students progress — in ways which may not always be immediately apparent — from elementary to more complex control of writing, and as they learn to make meaning in many different written forms and for an expanding range of purposes.

However, the point is not only that writers differ from each other in their methods of composing and revising, in solving problems encountered in writing, in rehearsing and shaping the meanings they wish to express. Often, differences in individual writing behaviour become apparent over time. Development does not occur in a linear sequence, with identifiable levels within this sequence. Rather, there might be evidence of students achieving control over new forms and processes in a variety of ways, sometimes appearing to take big steps forward, or at other times seeming to regress. This recursive growth pattern may show up when a writer wrestles with a specific problem, such as how to handle flashback sequences within a story, or attempts to master a previously untried form — for example, a scientific report, or a feature article for the school newspaper.

Attitudes to writing vary, too, with writers being more highly motivated and enthusiastic at some times than others. For these reasons, it is essential for teachers to look at a wide range of evidence when describing individual development: collections of writing made over time; pieces of writing from different periods of the writer's work; writing for various purposes and in various forms; recorded observations of the writer in action; draft writing and finished pieces.

Evidence covering this range can only be gathered when the teaching program gives learners access to a variety of contexts for writing and a supportive classroom environment.

CONTEXTS AND ENVIRONMENTS FOR WRITING

Evidence of development in writing, in a number of dimensions, derives from informed observation of writers in action in a variety of classroom contexts, as well as from responsive reading of a range of draft and finished writing. In Chapter 7, Students at work, we explore the drafts and final version of one piece of writing, in the process raising a number of important questions which teachers frequently have to address in responding to students' writing.

In this chapter, we have focused attention on the contexts and environments in which we believe students learn best, and described a range of writing activities which help to create such contexts. Parallel with this, we note signs of development in writing abilities which can be observed as students are encouraged to write for many purposes. The activities described throughout this chapter are appropriate for a wide range of students, though some are more suitable for younger and some for older students. Many of the activities can be adapted in various ways to meet the needs of particular students.

In general, the activities will involve students in taking increasing responsibility for their own work, in writing for real purposes and real audiences, and in working in close cooperation with others. The environment should make students feel comfortable about working with others. For example, the furniture arrangement should be sufficiently flexible for students to work on their own, as well as in pairs or small groups. Appropriate resources, such as paper, word-processors, scissors, paste, dictionaries, thesauruses, a wide range of books, newspapers and magazines, filing cabinets and book-binding equipment should be easily accessible.

Writing activities integrate naturally with the whole English program, and are often not seen as separate components. For example, writing constantly involves reading — students read and re-read their own texts and the writing of their peers as well as a variety of published writing which provides a constant source of ideas and models. Often, reading will lead to writing, perhaps to speculation about what might occur after the end of a story, or to imagining what a minor character might have thought of the events in a novel. There will be a great deal of purposeful talk produced in the course of these activities, as students share their responses to other people's writing and their intentions for their own work. These interconnections between reading, writing, talking and listening are characteristic of classrooms where there are many opportunities for active use of language.

The goals of the writing component of the English program should be directed towards purposes which are strongly connected with the real world and the needs and interests of students. For example, rather than asking students to choose from a random list of 'writing topics', writing tasks can be related to the student's own experience: of reading; of particular encounters with others; of experiences in different curriculum areas; of events and memories which are of significance. Various purposes for writing will also be generated through sets of connected activities that might be called projects or workshops (see Chapter 3, The whole context and Chapter 7, Students at work) or from starting points other than writing itself.

Purposes for writing can include:

- informal, reflective writing in a reading log book, which will serve the important purpose of helping the reader develop a considered response to particular pieces of literature;
- an individual's report of the school swimming sports for the school newspaper, which will involve the gathering of certain information, and the presentation of that information in ways which will be accessible to the particular audience of the school community;
- a letter to the author of a novel that has been of special interest to the whole class, which may establish a contact the group will value;
- a letter to the manager of the local radio station seeking permission to visit, a practical outcome of which might be a class excursion;
- a statement from members of a group presenting a point of view on a current issue — for example, logging in a nearby state forest, or the wearing of school uniform.

These are all examples of the kind of real writing tasks which can challenge students to stretch their writing abilities.

Underlying all of these activities are assumptions about values and ways of learning in general. In working, writing classrooms, students have opportunities to share, to cooperate, to collaborate and to help. Participation in such processes assists students to recognise the value of cooperative learning in their own development as writers. The validity of their own and others' experience is respected, as a powerful source of ideas for writing. The nature of the activities reflects the significance of an acceptance of these values in fostering growth and learning.

DIMENSIONS OF WRITING PROCESSES

From the earliest years of schooling, it is important to make the connections between learning, teaching and assessment at all points in the writing process. There are many dimensions to this process, and to the development of ability as a writer. In describing the range of writing activities on which this chapter is based, we have constructed a scenario, based on different aspects of the writing process, for observing developing writers in action.

In a major study of writing development in the UK, Andrew Wilkinson (1986), recognising that 'in studying the competence of a writer to use language it is no use taking one example only . . .', took groups of students aged 7, 10 and 13 and collected four compositions from each of them. Devising a systematic way of analysing this body of writing, the researchers argued that:

> If we were to look at the writer as a developing being we felt we must be as comprehensive as possible and look at the quality of thought, of the feeling, and of the moral stance manifested in the writing, as well as at the style. Matters of punctuation, spelling, grammatical correctness are of course important, but these are commonly marked anyway. We wanted to look at other ways of assessment.
>
> (Wilkinson, 1986, p. 14)

The team devised four models to serve as systems for analysing the writing sample, in the fields of cognition, affect, morals and style. This work offers one example of the complexity of the task of making valid assessments of writing development, and the need to consider a variety of dimensions.

A reliable picture of the writer in action can only be built up from a series of snapshots of what is involved in making meaning in written language. A set of statements encompassing many dimensions of writing will provide us with multiple lenses to observe active learning writers, and to capture the reality of what is happening. The dimensions we have identified have been clustered under the following headings:

1 Early development
2 Writers in action
3 Writing to communicate ideas, feelings and information
4 Generating and developing topics and ideas
5 Managing different forms of writing
6 Writing for many purposes
7 Managing stylistic features
8 Developing awareness of audience
9 Mastering conventions — punctuation and spelling
10 Learning systems of written language
11 Revising and proof reading; presenting finished work
12 Attitudes to writing
   Taking responsibility
   Self-evaluation
   Interaction with others

In order to demonstrate how teachers can observe these aspects of writing, we have described in the following section a number of activities relating to each of the twelve dimensions identified above, and listed the signs of development and learning which are likely to be fostered by these activities, and likely to become apparent amongst groups of students engaged in these or similar activities. This section is followed by some accounts of a series of classroom episodes with a broader focus, in which development is likely to be evident in many of the dimensions listed. Both sections are intended as an *aide-mémoire* to teachers as they address the large number of considerations involved in responding to development in writing.

The purpose of both sections is to illustrate how much knowledge of writing development can be gained from observing work in progress, as well as from the evidence of the quality of the finished product. A responsive approach to assessment values the insights into the ways individual students approach writing, because it enables teachers to offer specific responses to learning needs. The responses offered to finished pieces are highly significant, in celebrating fine writing and recognisable progress, but these responses must be supported by understanding of many aspects of the writing process. When students become comfortable with the notion that there are many interrelated aspects of writing, and that they can attend to only some of these at any one time, they become more confident writers. Fluency and control then grow from this confidence. The metaphor Pat D'Arcy (1989) offers of a writing as a 'journey' is a useful one to explore with students, as it helps them to understand writing as a learning process.

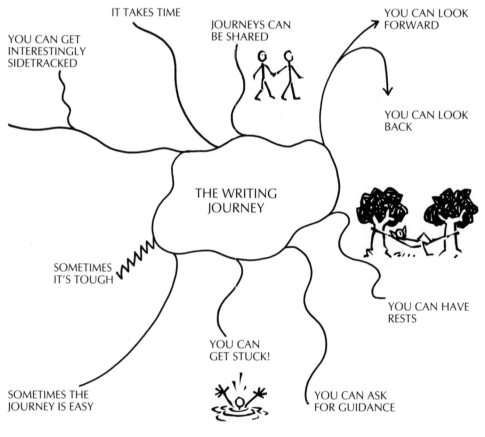

(D'Arcy, 1989, p. 27)

The activities which follow offer only a sample of the possible range. Within the context of the kinds of projects described in Chapters 3 and 7, these activities help learners to develop a repertoire of writing strategies that will enable them to cope flexibly with writing for the many purposes which they will encounter throughout their education, and in the world beyond school.

1 DESCRIBING EARLY DEVELOPMENT

Contexts for observing development

- Take a class of beginners to visit the local supermarket. Then ask them to make display cards, like those seen in the supermarket, for items in the classroom. Notice the range of responses — drawings, scribble, invented spellings, whole words.
- Establish a class letterbox and encourage the children to write to each other and to the teacher.
- Give children constant access to a wide range of picture books and story books, and set aside regular times for silent reading.
- Help each child to build up a personal word bank of favourite words.
- Foster the natural links between writing and drawing, encouraging students to draw, then to write about their drawing, or to label features in a drawing, or to tell the teacher, acting as scribe, what they would like to say about the drawing.
- Keep a picture file of news events and interesting photographs or other illustrations as a source of ideas for writing.
- Talk regularly with individual children about their writing — extend ideas verbally, and then encourage them to write about the things that were talked about.

Signs of achievement

- demonstrating understanding of the ways print in the everyday world conveys meaning
- using words which fit the meaning
- using approximate spelling to achieve meaning
- talking about matters which are seen as potential subjects for writing
- scribbling and drawing to express ideas
- distinguishing between drawing and writing
- using own symbols to write
- offering language for others to transcribe in writing
- understanding that writing goes from left to right and from the top to the bottom of the page
- understanding concepts of linearity and uniformity
- using letters or letter-like shapes
- understanding letter/sound relationships
- writing clusters or combinations of letters

- inventing spelling for needed words
- identifying small differences in letter shapes
- using spaced clusters of letters to create sentences
- knowing the names of letters, both upper and lower case
- making connections between drawings and writing
- recounting experiences while 'reading' own writing
- telling a story while 'reading' own writing
- using oral language to fill in the gaps in writing
- understanding that writing conveys meaning
- using conventional letter formation
- writing legibly enough for others to read
- writing single known words
- writing simple sentences using approximated spelling
- reading own writing to others
- reading what others have written.

There is, to some extent, a developmental sequence within these statements and, by contrast with the sets of statements which follow, they describe points in an individual's development which, once passed, do not recur. For example, the knowledge of the names of letters becomes internalised, and once writers have learnt to write single words they go on to write sentences. However, other items in this list describe attitudes and characteristics which persist, no matter what the age of the writer. The interest in what others have written remains a useful measure of an aspect of the writer's interest in writing, and it is always important to write legibly enough for others to read.

2 WRITERS IN ACTION

Classroom contexts
- Make time in class to watch the students as they work, for example when they are working in pairs or groups, or on their own. Standing quietly in one place, teachers can note the patterns of activity in the room; or roving around, can become the reader over the shoulder. If students have regular access to computers, it is interesting to watch for ways in which they may take advantage of the flexible writing strategies which the word-processor offers.
- From time to time, create an opportunity to review a student's whole writing folder. Ask about how a particular piece developed, how and why revisions were made, and what advice others may have offered.
- Encourage students to use the look/say/cover/write/check process to learn new words.
- Using various page formatting computer programs can help students to see various possibilities for arranging writing on a page. By this method, produce a class newspaper, to which every class member contributes.

- Keep a wide range of writing implements in the room: pens, pencils, textas, crayons, calligraphy pens. Have available sizes and colours of paper.

Signs of achievement
- learning to use a legible, attractive, personal handwriting style
- learning various forms of lettering
- writing quickly maintaining neatness and legibility
- using the word processor for entering, editing and formatting text
- writing easily for short periods
- arranging writing on unlined paper
- arranging writing on lined paper
- using print in the immediate environment to assist own writing
- using various means for checking the spelling of words used
- employing arrows, circles, crossing out, erasers, correction fluid, scissors and paste in revision
- maintaining a satisfactory handwriting style — letter formation, letter size, slope and layout
- using a personal word bank of interest words
- writing easily for long periods
- using references and resources, such as dictionaries, thesauruses, spelling checkers
- revising own writing
- helping others to revise.

3 WRITING TO COMMUNICATE IDEAS, FEELINGS AND INFORMATION

Classroom context
- In groups of four, students draw a map of an imaginary island. This island is to be the setting for a story written by the group. Individuals take responsibility for different sections of the story, using the map as a unifying device. Group members regularly read their drafts to the rest of the group.

Signs of achievement
- clearly conveying a sense of personal involvement in imaginative writing
- selecting and ordering events in logical and interesting ways
- developing a plot and resolving problems in stories
- using writing to organise ideas and information
- writing in detail about the feelings and ideas of other people.

Classroom context
- Students collected samples of writing which conveys information — articles from newspapers and magazines, sports reports, classified

advertisements, brochures, timetables, catalogues. They compiled a collection of these samples, noting the intended audience for each piece. Later, they developed some pieces of informative writing themselves, drawing on their direct experience or their research.

Signs of achievement

- expressing thoughts logically and succinctly
- expressing a well-reasoned point of view in writing
- writing clearly on complex issues
- presenting reasoned generalisations and recommendations
- expressing a committed point of view in writing
- adopting an independent line of thinking on personal and social issues
- using a wide range of relevant evidence to support views
- writing accurate records of tests, experiments, discussions
- expanding notes taken from talks, TV programs, films into detailed records
- writing an account of plans to carry out a task, scheme or project
- summarising information taken from several sources
- drawing conclusions about a series of events/set of facts
- expressing ideas with confidence and competence
- presenting a balanced overview of issues
- adopting various points of view on events and issues
- arguing logically towards decision and action
- displaying insight and understanding of people and ideas in writing
- evaluating arguments and opinions of others
- adopting a personal stance on issues
- formulating a single statement to express the central idea of a piece of writing.

Classroom context

Students were invited to list a series of loosely related memories, in a free association. In small groups, these lists were shared, and when the group's interest was sparked by a particular item on the list, the writer brainstormed an expanded version of the item — an event, a description or anecdote — which was later shared with the same group for further feedback. This established a peer response group which could offer informed response throughout the process of writing the piece, and to which the writer can share goals for the piece: 'In this piece I want to show what it was like when . . .', 'I really want to show what it felt like . . .'

Signs of development

- recollecting past experience through writing
- recreating past experiences in writing
- expressing personal attitudes and feelings in writing
- showing the ability to recreate personal experiences
- reporting on past experiences whilst maintaining a logical sequence of events
- drawing upon and clarifying personal experience
- communicating ideas and experiences clearly.

Related contexts
- Students read about a particular subject — say, coin collecting — and tell someone else about what they have read. They then make notes about what they told the other person, without referring to the original reading. These notes later become the basis for a piece of writing.
- Students make lists of ideas concerning a particular subject. They then use different coloured pencils to link related ideas. These related ideas are then set out on a branching tree design, which provides an organisational structure for a piece of writing.
- Individuals are invited to brainstorm lists of ideas on a common subject. These lists are then cut up into separate items, and, working in small groups, students cluster the items into related groupings. The clusters of ideas are then pasted onto large sheets of paper in some connected way — perhaps as a web, or a tree. Individual students can then use the structure to develop a piece of writing on the original subject.
- Talk with a group of students about interviewing other people to collect information, perhaps about the early history of the school. Work out the key questions the group is interested in for a group research project. Following the interviewing, students write up their notes under the headings of the key questions, which become the organising structure for the group report.

4 GENERATING AND DEVELOPING IDEAS AND TOPICS

Classroom contexts
- Encourage learners to draw on their personal experience and knowledge of the world in their writing by using a clustering strategy. Write a topic in which they are interested — dogs, the zoo, football, swimming — in the middle of the page, and around it write words and phrases which come to mind as the students think about the topic. This cluster then becomes the basis for a first draft of a piece of writing on the subject of interest.
- Students in one class worked in groups to brainstorm lists of their experiences at a recent school camp. Ideas and suggestions were accepted from all group members. They then discussed possibilities for presenting a report of the camp, and reached agreement on the nature of the report. Using the lists from several groups, the teacher worked with the whole class to construct a class report of the camp, drawing attention to some features of report writing, including the use of past tense, and the significance of the order in which events are described. Students then returned to their groups, to write reports based on the lists they had brainstormed. Some groups wrote their reports as wall stories, while two or three people wrote others using a word processor, each taking turns at using the keyboard.

Signs of achievement
- recollecting retained knowledge to use in writing
- brainstorming lists and clusters of ideas
- using past experience as a source of ideas for writing
- sharing in the construction of a piece of writing
- recounting experience in writing
- generating ideas for writing
- planning structure and detail on a given topic
- developing ideas in interesting ways
- expanding and elaborating ideas through appropriate use of detail
- using a wide range of specific, accurate information in writing
- writing a report of a shared experience.

Related contexts
- Journals, including those compiled in other areas of the curriculum, can provide many starting points and much useful material for writing. Students should be encouraged to write regularly in journals, recording and reflecting on personal experience, and to use their journals as a place for noting all manner of things — overheard conversations, observations, anecdotes, for example — which they might later use in writing.
- Encourage students to brainstorm ideas, and then to arrange these ideas into webs of connected ideas. The webs then form the structural basis for the piece of writing. For older students, there are various computer writing programs that can help them to develop the notion of a variable branching structure.
- Arrange for students to interview an older person in the community, to gather information on a matter of interest, such as the early days of the school, the Vietnam War, life during the Depression. Talk with the students about interviews, working out appropriate questions and ways of recording the information — notes, tape recorder.

  Students should then write to the person they would like to interview, explaining the purpose of the interview (for example, to prepare an oral history of the school,) and indicating that they will telephone to arrange a time for the interview.

  If students lack confidence about the visit, it may be possible to arrange for them to be accompanied by a parent-helper.

  After the interview, the students can write up their notes into a fluent piece, perhaps on the word processor. They will have a great deal of material, and will be able to focus more closely on how they want to express their ideas, instead of on what they want to say.

Signs of achievement
- developing topics for writing from a range of sources
- gathering information for writing
- sorting and organising information

- taking notes from interviews
- writing to explain
- developing a command of both serious and humorous topics
- relating a number of associated ideas in writing
- arguing a point of view through definition and analysis
- speculating and hypothesising on the basis of present information
- adopting a variety of stances on a particular issue.

5 MANAGING DIFFERENT FORMS OF WRITING

Classroom contexts
- One group of students planned a report in which they explained aspects of a topic they had chosen. Using a web or mental map, they brainstormed as many aspects of the topic as they could think of. After looking at their ideas arranged around the page, they 'bundled' or classified each aspect under certain subheadings. They wrote an introduction based on the subheadings and composed the piece using subheadings to signify particular aspects of the topic.
- Students collected examples of newspaper and magazine reports on an important event. In small groups, students looked at the different ways in which the event was reported. They chose another recent event or a personal experience and, using the models they had identified, wrote three different accounts.

Signs of achievement
- learning the skills of paraphrasing, note-taking, outlining and summarising
- selecting and ordering details
- organising ideas logically in writing
- using models of writing
- writing reports of events, incidents and experiences
- showing awareness of different types of writing
- using different forms of writing — stories, reports, letters — as appropriate
- writing a factual account maintaining logical sequence
- writing a story or report in the past tense
- writing factual accounts in both the first and third person.

Classroom contexts
- Students were asked to write a sequel to the novel which had been the focus of shared reading. When the class had read the novel, students talked in groups about likely futures for the main characters. A recorder in each group made notes of the discussion on a large sheet of paper. To justify their scenarios, students found details from the text of the novel to support their ideas. Details of characters and events from the novel gave clues to what might happen to the central characters beyond the last chapter. Students drafted their sequels and read them

aloud to members of their writing groups. Students were challenged by questions such as: 'What makes you think that?' and 'How could that possibly happen?'
- Students worked in a group to improvise a scene from a novel they had all read. On the basis of this improvisation, they wrote a script for a TV production of this scene.

Signs of achievement
- brainstorming ideas in a group
- talking about ideas before writing
- selecting appropriately related ideas and expressing them fluently
- using logical sequencing in story writing
- writing an original story within the framework of another story
- making predictions in writing
- writing about imaginative possibilities drawn from reading
- revising writing in terms of feedback from an informed group
- improvising to clarify ideas
- using knowledge of one media (television) to develop a text in another medium (script)
- collaborating with others in writing
- writing imaginatively and creatively
- writing in various forms
- writing for a variety of purposes
- achieving a clear and coherent structure in a particular form of writing
- using dialogue effectively.

6 WRITING FOR MANY PURPOSES

Classroom contexts
- Students draw a picture, ensuring that their partners do not see their drawing. They then write instructions so that the partner can reproduce the drawing accurately. After the partner has completed the drawing it is compared with the original. The writers can revise the written instructions in the light of the accuracy of the reproduction.
- Give students the basic outline of a story — setting, characters, problems — and ask them to:
  — fill in the details, and
  — plan interesting or unusual ways of starting and ending.
- Students investigate a place or person and note five or six interesting facts. They experiment with the order of these facts, making decisions about how they will order the facts in a piece of writing about their subjects.
- Students explain in writing how to do or make something from start to finish. These pieces are read to partners who are asked whether they have any questions not answered by the procedure described.
- Students brainstorm a list of 'hot' issues. They then choose one that

they would like to write about immediately. Students write their own view in not more than three sentences or fifty words. Then they write the opposing view, introduced by connectives such as 'On the other hand' and 'However'. Next they write a question or brief statement of the issue as a headline, and compose the whole piece using what they have written, building in new ideas and facts and using connectives.

- A group of students writes a series of captions for the photos of the class trip, the swimming sports or some other recent school event. The photos and captions are displayed on the school notice board.
- Students are asked to prepare a biography of an older person they know well. They also read a number of published biographies while they are researching their own subject, keeping a log of the features they encounter in their reading.
- Students read a short newspaper report of a dramatic event and then rewrite the report as a poem, working in pairs or groups.
- Students are challenged to write in ways which will persuade people well known within the school to change their allegiance to a particular football team. Offer an award for the most persuasive piece of writing.
- Students take part in a letter exchange — perhaps as electronic mail — between parallel classes in different schools.
- The class takes responsibility for the production of a school newspaper, which will contain all the features of a regular newspaper — feature stories, sports reports, editorial opinion, cartoons, and so on. The paper must convey a lot of information of interest to the general school community. Their responsibilities include the writing of headlines and captions for photographs.

Signs of achievement

- writing for a range of purposes
- writing for a variety of audiences
- collaborating with others in writing
- developing coherence in writing
- writing personal and business letters
- writing to persuade
- writing to inform
- writing narrative
- developing sequence and structure in writing
- reporting on past experience whilst maintaining a chronological sequence of events
- writing a set of instructions
- making written notes for various purposes.

7 MANAGING STYLISTIC FEATURES

Awareness of style in writing is developed from the earliest encounters children have with written language. In the classroom, they should have constant access to the widest possible range of literature, which they should be encouraged to read for themselves, as well as having it read aloud to them. This should include informative, persuasive and technical writing as well as many different forms of literature — stories, novels, scripts, poems. Reading aloud in the classroom enables children to hear and internalise the patterns and rhythms of written language, and to develop a sensitivity to language.

A continuous conversation about language builds on the enjoyment of discovering new words and new ways of saying things, and extends students' knowledge of the potential of language. A class bulletin board of interesting pieces of writing encourages students to build a collection of interesting samples of writing in their writing folders.

The classroom climate should encourage students to take risks with new ways of saying things, perhaps telling a story from a different point of view, or using a different tone. Not all the experiments should be expected to work; what is important is to make discoveries about writing by playing with all sorts of possibilities.

Classroom contexts

- In one class, students were asked to write a poem based on events or people in the news. When they had collected several newspaper clippings, they made lists of important words and phrases reporters had used to describe the events in the clippings.

  Students constructed poems from these lists by writing in their own words and phrases so that connections were made between separate events, different people or various scenes.

- After looking at a newspaper report of a sensational event, students talk in groups about the reported order of events and details, and why the journalist used this order. They then work out possible reasons for this order of presentation.

Signs of achievement

- understanding the significance of sequence in creating meaning
- creating atmosphere and mood through descriptive language
- choosing appropriate words to create mood and tone
- using varied and imaginative content
- writing in imaginative and interesting ways
- elaborating ideas through appropriate detail
- choosing appropriate words to match thoughts, ideas, and feelings
- placing words in context
- writing effective word pictures
- using an extensive vocabulary in writing.

8 DEVELOPING AWARENESS OF AUDIENCE

Classroom contexts

- Over several sessions, students browsed through and read, or re-read, a large collection of picture books. They were encouraged to discuss the way the pictures and text work together to create meaning, and how sometimes the pictures extend the meaning beyond the written text.

Students also talked about the wide range of topics which can be addressed through the medium of the picture story book. Students then started on the task of writing their own picture story books, for a known audience — younger children in the same school, at a nearby pre-school centre, or younger members of their own family. At different points in the drafting and revising of their stories, they visited the children they were writing for in order to estimate the effect of their work. Finally, the picture story books were read to the intended audience, and kept in a permanent collection.

This activity took a long time, and involved much related reading and discussion — it was a major project. In some cases, it is a good idea to allow students to work in pairs on this project.

- Students each wrote a short piece of about two paragraphs, and exchanged pieces with a partner. The reading partners made up a list of all the questions that they, as readers, would like answered. The writers then revised the piece in the light of these questions, providing the extra information required by the readers. This activity helps to identify the ways in which writers have to anticipate readers' questions.

Signs of achievement
- writing for a variety of audiences
- writing for a known audience
- varying choice of words and sentences for different purposes and audiences
- writing for younger children
- using various sentence structures to achieve shades of meaning
- writing in particular ways according to audience
- combining pictures and text to create meaning
- developing ideas for writing that suit various audiences
- valuing the advice of others
- convincing the reader of knowledge of the subject
- showing awareness of the needs of the reader.

Related contexts
- Provide students with some statistical information, perhaps on the nutritional value of fast foods. Ask them to write two different 100-word paragraphs to two very different interest groups: perhaps one to the owner of a fast food chain, the other to a group of heart patients on a low-fat, salt-free diet.
- Brainstorm, with the whole class, a list of reasons why people write. Ask students to collect, from various sources, examples of writing which match these reasons. Students then compile a personal list of purposes for writing, and try over time to write pieces which fulfil these purposes.

- Ask a group of students to write a series of letters to the local paper on a matter of local interest.
- Negotiate a work plan with students which requires them to present a folder of writing, containing a specified number of pieces covering a range of different purposes.
- As a class project, compile an anthology of students' writing. Having their writing published heightens students' awareness of the importance of the audience. Ways of publishing writing within a school include contributing to a school or class newspaper, to anthologies, or to a book of class stories. Beyond the school, there are other avenues for publication, such as local newspapers.

  One school requires its senior students to have three pieces of writing published as part of the assessment for the course. Students write sports reports, letters to the editor, reports of newsworthy events within the school and so on. Another large primary school regularly publishes students' writing in the weekly parents' newsletter, even serialising some long stories.

9 MASTERING CONVENTIONS — PUNCTUATION AND SPELLING

Classroom contexts

- Students keep a look/say/cover/write/check page in their writing folders, so that they can have ready access to it when they are writing.
- Frequent reference to the ways punctuation is used in published writing helps students to recognise the significance of clarifying meaning through punctuation as well as through vocabulary and syntax. Students collect, from a variety of sources, interesting examples of ways in which all the major punctuation marks can be used. Then, in small groups, they compare their collections. This generates talk about common usage of punctuation marks.

  Imitation of the punctuation and syntax of a published author can stem from this activity, developing students' abilities in using the conventions of written language. For example, a senior class reading David Malouf's *Fly Away Peter* wrote descriptive pieces that imitated the first page or so of the novel. Students were asked to picture a scene that they knew well and to imagine from their own experience the things that could change this scene dramatically, such as a storm, a loud explosion, a plane flying overhead or an invasion of tourists. They then wrote pieces using the same sentence structure, punctuation and paragraphing as the first page of Malouf's novel.

Signs of achievement

- recognising patterns and groups of letters
- recognising the sequence of letters within words

- using look/say/cover/write/check for spelling
- attempting to spell new and difficult words
- learning accurate spelling by successive approximations
- finding correct spelling for approximations
- showing control of spelling in a variety of writing contexts
- using commas, full stops, question marks, inverted commas, apostrophes
- writing a variety of sentences
- using punctuation to create meaning
- showing controlled and flexible use of the conventions
- using punctuation accurately in own writing
- understanding how punctuation affects meaning.

Related contexts

- Students build personal banks of words that they want to use in their writing, have difficulty in spelling, and discover in reading.
- When students are confident to use an approximate spelling for particular words, the teacher can talk with them about the value of having used the best word to carry the intended meaning, and ways in which the spelling can be verified. 'Bloke' may well be more effective than 'man' in a piece of writing, even if it is spelt as 'blokk' at the first attempt.
- The word processor can be used to help students see the effects of punctuation on meaning. A small group of students can experiment with deleting all punctuation from a passage of text, and trying to read it aloud. They can try out various different ways of punctuating the passage until they are satisfied that the meaning can be clearly understood.

10 LEARNING OF SYSTEMS OF WRITTEN LANGUAGE

Classroom contexts

- Students worked with a partner to write a coherent story, taking turns to write alternate sentences. To do this, they needed to focus very precisely on the overall coherence of their writing. The discussion which occurred naturally as they composed the story develops awareness of the ways in which coherence is achieved. Continuous story writing can also be undertaken by groups, each group in turn building on the story.
- Students collected newspaper articles as a major series of events unfolded — in this case, events in China in June 1989. Groups chose one article that they thought provided a clear picture of what had actually happened. In their logbooks, students listed the various events that the article described. They were asked to examine how the reporter had managed to fit so much information into the article. What strategies in the use of sentences and paragraphs had enabled the writer

to provide this information? The class together looked at specific examples of sentences where various pieces of information had been combined. Each group was asked to compose a newspaper report that would summarise events as described in the series of newspaper articles they had collected.

Signs of achievement

- placing sentences in their logical sequence
- writing a number of paragraphs in logical sequence in narrative mode
- writing various sentence beginnings and making appropriate choices
- using singular and plural forms of words
- writing in sentences and paragraphs
- writing coherently and logically
- constructing paragraphs that elaborate and support the main idea with examples and reasons
- writing a number of paragraphs in logical sequence in narrative/non-narrative mode
- using appropriate tense in writing
- using different kinds of connectives
- linking ideas in writing.

Related contexts

- To help students write sentences meeting given restraints, and then to evaluate sentence completeness, they can be asked to make up sentences in which each word starts with the same letter. (The sentences can be nonsensical, but need to be grammatically correct.) In small groups, or with the whole class, the sentences are discussed to determine their completeness and grammatical correctness.
- Ask students to take a piece of their own writing, to cut it up and then to arrange the sentences in a random order. (This can be done with scissors, or on the word processor.) Another student is then asked to arrange the piece in a logical order. When the original is compared with the rearranged version, possible variations in logical sequence can initiate discussion of how the logic of the piece was achieved.

  A variation is to separate a piece into paragraphs, and to see if another student can reassemble the piece into a logical order. Often the writer will discover that the inclusion of tighter links between the paragraphs will help others to recognise his or her desired sequence.
- Students work in groups to compile a list of words which help to connect ideas in a piece of writing. They discuss and list words such as: moreover, again, otherwise, however, finally, next, for example, in other words, eventually, under, below, therefore, similarly; and then talk about the function of these words. For example, 'moreover' can be used to add ideas, while 'therefore' shows a conclusion. Another list of the uses of these words can be developed by the group — to add ideas, to show order, to compare and so on.

11 REVISING AND PROOFREADING, PRESENTING FINISHED WORK

Classroom contexts — revising

- Students took a completed piece of writing, and rewrote the introduction. Then they were asked to write a third possible introduction. Each introduction was to be as different as possible from the original one. Students then shared their introductions in work with a small group and developed a group consensus on which introduction worked best in the overall context of the piece.

  This activity encourages students to experiment with a range of possible approaches, and often leads to interesting developments when students write their own pieces. Students revised their introductions and planned stories to develop from them. Each introduction was read to a small group whose members were asked to say what they thought might happen in a story with such an opening.

  Each student then drafted and revised a story based on this opening.

- The writing conference, between teacher and student, or amongst other members of the community of writers within the classroom, is a supportive and encouraging context for revision. Within a conference, a friend can say: 'You need to say more about the dungeon master', and help the writer to see where extra information is required. In a conference, the teacher can advise a student on the appropriate way of setting out dialogue in writing, by referring to examples in books the student is reading, and by reworking pieces with individuals. As described in Chapter 7, peer response groups also provide a productive context for revision and editing at various points in the composition of a piece.

Signs of achievement

- writing openings that arouse interest
- understanding how writers use introductions
- planning detail and structure
- expanding and elaborating ideas through appropriate use of detail
- accepting ideas from other people
- listening to advice about ways of writing
- formulating alternative ways of expression
- completing major structural revisions of a piece of writing
- rewriting, clarifying meaning and diversifying language
- rewriting to achieve precision and vividness
- revising and paraphrasing own sentences and paragraphs
- polishing and redrafting writing by reordering, changing words, tightening structure
- reordering material to catch a reader's interest
- creating a context for adding material while maintaining coherence

- integrating new ideas and information into a text
- eliminating redundant words
- adding illustrative examples
- changing sentences to match the writer's intention — to convey mood, appeal to emotion
- writing different versions of sentences
- acting on advice offered by others, e.g. when extra information is needed
- using a variety of strategies and resources for revising.

Related contexts

- When students are encouraged to paraphrase their own work, they develop a range of possibilities to consider.
- Another way of discovering alternative possibilities is to have students take a piece of their own writing, and delete some words — perhaps all the descriptive words. They then ask other students to complete what is really a 'cloze' exercise, and so collect a set of other words which make sense within the passage, amongst which they may discover a fresh approach. (The computer makes this a very simple activity to organise.)
- Work with the whole class to build up a list of reasons a writer may have to change a sentence — say, to make the sentence funnier/scarier/sadder; to try to communicate to a younger person; to add content; or to try to appeal to reason or emotion. This list can be kept in individual writing folders as a handy guide to revision.
- Make a checklist for revision:
  — My goals for this piece are to . . .
  — Here is the main idea, or argument . . .
  — I see the following problems with the piece, and would appreciate your advice . . .
  — My plans for revising this draft are . . .
  The student can give this to a friend, or to the teacher, or use the checklist as a guide to personal revision. The opportunity to explain or describe goals and problems is an important aspect of revision.

Classroom contexts — editing

- Encourage students to proofread each other's writing — in this way they will also learn to proofread their own writing more effectively.
- Create occasions when it is particularly important for a piece to be properly proofread, perhaps for publication in the school newspaper.
- Offer students a checklist of things to look for when proofreading; this list can be kept in the writing folder or file for ready reference.
- Invite professional writers to talk about the importance of accurate proofreading, and to explain the strategies they use.
- Encourage students to read their work aloud to someone else — in the process of reading they will become more aware of errors which need attention.

Signs of achievement
- proofreading own writing for legibility, clarity and accuracy
- proofreading for meaning as well as accurate use of language
- undertaking simple revision and proofreading for legibility, spelling and meaning
- referring to dictionaries and thesauruses to check spelling and word choice
- proofreading and presenting work for publication.

12 ATTITUDES TO WRITING: RESPONSIBILITY, SELF-EVALUATION, INTERACTION WITH OTHERS

Classroom contexts — responsibility and self-evaluation
- Students make a selection of the best pieces of writing they have done in a certain period of time. When they gather these pieces into a folio, they can enjoy a real sense of achievement. They can be asked to write a short introduction to the folio which gives the reasons for their choice, and to say why they were perhaps more satisfied with one piece than with another.

Related contexts
- Encourage students to read widely, and to consider how writers use language and solve problems in their writing. Frequent discussion of others' writing provides a perspective on the writer's own work.
- Sometimes ask students to keep a record of the development of a particular piece from the very first rough idea until the finished product, stapling all notes and drafts to the back of the finished piece. Review this record with the student in a writing conference, together with all of the drafts. The discussion will illuminate the ways the writer has approached the task, and indicate the growth that has taken place.

Cooperation
- Writing is often a social experience, and growth in writing ability occurs in contexts where students know that their ideas and experience are valued, and where they are confident to share their work with others, at any stage of writing. Opportunities for collaborative composition enhance this confidence.
- Validate the students' work by displaying folios of work, by reading work aloud to the class, and by encouraging students to publish some of their best work.
- Encourage cooperative situations for writing, wall stories or co-authored productions, for example. When a Year 12 student and a primary school student wrote a story together, each learnt from the other.

- Offer students models for responding to each other's writing, demonstrating the value of detailed comment rather than a general acceptance. It's better to point out that the sequence of events in the hitch–hiking episode is confusing before: 'How did he pick you up?' than simply to say: 'I don't understand'.

Enthusiasm

A program which provides support for students at all stages of the writing process, which recognises and makes use of the different approaches of the different writers in the group, encourages positive attitudes to writing, which promote growth. When writing for real purposes and audiences, students are likely to enjoy writing and to be prepared to tackle new challenges.

- If a student is reluctant to write, talk about experiences beyond school. If the student was involved in a successful Jamboree of the Air, or a hiking activity, suggest that this might be a basis for a piece of writing. Offer to act as the scribe to help get the piece started.
- Ask students to write a 'choose your own adventure' story, exploring as many options as possible. Make sure they try the story out with different readers, and that they try to be really adventurous in the possibilities they offer the reader.
- Students can write an alternative ending to a novel, or write a sequel about events after the novel ended, or write a version of what might have happened in one of the 'telling gaps' in the story (for example: 'Why did Max decide to return to his very own room, where his supper was still hot?'). This sort of writing helps the student to reflect on the reading, and often provides a framework for writers who find it hard to start writing.

Signs of achievement

- developing a reflective, critical attitude to own writing
- adopting an objective view of own writing
- building a wide background of reading which provides an informed perspective on own work
- describing why one piece is more effective than another
- explaining goals in writing a piece, and indicating the extent to which these goals were achieved
- accepting advice on ways of improving writing
- making a selection of the best writing done over a period of time
- indicating which aspects of a particular piece were successful and which were not
- keeping personal records of progress and development.

Cooperation

- contributing to group/class stories
- drafting and revising in collaboration with peers and teacher

- talking with adults to gain information and ideas
- giving constructive assistance to other students
- sharing information and ideas with others
- assisting others to evaluate their work
- valuing advice offered by others
- acting on advice offered by others
- participating in revision of partner/group/class stories
- participating in the making and revision of group/class stories and poems.

Enthusiasm
- showing enthusiasm for writing
- actively engaging with writing tasks
- experimenting with ideas and language
- being resourceful in gathering information
- being firm and confident in adopting a point of view in writing.

EPISODES FROM THE CLASSROOM

As in the preceding chapters on talking and listening, and on reading, these episodes are presented to show the range of signs of language learning that can be observed in such situations. While the emphasis of these episodes is on ways of writing, teachers will also recognise that learning about written language and how to use it is generated by talking, listening and reading. The signs of learning observed in students' participation will therefore range across the language modes.

EPISODE ONE: JOURNAL WRITING AT YEAR 2

The teacher talked with the students about keeping writing journals — personal notebooks in which they could write regularly, about anything which seemed important to them. The teacher explained her willingness to respond to the writing in the journals, if invited to do so. A special time for journal writing each day was nominated.

The journal writing venture was 'launched' when the teacher gave each student a new notebook, with a brightly coloured cover. Students were able to choose a favourite colour, thus establishing the individuality of the journal from the start. They were free to write, to draw, to make lists, to write about their day's experiences, to write about books they had been reading, funny experiences, jokes, or to write in detail about particular incidents and feelings. The idea of the journal as a place for 'thinking on paper' was talked about.

During journal writing time, the teacher also wrote in a journal, and from time to time shared excerpts from this journal with the students. This modelling suggested a range of possibilities to the children, and helped journal writing to become an established part of this class's routine.

Once established, journal writing extended this class's interest in writing. Journals were sometimes used as sources of ideas for more extended pieces of writing. Some children asked to take the journals home to write more than they had time allocated for in class. When invited to read the journals — and most children offered this invitation — the teacher wrote comments and questions, and many of the children replied to these in subsequent entries, thus establishing a written dialogue.

Signs of achievement
- writing for enjoyment
- writing for self as audience
- coming to terms with new experience and information through writing
- writing to learn
- exploring new ideas in writing
- demonstrating a preparedness to write regularly
- showing ownership of writing
- using a personal journal to reflect on experiences in everyday life
- developing fluency by writing regularly
- discovering value in writing as a way of making sense of experiences
- making connections between past experience and new experience and knowledge
- thinking through writing
- recording significant personal experiences
- writing in a variety of ways — lists, notes, descriptions
- developing a point of view on a variety of issues
- understanding the value others place on personal writing
- using a journal as a source of ideas for writing.

EPISODE TWO: TALKING ABOUT WRITING AT YEAR 3

Three children formed an editorial group to review the most recent drafts of their reports on the excursion to the dinosaur exhibition. Since the whole class had been on the excursion, there had been a lot of talk about dinosaurs and other extinct animals. Lists of 'dinosaur' words were displayed in the classroom; there were pictures collected from various sources, and some papier mâché models made in art lessons.

The written reports are intended for a class book on the excursion. Everyone's report will be included. These three children have already discussed earlier drafts of their reports and various suggestions for improving them were made. In this session, they are doing a final editing check prior to their reports being entered, by the parent helpers, on the word processor for printing and publication. Attention is focused on spelling, punctuation, sequence and accuracy of expression.

Each child reads her report in turn. The other students listen to check that the order makes sense: 'Didn't we look at the big dinosaur first?', 'That's when the man told us about what they ate'.

The short reports are then passed around the group for everybody to read. As the student editors focus on each piece, the necessary corrections are marked on them. At this point, we hear questions such as:

- 'Shouldn't this be a full stop?'
- 'You haven't spelt "tyrannosaurus" properly. See . . . on the list over there . . .'
- 'Shouldn't it say what colour it was?'

Signs of achievement
- understanding that writing conveys meaning
- showing interest in reading what others have written
- developing fluent, legible handwriting
- using print to convey meaning
- developing awareness of different ways of writing
- gathering information for specific writing purposes
- developing the ability to write a factual account maintaining logical sequence
- developing ideas in interesting ways
- recognising words with familiar meanings
- using knowledge of print to learn other words
- self-correcting when reading does not make sense
- anticipating high-interest words using consonant cues
- reading silently with understanding
- carrying out research tasks
- developing ability to use specific, accurate information
- collaborating in action with others
- using speech to plan and carry out specific tasks
- recognising and expressing problems and their solutions
- sharing ideas with others clearly and logically
- expressing an opinion when answering a question
- making a simple analysis of a situation, with supporting reasons
- respecting others' ideas
- using speech effectively to comment on text
- answering questions by providing information
- asking clear and thoughtful questions
- showing tenacity in pursuing ideas
- participating effectively in task-oriented discussions

- demonstrating tact in resolving disagreements
- understanding the purpose of writing a report
- considering the needs of readers.

EPISODE THREE: FACTUAL WRITING IN YEAR 5

The Year 5 class made lists of topics they wanted to write about, and had contributed many ideas to a class book which provided a resource for students during the year. The topics came from the children's experience and interests, from classroom reading and from talking with others. As the year progressed, more ideas were added to the lists and to the class book. The children were encouraged to think of ideas from their work in all areas of the curriculum, and gradually it was clear that a variety of forms and purposes for writing was accumulating. As well as finding topics for stories, students wanted to write about such matters as:
- TV programs
- Australian scenes and places
- bikes and skateboards
- strange events, and
- the Olympic Games.

When asked what they wanted to do with topics like these, students responded with such comments as:
- 'Describe what really happened'
- 'Teach someone else how to do this'
- 'Give some more information'
- 'Say what I think about this'
- 'Describe the scene'.

The class had read and talked about a number of topics connected with a project on Australia. This was planned as an integrated project which would:
- extend knowledge
- provide opportunities to draw on personal experience
- provide opportunities to investigate topics of interest
- involve students in group activities, and
- create a context for writing in various ways.

In reading and through library research, students had found and were shown some factual accounts of Australian scenes and sights. It was decided by mutual agreement to look at travel literature and to choose a particular place to write about. Each group was to choose one place. The purpose of the activity, in addition to reading different kinds of text, was to provide experience in ways of communicating clear and interesting factual information so that readers might be interested in visiting these places. Several pamphlets and posters, obtained from local travel agencies, were displayed in the classroom, and students also looked at pamphlets and brochures.

Each group was given a number of cards on which to write a single fact about the place they had chosen. They were asked to write at least 10 facts and then to sort out the cards that seemed to go together; that is, the cards that described facts which were related in some way: 'What things go together?'.

The students were then asked to look at each pile which, in most cases, comprised two or three facts. 'Write a sentence about each set of cards. What is each set about?' From this activity, students were able to classify aspects of the place they had chosen. At this stage, each student formed a partnership with one other member of the group and began to prepare a publication advertising the attractions of the places they had selected.

They looked at travel brochures and decided where they would put each set of facts, and what they would say on the front and back pages. This led to some persuasive talk based around two or three interesting features of the material. Some pairs chose to begin their publication with the most exciting feature.

Some groups chose a simple leaflet, using front and back of an A4 sheet; others developed four- or six-page pamphlets folded from one A4 sheet. Whatever the number of pages, students had to decide where they would put each set of facts. They drew maps and illustrations and obtained relevant magazine pictures to go with their texts. One or two of the partnerships made up stories based on the facts they had found — another way of persuading readers to go there. Several groups chose to use word processing programs, in order to create various kinds of type styles for the headings and subheadings, and to vary the text throughout the pamphlet.

All material was displayed around the room and the students talked about which of the publications were the most effective. This discussion helped to promote the idea that there are many ways to persuade people to take a course of action.

Signs of achievement
- working in collaboration with others
- collecting a range of factual information
- sorting information
- selecting and ordering information
- writing narratives based on facts
- generating ideas from previous experience and research
- writing in different forms
- writing for a range of purposes
- reading various models of travel literature
- planning writing with others
- recognising ways of persuading in writing

- using maps and illustrations to extend and support writing
- using the word processor
- reflecting on the effectiveness of the writing.

EPISODE FOUR: COMPILING AN ANTHOLOGY AT YEAR 8

A whole term's work in English was devoted to the development of personal anthologies of writing, including a range of writing selected from various sources, and a selection of the students' own writing. The students had seen the anthologies produced by the previous year's class when they had been displayed in the school library, and were eager to produce their own.

There were some set requirements for the anthology: the total number of pieces, and the number of pieces of their own writing which were to be included. The intention was to develop a collection of different kinds of writing — narrative, poems, technical writing, reports, newspaper writing, instructions and so on. The students were also asked to develop a table of contents, to give the source of each piece of writing included in the collection, and to write an introduction to the anthology, in which they explained their choice of theme, and how they had gone about collecting the material. In a short conclusion, they were invited to reflect on what they had learnt from the experience of compiling the anthology.

Students chose a linking theme for their anthologies — animals, war, relationships, the future, sport. As much class time as possible was spent in the library during this project, and librarians gave extra support to students as they browsed around the library shelves in search of material, answering questions such as: 'Where can I find a poem about sport?', 'Is there any factual information about . . .?'. This research time gave students an opportunity to become really familiar with the full resources of the library, to learn to use tables of contents and indexes effectively, and to do a lot of incidental reading as they hunted for the material they wanted.

All writing in the collection had to be reproduced by the students, either in their own best handwriting, or on the word processor. Many students learnt how to make very good use of the word processor in the course of this project.

The teacher's role for most of the time was to work one-to-one with students, offering advice and support in the selection of material, and in the drafting and editing of the students' own writing. This created many valuable learning situations.

The final presentation of the anthologies was a matter of pride for all students, some making books out of brightly coloured paper, bound together in a variety of ways, others using scrapbooks, others using plastic display folders. Many of the collections were illustrated. All were read avidly by other class members, both while they were being compiled and when they went on public display in the library.

Signs of development

- managing an extended project
- organising own work time
- becoming familiar with the resources offered by the library
- reading a wide range of different kinds of writing
- learning where to locate different kinds of writing
- developing an awareness of differences between writing intended for a range of purposes and audiences
- experimenting with writing for many purposes
- in the process of reproducing other people's writing, becoming familiar with possibilities of tone, form and style
- producing a range of finished writing for different purposes
- drafting and revising with care
- proofreading with accuracy
- presenting finished work in an attractive way
- practising handwriting skills
- developing competence in using the word processor
- compiling an interesting, readable and coherent collection of writing
- sharing finished writing with a wide readership.

EPISODE FIVE: DIARY WRITING IN YEAR 10

Students kept a diary for five weeks in the first term of the year. They were asked to make entries each week and were given 10–15 minutes' class time to do this.

In the diary, students were asked to:

- write at least five entries each week in the time given in class;
- write down whatever seemed important or interesting on that day; and
- decide what would be shown to others, and read other students' diaries only when invited.

At the same time, the class was reading *The Diary of Anne Frank* and other published diaries.

There were opportunities to talk about this book with other people, and to explore some of these questions:

- What did Anne Frank think was important to write about?
- Why do you think she wrote in the form of letters addressed 'Dear Kitty'?
- Now that you've seen the video on Amsterdam in the war years, do you think you would have acted differently in that situation?

Students were asked if they had access to diaries, letters or other personal writings belonging to people in their family, and invited to share these with a group.

At the end of the five weeks, students were asked to look back over their diary from a reader's point of view. These questions provided a focus for this review:

- What things in your diary would other people not understand? Why not?
- What would you have to do to make these things understandable?
- Were you talking to anybody in particular when you wrote any of the pieces? Explain.
- What do you think would most interest other people?
- Are there many connections between things you have written?
- What do you see in your diary now?

They were then asked to select some pieces from the diary to read to other people, and to listen to their responses, noting the pieces in which the listeners seemed most interested. They then rewrote these passages as a connected piece for the group, and read it to the group to find out:

- what they thought the piece was about, and
- whether or not that was what the writer intended.

These pieces were used as the basis of a folio of writings based on the diary. These ideas suggested some starting points:

- Write about one of the events from the point of view of someone else involved (e.g. your parents?).
- Write a report of one event in the diary for the school newspaper.
- Memories — do the events in your diary remind you of past experiences?
- What happens next? Predict the next few months in your life.
- If you've written about a problem in your life, did you solve it? If not, what do you think you might do about it?
- Did you write about something in the community that you feel strongly about? If so, state your case to classmates.
- Write a letter replying to one of the entries in another person's diary.
- Write a piece for your autobiography telling what happened in this stage of your life.
- Read Robert Frost's poem 'The Road Not Taken' and write a piece entitled 'A Road I'd Like To Take'.
- Select fragments from your diary and shape them into a poem.

Signs of achievement
These signs of development were observed in the activities of individual students who worked on this project:

- writing for an extended time
- expressing feelings
- clarifying personal experience

- evaluating others' opinions
- explaining ideas and views
- writing about other people's feelings and opinions
- selecting and ordering events in logical and interesting ways
- recounting experience in writing
- generating ideas for writing
- developing ideas and topics for writing
- writing from different points of view
- writing for a variety of audiences and purposes
- writing accurate reports of events and experiences
- writing a personal letter
- writing a story or report in the past tense
- writing factual accounts in both first and third person
- using writing to make predictions and to speculate
- writing in imaginative ways
- using an extensive vocabulary
- developing and elaborating thoughts through appropriate detail
- using language to match original ideas
- listening to other people's ideas
- varying syntax to suit audience and purpose
- varying choice of words to suit audience and purpose
- using word pictures to convey feelings and experiences
- showing awareness of how different readers might respond to a piece
- adopting different voices for different audiences.

All the signs of development listed in this chapter have the potential to be used with students as the basis for reflection and self-evaluation.

■ ASSESSING ACHIEVEMENT

As in Chapters 4 and 5, we offer three tasks which can be used when it is appropriate to make a specific assessment of achievement in writing at a particular time. These tasks can be adapted for a number of year levels. Teachers can utilise the signs of achievement listed for each task to develop criteria to assess levels of performance, if necessary. The precise requirements of these tasks, and the criteria by which their effectiveness will be judged, should be known to students at the inception of the process.

TASK 1: WRITING FOLIO

This task involves the compilation of a folio of finished writing, demonstrating the student's capacity to write for different purposes and audiences. The number of pieces, and the range of purposes and audiences for writing to be included in the folio, are specified. Finished writing is writing which has been carefully shaped to meet the writer's intended purpose and is, as far as possible, error-free.

Students can be asked to write a brief introduction to the folio, explaining the origin of each piece in the collection, and the purpose and audience intended for each piece. In this introduction, they could also comment on how they went about preparing the folio, how they consulted with others about work in progress, and what writing problems they had to overcome.

It is useful to make it a requirement of the task for students to include notes and drafts for each piece in the folio, providing evidence of the development of the piece.

Signs of achievement

- the presentation of a range of writing for different purposes
- the appropriateness of the writing according to the intended audience and purpose
- the complexity and interest of ideas explored in the writing
- control of a variety of structure and organisation of writing for different purposes and in different forms
- the cohesion of each piece
- evidence of revising and editing for improved work
- imaginative organisation of material
- expressiveness and fluency in the writing
- the ability to make appropriate choices of vocabulary, tone and style
- imaginative and striking use of language
- control of the conventions of spelling, grammar and punctuation.

TASK 2: RESPONSE TO A TEXT

A single piece of writing, expressing a response to a text, provides interesting evidence of students' capacities to organise and express their 'reading' of a well-known text to others. The task requires close and detailed knowledge of the text, and the ability to structure a logical discussion, to argue a case, to write an imaginative extension to the text, and so on.

The prompts for writing in response to a text can vary:
- (arguable proposition about a text) 'Is this how _____ seems to you?'
- (arguable proposition about a text) 'Discuss'

- Write a further episode to be included in the course of the text, perhaps focusing on the actions of a minor character.
- Write a sequel to a play or novel.
- Write a series of letters which could have been exchanged between the characters in a novel.
- Present a point of view on an issue raised in the text.

Signs of achievement

- close and detailed knowledge of the text
- evidence of a close personal contact with the text
- a willingness to explore and be challenged by ideas in the text
- an appropriate response to the given prompt
- responsiveness to the tone and style of the text — reflected in the language of creative responses, or in references to language in more analytic responses
- the ability to give shape and cohesion to a piece of writing
- effective sequencing and structure
- expressiveness and fluency
- language appropriate to the writing prompt
- imaginative use of language
- control of the conventions of language.

TASK 3: RESEARCH REPORT

When students work with a group, or alone, on the investigation of an issue of interest to the group, perhaps relating to changes in the environment, they can be asked to present a written report which will give specific evidence of achievement.

Before undertaking this task, students should be familiar with report writing, and have explored a range of written reports in class. Aspects of report writing, such as the frequent use of the present tense in scientific reports, the way a report is often structured to begin with a general view of the issue, the use of subheadings, the possible use of charts and diagrams, and ways of referring to sources of information should be discussed.

An approximate word length for the report should be specified.

Signs of achievement

- ability to identify significant issues
- clear formulation of the issue on which the report is focused
- evidence of thorough research leading to knowledge and understanding of the issue and background information
- ability to select significant information
- synthesis of a range of information
- imaginative and thoughtful organisation of material
- control of structure and sequence within the report

- the development of a coherent perspective on the issue
- clear, precise and concise use of language
- control and use of specialist language relating to the issue
- appropriate tone and style
- effective use of subheadings
- appropriate use of charts and diagrams
- control of the conventions of written language.

As in the earlier sections on talking and listening, and on reading, we offer a number of formats for recording development of writing abilities (pp. 164–7). These writing checkpoints are intended to provide possible models for describing signs of developing abilities observed in various classroom contexts. By using formats such as these, we can build up a profile of learning based on the evidence of classroom activity.

These sheets could be used in combination with students' own records to describe development in writing. If copies of these formats were used to record writing behaviours demonstrated by students over several pieces of writing, these records could eventually provide a comprehensive picture of the development of each student's writing abilities. As students plan, compose and finish various pieces of writing, new signs of learning might gradually be observed and noted, yielding an accumulating record.

▪CONCLUSION

In these three chapters on talking and listening, reading and writing, we have illustrated a range of signs of development in each of the language modes that might be observed and described when students are working on various classroom activities. In part, our purpose has been to show how wide the range of opportunities for language learning needs to be if valid and fair records and reports of development are to be produced. We suggest through the selection and presentation of the classroom episodes that this is the kind of experience students need, and the kind of experience which validates general statements about individual students' language development.

If we can describe development in each of the modes from classroom experiences such as these, we can achieve standards of assessment that are:

- precise — based on accurate observation and recognition of signs of development;
- fair — based on the work done and the goals achieved;

- comprehensive — based on a range of activities and contexts; describing strengths and weaknesses, goals achieved and not achieved; drawn from across the language modes, a balanced summary of development in talking, listening, reading and writing.

The description of these signs of development facilitates discussion with students about their own perceptions of their development — that is, about what they think they have achieved in English — and new goals for working and learning can be negotiated from this basis. Description of signs of development also establishes an agenda of items for recording and reporting, providing the kind of evidence upon which accurate general statements about individual students' work and development can be communicated to parents.

We hope that this section on the language modes illustrates how professional knowledge can be enhanced by observation and description of signs of development. Recognising a wide range of development among students working in various classroom contexts provides an accumulating resource for setting new goals and for planning and managing new classroom activities. The sensitivity and responsiveness of professional knowledge to signs of development depends on this continuous enhancement of the focus of our observation in classrooms.

This improved focus can be employed to recognise and describe a wide range of development in English and in other related aspects of learning, in particular classroom projects and the development of individual students. An example of the use of this enhanced focus is described in the next chapter.

Writing 1

Name: _____ **Year:** _____ **Date:** _____

Signs of development

Examples:

- explains ideas expressed in scribble and drawing
- shows understanding that writing conveys meaning
- distinguishes between drawing and writing
- experiments with own symbols to make marks on paper
- suggests words and ideas for others to transcribe
- writes strings of letters
- uses letters of the alphabet
- writes clusters or combinations of letters
- writes single known words
- uses approximated spelling for words
- writes simple sentences using approximated spelling
- spells with sufficient accuracy for the meaning to be clear
- writes from left to right and top to bottom in lines on the page
- can use drawings to help map out a draft of a piece of writing

- can brainstorm ideas for writing
- can talk with others about ideas to use in a piece of writing
- recounts experiences while reading own writing
- fills in the gaps in writing by talking
- makes some attempt to organise ideas to produce meaning
- recognises that some aspects of a piece of writing are more important than others
- recognises that writing can be used to explore and reflect on experience
- uses writing to convey information
- can state an opinion in writing
- recognises that a first draft may be improved by rewriting it
- recognises that editing may reduce error and inconsistency
- punctuates with sufficient accuracy for the meaning to be clear
-
-
-

Date	Comments

Writing 2

Name: _____ Year: _____ Date: _____

Signs of development

Examples:

- uses writing as a tool to speculate, plan, reflect, report, invent, instruct, explain, inform, argue
- uses writing to help solve problems
- can find ideas for writing from own experience
- shows an awareness of what readers may need to know
- can shape a plot for a story
- can develop characters, setting and incidents
- writes simple sentences using appropriate punctuation and word forms
- uses paragraphing to help structure a piece of writing
- writes sufficiently legibly for others to read
- is developing a fluent, legible handwriting style
- makes use of print in the environment
- can use a wordprocessor to enter, edit and format text
- writes about real and imagined experiences
- experiments with organising material in different ways
- is interested in different kinds of writing
- creates characters and atmosphere in writing
- includes thoughts and feelings in writing

- writes to give/ask for information
- uses direct speech in writing
- arranges information in a way that makes sense
- uses a variety of ways of conveying information
- uses different kinds of sentences
- is developing varied forms of sentence structure
- follows the usual rules of punctuation
- usually spells accurately
- is able to use a variety of methods to check spelling
- is prepared to work on one piece for an extended time
- drafts and clarifies a piece of writing, perhaps several times
- edits own work
- can help another person to edit work
- proofreads own and others' work
- recognises where writing needs revision
- reads through own writing and eliminates mistakes
- is interested in feedback on own writing
- is able to give feedback on others' writing
- is interested to read what others have written
-
-

Date	Comments

Writing 3

Name: _____ **Year:** _____ **Date:** _____

Signs of development

Examples:

- writes easily for long periods
- writes fluently, maintaining neatness and legibility
- can make effective use of word processor in planning, drafting, revising and presenting finished work
- spells accurately
- uses punctuation to help communicate meaning
- chooses words to suit purpose and audience
- chooses sentences which suit the purposes of the writing
- uses resources — dictionaries, thesauruses, style manuals
- draws on a wide vocabulary
- is appreciative of the various ways authors use language
- draws on personal experience as a reader in making choices about writing
- requests and acts on feedback from listeners and readers
- can select and order events, ideas and information in various ways
- can develop characters, setting and incidents
- formulates a single statement to express the central idea of a piece of writing

- is able to collaborate with others in major writing projects
- makes notes in writing
- uses writing to organise ideas and information
- gathers and organises information for writing
- writes plans to carry out tasks and projects
- reports accurately on events, incidents and experiences
- can present arguments in writing
- uses evidence to support arguments and opinions
- can justify a decision in writing
- can offer an overview of different positions on an issue
- includes detail helpful to readers
- revises words and sentences for clearer meaning
- can write letters for a variety of purposes
- has developed a legible, fluent handwriting style
-
-
-
-
-
-

Date	Comments

Writing 4

Name: ———————————— **Year:** ————— **Date:** —————

Signs of development

Examples:
- can achieve coherence and structure in a piece of writing
- is interested in the precise uses of language
- explores new forms of language — poetry, science fiction, technical reports, etc.
- organises the presentation of an argument to make overall sense
- orders ideas and information to achieve particular effects
- can choose to write from different points of view — as narrator, observer, commentator, participant
- writes in detail about the feelings and ideas of other people
- writes clearly on complex issues
- presents a balanced written overview of issues
- argues logically towards decision and action
- uses writing to secure action
- uses a wide range of relevant evidence to support views
- can summarise information taken from various sources
- expands notes taken from talks, TV programs, films into detailed records
- can control the mechanics of writing

- controls spelling in a variety of writing contexts
- expands and elaborates ideas through appropriate use of detail
- creates mood and atmosphere through descriptive language
- varies choice of words and sentence structures for different purposes and audiences
- argues a point of view through definition and analysis
- can speculate and hypothesise from present information
- writes creatively using a wide variety of words
- displays logical organisation of ideas in writing
- varies syntax to suit mood and atmosphere
- uses various sentence structures to achieve shades of meaning
- integrates new ideas and information into text
- revises and edits by reordering, changing words, tightening structure
- writes for a variety of purposes and audiences
-
-
-

Date	Comments

7 OBSERVING STUDENTS AT WORK

In this chapter we describe a classroom episode, a project undertaken by a Year 10 class, that offered opportunities for observing a wide range of evidence of development. This account of classroom action illustrates:
- how a connected experience of language in its various modes can be provided by a variety of classroom activities;
- how, from this connected experience, many signs of development can be observed — across language modes, in ways of working and in attitudes to learning and to work;
- how opportunities for observation occur within such a context;
- how real evidence of development can be gathered from classroom action; and
- how these observations might be described, with particular reference to the work of one student.

In focusing on this episode in a Year 10 classroom, we can note a large number of observations of the widely varying abilities and attitudes that students of this age range often exhibit. We can show from this context how broad and flexible a professional focus on and description of development needs to be. It is also possible to focus more sharply on the planning and managing activities required when working with students and observing what they do.

This classroom episode, like the project 'Taking A Trip' which was described in Chapter 3, shows the ways in which connections between the various modes of language can be constructed and managed within the scope of an extended program of work or project. Although the major focus of this book is on assessing language development, it is obvious that classroom action where students use language in various ways also demonstrates many other features of development.

:A ROAD I'D LIKE TO TAKE

I shall be telling this with a sigh
Somewhere ages and ages hence:
Two roads diverged in a wood, and I —
I took the one less travelled by,
And that has made all the difference.

(from 'The Road Not Taken', by Robert Frost)

DEVELOPING A SENSE OF AUDIENCE WITH YEAR 10

1 What makes you think that all your ideals will come together?
2 Why is a good career necessarily related to a good life?
3 Why do you ignore 'all minor hiccoughs'?
4 Is success that important?

These were the questions asked by a Year 10 student after reading a piece of writing drafted by a classmate. Reading another person's writing and asking questions about it was part of an activity in which students responded to Robert Frost's 'The Road Not Taken' by writing on the topic 'A Road I'd Like To Take'. The activity was planned in order to promote, among other things, an awareness of audience in writing.

Students in this class were accustomed to helping each other with pieces of writing. However, experience of responses from others needs to be regular in order to promote acceptance of the idea of audience in writing. So it was considered necessary to implement a simple strategy that would give a focus to talk between peers about writing and an agenda for revision. This was also planned as a way of providing experience for students in the role of reader-listener-audience, an experience that would assist the readers in their own writings as much as it would help the writers to whom they responded.

Control over writing is generated by experience at making predictions about what a reader might expect or anticipate, and by making such predictions in the role of readers of texts. Audience and purpose are intricately connected to reader response and there are therefore many strategies that might promote these abilities.

Students themselves form a natural, interested audience for each other's writing, and so the activity was designed to:
• provide students with opportunities to write in different ways;

- respond sensitively to other people's writing;
- promote knowledge of strategies for revising writing;
- give students experience of different roles in classroom activities; and
- promote awareness of audience when writing.

These concerns all stem from professional knowledge of how people learn to write. A major focus for the activity was the provision of a strategy for revision of writing using peer responses: where peers are readers as well as writers, a context for purposeful revision can be established. Further, if students are invited to ask questions about each other's writing, an agenda for revision might be provided: the questions form constructive suggestions about which the writers need to make decisions.

The plan of work which encompassed this activity had been designed to extend students' learning and language in certain directions; that is:

- responding personally and sensitively to a range of texts;
- writing for an audience;
- drafting and revising their writings; and
- revision strategies.

The teacher needed to be able to:

- create a context in which students would have opportunities to develop these abilities;
- observe and describe students' abilities.

CLASSROOM CONTEXT

As part of a project on People, starting with the novel *The Untouchable Juli* by James Aldridge, a Year 10 class read the poem 'The Road Not Taken' by Robert Frost. The poem provided an end-piece to discussion and writing related to:

- the novel;
- newspaper articles about people; and
- various poems.

Initially, the students' work had focused on the theme of people. From their discussion of the experience and feelings of the different people they had read about, students were asked to think of a number of general ideas illustrated in the texts they had explored. Group discussion of these possibilities produced suggestions such as loyalty, family, Australians, identity, relationships and aspirations. The resources for the theme provided a path by which students tentatively explored the territory of relationships and community and personal values.

Students in this class were accustomed to working in a workshop setting. This setting had been generated by introductory activities early in the year and had operated in projects prior to the focus on people. In this setting, students are encouraged to work towards the completion of a range of connected tasks described in work plans. Students' work is related to the achievement of different kinds of goals such as:

- reading and talking about a range of texts;
- writing for various purposes, including in response to reading and viewing; and
- completing tasks by set deadlines.

Some tasks — such as the completion of a writing folio or presentation of a collage of newspaper clippings — are mandatory; others — such as the choice of subject for writing, or the selection of poems for readings — are decided by the students. During these activities, students are asked to complete a workshop record in which they plan and record the tasks they will undertake in each session devoted to the project. An example of this workshop record, completed by students working on the project which included reading, talking and writing about the poem 'The Road Not Taken', appears in Chapter 8.

While working on earlier activities and projects, students had developed a number of records of their work. These records included:

- a *workbook* — where goals, plans, exploratory ideas and thoughts were recorded;
- a *reading log* — stored in the workbook, a range of responses to novels, poetry and other texts;
- *drafts of writing* — again stored in the workbook;
- a *writing folio* — the collection of finished writing;
- a *writing folio record* — a record of drafts of writing; and
- a *workshop record* — a record of what students did each session.

Group discussions and reports, especially when shared with the whole class, and conferences and discussions with individual students, produced further evidence of students' abilities.

One considerable advantage of working with students on projects conducted in a workshop setting is that the teacher has opportunities to talk with individual students, to observe what they are doing, and to make notes about these observations.

Such a wide range of evidence, especially that generated by students' involvement in the record-keeping, enabled the teacher to observe and record the work and development of individual students. Over many such activities and projects, the work of all students in this class could therefore be observed and described.

These notes and comments were recorded in a teacher's record book on blank pages allotted to individual students. Such records are particularly useful in monitoring individual students' development and as a basis for writing more summative descriptions of their work and achievement. Also, sharing these comments with the students concerned can provide a basis for negotiating with them about what can be said in their reports.

RESPONDING TO THE POEM

The poem 'The Road Not Taken' was explored in the following way:

1 The teacher read the poem to the class and asked students to think of questions about the poem — anything that came to their minds.
2 Students then read the poem silently.
3 Students were asked to write a list of questions that came to their minds about the poem and they generated a large number of questions. When they ask these questions — for example, about the meanings of particular words, the layout of lines, the feelings they receive from reading the poem — they are exploring the language of poetry in an open and personal way.
4 These questions were then shared with the whole class. A quick round-up of questions from various students in the class indicated a range of concerns and ideas, and also suggested that students were making their own meanings from the poem.
5 Small groups were formed to discuss the questions.
6 Each group reported to the class by providing answers to as many of the questions from members of their group as they could.
7 In their workbooks, students wrote answers to two of their own questions.
8 In the first 10 minutes of the next session, students were asked to draft a piece of writing on the topic 'A Road I'd Like to Take'.
9 Students read their pieces aloud to a partner who was given the task of asking questions about the piece.
10 The writers wrote the questions at the end of their pieces and considered what action they would take about them.
11 These questions thus provided an agenda for elaborating and explaining what they had written — a strategy for revision.
12 The writings were revised until the writers were happy that they had answered their partners' questions. In some cases, they decided not to answer one or two questions because, as they said, they wanted to leave things for the reader to think about.

The students were prepared for the role of listener/reader by reading and asking questions about the first chapter of the novel, about people in a file of newspaper articles, and about the poem. Because students had had prior experience of responding to texts in these ways, they were accustomed to asking questions and shaping their own ideas about what a text was saying.

In a study of the effectiveness of peer response groups, Karen Spear (1988) concludes that:

• students should be encouraged to become peer collaborators and therefore to move away from the role of teacher-surrogate;
• harmonious, trusting relationships between writers and their response groups are essential to the effectiveness of sharing and revising writing;

- peer response groups have a vital role to play in the promotion of awareness of audience;
- experience in responding to text in personal and exploratory ways helps students to suggest ways of developing the writings of other students;
- experience of personal and exploratory responses to other people's writing often helps the reader-listener as much as the writer.

(adapted from *Sharing Writing — Peer Response Groups in English Classes*)

Spear argues that students appear to need experience in controlled situations, such as single writing activities or writing from a common experience or pool of information, before they can respond to different kinds of writing. This is because 'with a common database, students find it relatively easy to see what works and what doesn't in each other's writing'. (p. 90)

The work plan, the novel and the various other texts explored by the class provided such a common database. Focusing writing on a common task — responding to a poem through writing about 'A Road I'd Like To Take' — also provided a context where strategies for revision could be based on shared knowledge of a writer's purpose.

If students understand the purpose of another student's writing, they can be receptive, supportive and critical of that writing. The shared experience of classroom activities, the common task, and the shared understandings of the purpose of the writings work together to create an agenda for revision.

OBSERVATIONS AND OUTCOMES

What was observed about students' work in this context? The effectiveness of the activity could be gauged by whether or not the listeners asked questions that writers felt they had at least to consider, if not take action to answer them. All listeners asked at least two questions and therefore all writers had clear decisions to make about their pieces. A few students immediately drafted lengthy explanations in answer to the questions their listeners had asked. Others preferred to build in words and phrases that clarified what they had originally written; and other students did not act on the questions because, as they said, they didn't think the questions of sufficient importance to warrant action.

One or two students were well aware of their 'rights' as authors to leave their writings deliberately vague in one or two spots. 'Let the reader work out what I mean', 'Surely readers can answer that question for themselves', they said. Also, since they were writing about their own futures — not all that clear to students of 15 or 16 — it was impossible to answer some questions with the same certainty as in the case of, for example, a report of a major event or personal experience.

This writing task proved difficult for some students in this class. Some students didn't have clear goals and, at first, didn't think they could write about why this was so; some focused on narrow, materialistic concerns which were readily challenged by their readers. In many ways, writing such a response to Frost's poem entailed an exploration of values by students in ways that they hadn't really encountered before. This was the kind of exploratory activity that often helps the teacher to recognise the variety of development among students in a class. Some students were clearly not ready to write about this topic: they had thought about the road they'd like to take, but in some cases couldn't write about it in detail, or preferred not to. All recognised, however, that they were dealing with a metaphor for the decisions they'd need to take about their lives. This range of development was illustrated by the work students did in responding to their readers' questions.

FOCUSING ON INDIVIDUAL STUDENTS

To provide more detailed observations of the work of individual students, the teacher:
- chose six students of varying abilities and attitudes;
- listened to their group talk from a distance;
- included them in discussion volunteered in the classroom; and
- where necessary, completed the notes after each session.

Time for the teacher to observe and record examples of these students' work was created by the need for them to write, talk with a partner and revise their writing — activities to which, as described earlier in this chapter, they were accustomed. During these activities, anecdotal records were kept on the work of this sample of students.

What questions did these writers consider and what action did they take? Here is a sample of the questions and decisions made by the students whose work was most closely observed. The pieces of writing sampled here were unfinished, with problems of spelling and syntax left for later revision. The main focus of the sample is the quality of listening and questioning, and on the extent of decisions made by the writers to such responses; that is:
- Did students write freely and fluently on the topic?
- Did the listeners listen attentively? Were their questions relevant?
- What action did writers take on the basis of the questions asked?
- To what extent did writers show awareness of the need to revise by expanding, elaborating, and integrating?

Sample questions asked by listeners were as follows:
- What positive results would you like to achieve?
- Why do you choose these two roads?
- Which road would you like to take?
- Why, as a game fisher, wouldn't you get married?
- Why become a landscape gardener after years of education?
- What if you don't become a landscape gardener, what will you become?
- Will you finish Year 12?
- What do you believe would be the main thing to keep you happy?
- Would your job be very hard?
- How would you like to achieve happiness?
- What would come first in your life?
- Why would you take this road?
- Would you use people on your way to success?

One student responded to the task by writing in an apparently literal way about roads and travelling in fog and darkness. This was a highly descriptive piece that created mood and atmosphere very effectively, and left the reader in no doubt that the writer was vividly extending the metaphor of the road to talk about his life so far and his future. Here are the questions this writer was asked by his listener:
- What is the road going up?
- Why is it dark at the moment?
- Why does the scenery change so much?
- Why does the road already covered seem endless?

This student carefully considered the questions he was asked but took very little action when revising his writing. He integrated material that responded directly to the first and second questions but did not elaborate these new thoughts. If he had made wholesale changes to his piece — for example, starting with new sentences that gave reasons for how he felt — the gloomy atmosphere he created might have given place to a more reasoned and probably less interesting piece.

What then were the kinds of learning observed in this context? Here is a sample of the notes made by the teacher about individual students' work on this activity.

These notes were recorded in the teacher's journal and were part of an accumulating record of evidence of students' work and development. They suggest that certain questions — certain likely signs of development — provided a focus for observation and therefore for the text of the records. Some notes describe personal responses, attitudes and ways of working; some specifically refer to goals of working and learning in English; and others express the unexpected signs that are often observed in students' responses to tasks.

An example of a continuous prose report based in part on such records and discussed with the student is given on p. 238, Chapter 6.

Jason

7.9 Asked several questions about the poem. Listened to others' ideas and was able to answer his own questions. Contributed sensitively to discussion.

8.9 Worked on his responses to the poem in his workbook — writing showed detailed knowledge and understanding

11.9 Wrote for an extended time on his draft. Willing to share it with others. Read aloud to Ben.

12.9 Had revised his draft by answering Ben's questions. Able to manage revisions of writing. Can explain ideas with examples.

Jim

7.9 Found difficulty in focusing on poem — would much prefer to go on with computer studies. Hesitant to question poem. Group dominated by another student.

8.9 Writing on the poem — highly personal response. More interested in personal views than in group.

11.9 Wrote very slowly as usual. Not keen to share ideas but happy to listen to Chris's piece. Listened attentively. Probably had the most difficult task in class — Chris's piece highly descriptive and dense. Managed to ask two challenging questions.

12.9 Still hadn't finished first draft — help needed from Chris and Damien but not been to accept it. Held them up. Needs to think a lot before writing? Is being with Damien really a help to him?

Sam

7.9 Still recovering from the school play? Still makes comments on task and text? Followed instructions after prompting. Had many questions to ask about the poem. Group answers were interesting — Sam made quite a contribution.

8.9 Workbook notes on poem — a bit scratchy. Didn't write all that he talked about.

11.9 Wrote for fifteen minutes on topic. Very happy to read aloud to Brendan — gave him something to think about. Pessimistic piece.

12.9 Expanded piece. Didn't put in new sections — just added words here and there. Able to intergrate material concisely.

ONE STUDENT'S WORK

Here is a collection of one student's writings completed during this activity. It is offered as an example of the kinds of drafts, questions and revisions that were generated in this context.

Peter is a student who needs the kind of values clarification implicit in activities of this nature. Like many Year 10 students, he is gradually working out a set of guidelines for his own behaviour and developing considered views on important issues such as marriage, or relationships with the opposite sex. Further opportunities for students to explore these concerns and to hear the responses of a reader can be built into future activities: for example, writing a sequel to a novel such as Harper Lee's *To Kill A Mockingbird* or explaining how he would have handled Jack in Golding's *Lord of the Flies*.

Peter's work on other writing for his folio sprang from a number of original ideas that suggested considerable creativity, imagination and social concern. However, it was clear to the teacher that he, and many other students in his class, needed greater experience in the kinds of exploratory activities that making decisions about writing involves. If, for example, he was prepared to make changes to his drafts of writing — to explain his thoughts, or to include new material, especially in response to the ideas of other people — this behaviour might indicate a growth in the sensitivity with which Peter viewed his particular world and the people around him. These signs of development would have been as significant to his personal growth as to his language abilities.

Peter also needed experience in situations where he could work without close supervision. In previous years, he had developed a reputation as someone who needed constant prompting to start and complete set tasks. Could he manage the tasks and activities in this workshop setting? Would he undertake responsibility for his work?

The extent to which students took advantage of opportunities to redraft, talk with others about their work and revise varied greatly. However, the example of Peter's work is reasonably representative of the activities that occurred while students were engaged on this task. This example is provided to illustrate how opportunities for composing a piece of writing with the help of peers can offer perceptive observers significant evidence of students' development. Peter's first draft, including the original technical problems, is reproduced here.

A Road That I Would Like To Take
(Peter's first draft)
(11 September 1989)

The road that I would like to take is to go out into the real world with out any hassles or difficulties about my life. I would like to live a carefree life with a steady income and be able to do what ever I please within certain guidelines. For there has got to be these guidelines or it will lead me to trouble which is

what I dont want. I would like to live a life of of sporty and non–stop activity and generally socialising. I would not like to be married or
I feel this way because
heavily commited unless it involved a large proportion of wealth. For it would lead to stress and breakdown in my life.

I feel this way because I have learned through my years of experience that whenever I am faced with difficulties in life I crack, and go through some unenjoyable fazes a which cause me to get into trouble.

Questions (from Ben):
• Why don't you want to be married?
• What are the guidelines?
• Do you think these guidelines are important?

A Road That I Would Like To Take
(Peter's second draft)
(October 1989)

The road that I would like to take is one that is carefree and not restrained. I would like to leave school with a definite pass and with no problems arrising around me. After I leave school I would like to travel up north for a year and discover new people and fascinating sight sites. Then I would like to return to the real world and get myself a steady job and live unmarried unless I ran into a very wealthy and good-looking women. I don't want to be married because this would lead to stress and conflict and cannot handle stress and this would lead to a breakdown in my life.

I feel that I would like to take this path because I would like to enjoy the freedom that I have been deprived of in my childhood, and I would like to be able to do anything I please within certain guidelines, which would be along the lines of keeping out of trouble with the law, because I have learned through my experience in life about myself that whenever I am faced with difficulties in my life I crack under pressure and go through some trecherous fazes, and cause me to get into trouble, which is not what I want.

What changes did Peter make to the piece? The questions asked by the listener have prompted explanations of thoughts rather casually described in the first draft. It seems that the questions have given the writer something to think about.

Quite apart from developing writing abilities, the experience of being asked questions about his future was valuable and necessary for this student. His listener was naturally interested, as a friend, in the kinds of guidelines that Peter would live by, and why he wouldn't be getting married. From the teacher's observations of this class, it appears that classmates were trying very hard during the year to convince Peter to behave himself — for his own good.

One of the benefits of writing a piece about one's future is that, like writing a sequel to a novel, it helps the writer to clarify personal values through the aspirations and ideas expressed. Having listened to his draft, Peter's listener took the opportunity to challenge him about his quest for freedom. From this perspective, the second draft displays signs of a growing recognition of personal responsibility.

In this student's writing, the listener's questions prompted two major alterations:

- to say why he wouldn't get married, and
- to describe the sort of guidelines he would follow.

There are many other incidental revisions which have also changed the character of the piece. Words such as 'not restrained', 'fascinating sites', 'take this path', 'deprived of' and 'trecherous' have been added, giving the piece a greater sense of purpose. The second paragraph contains structural problems but this has been expanded in an effort to explain the writer's views. Perhaps Peter could not pay attention to sentence structure in the second draft because he was intently focusing on explaining his ideas.

A major structural revision has occurred in the point about following 'certain guidelines'. This has been shifted to the second paragraph, making both main ideas — living a carefree life and following guidelines — stronger for their separation. In this way, the piece is developing a greater sense of direction and at the same time elaborating ideas for the reader.

As part of their work requirements for the following term, students were asked to complete a folio of finished writing. Peter wished to include a third draft. The development of the first and second drafts had been achieved through Peter's own thinking and writing, and through consideration of his listener's responses. At this stage, he asked the teacher to suggest further ways of developing the piece so that it would be ready for inclusion in his folio.

With personal writing such as this, it is appropriate that writers explore their own ideas and feelings as far as they can without a great deal of help from the teacher. Peter didn't want the teacher to see his piece until he decided that the time was right. Response from the teacher posed particular problems because, although Peter had clearly developed the piece from first thoughts to a more detailed explanation in two well-structured paragraphs, using a widening vocabulary, the draft still needed a fair amount of work before it could be considered 'finished'. In this situation, the question facing the teacher-reader is:

- How can I help this student develop his piece?

Having read the first and second drafts, the teacher could see three main areas of development:

1 use of language and conventions

The writer's use of language had expanded and gained greater variety to match the thoughts and feelings he was trying to explain, but there were problems of spelling and sentence structure and a lack of variety in the use of tenses. The sameness of the tenses was, to some extent, stimulated by the topic: to describe the road he would like to take, Peter needed to use verbs which conveyed the conditional future; but at this point he had not considered other possibilities that carried similar meaning.

2 depth of detail

There are signs that the writer has paused in his journey along this road and considered why or how he might achieve his goals. The challenging questions from his listener have promoted further explanation of ideas and feelings such as marriage and 'guidelines'. The term 'the real world' could have been explained: this seems to relate to Peter's idea of freedom which he feels has been denied him in childhood. How did he intend to achieve an accommodation with this 'real world'?

A problem here was how far it is possible for a Year 10 student to explain wishes for his future. In the minds of Year 10 students, ideas such as 'marriage' and 'freedom' might loom as likely or possible destinations to be reached or paths to be avoided, but explaining them in detail forces choices on students not yet ready or sufficiently experienced to make such decisions. Should these goals be left in the shadows? Is it not enough that a student of this age perceives some of these possibilities? Are there other possibilities he has not considered (for example, tertiary education?)

3 values

The student who listened to Peter's reading of his piece was clearly interested in Peter's comments about marriage and women. 'Why don't you want to be married?', he asked. This question challenged Peter to explain his ideas more fully. However, in doing so, he exposed some personal attitudes — all contained in the section 'unless I ran into a very wealthy and good-looking women' — that the teacher, after reading the piece, felt bound to respond to. Much personal writing, especially when students are asked to consider their own futures, or write sequels to novels, involves an exploration and clarification of personal values that can create and sometimes dominate the agenda of consultations between writer and teacher. Peter's attitudes to women and money as expressed in his piece were signals for a gentle but challenging response from the teacher: challenging, because in the interests of his own personal development, Peter needed to continue to explore these values in his own mind; gentle, because the writing of this piece was an opportunity for Peter to explore and clarify his values rather than, if he felt that these were unacceptable thoughts, to edit them out. Because students continue to regard teachers as evaluators, too heavy an intervention could influence the writer to abandon lines of thought that he ought to explore. The response from the teacher had to value Peter's work and the honesty of his ideas and feelings, and to help him explore thoughts about his future more fully, both in the piece and in his own mind.

These three areas, then, provided an agenda for consultation between Peter and his teacher. The conference began with some comments from the teacher, noting and praising several ways in which Peter had developed the piece so far. For example, one of the opening comments from the teacher was: 'I like the way you developed each paragraph. Why did you do that?'

Peter's response indicated that his work on the draft had stemmed from the questions he had been asked by his listener. He felt that these questions had helped him to think more deeply about his ideas. They had prompted some further explanation in each paragraph. These and other opening exchanges established a supportive context in which Peter was willing to talk about his piece and his plans for developing it further. He had been considering introducing a middle paragraph explaining his ideas on marriage, but he felt that this would make the first paragraph too brief. This remark provided an opportunity for the teacher to comment: 'What about further study? Do you intend to go to college or university? You haven't mentioned that.'

It was agreed that Peter could expand the remaining first paragraph in this way. Then followed a discussion about what would constitute the new second paragraph. Peter felt that he needed this new section to describe his views on marriage. Again, this comment provided an opportunity for the teacher to ask: 'Do you think you could put this a different way?'

The aim of this question was to help Peter rethink his attitude. If he could think of a 'different' or 'better' way of putting it, this might encourage a moderation or change in his attitude. Talking with Peter, the teacher felt that there was nothing deliberately sexist or insensitive about this attitude. Nor was it simply a case of adolescent bravado. Peter was genuinely apprehensive and uncertain about relationships, as are many young people of similar background. (There was also other evidence, known to the teacher, to suggest that Peter had been deprived of close relationships, and hurt by the few in which he had been involved.)

In the course of the conference, these and other matters were raised through a carefully guided discussion. There was little time to talk about the use of language or conventions, or the lack of variety in the verbs. It was more important for Peter to continue to develop his thinking on paper. Also, if Peter considered his ideas more deeply and described them more fully, it was likely that problems of an appropriate range of vocabulary would be overcome. The need to find and use new and better words and structures to express his ideas and feelings was inherent in the task of developing his piece. However, conferences such as this, held at the student's request, can provide the moments for modelling and demonstrating various kinds of language — especially the choice of words — that the writer could use in the piece. One example of this is given in the question about tertiary study described above. The question:

'Do you intend . . .' was aimed at providing Peter with another possible way, apart from the words 'would like' and 'want to be', of stating his goals. Another example occurred when the teacher, noting the significance of Peter's phrase 'trecherous fazes', made this comment: 'I like your phrase "trecherous fazes". What happens then? Do you get angry or depressed?'

In the third draft Peter adopted these words and translated them as 'trecherous fazes of anger and depression'.

This new draft is reproduced below, with teacher's comments describing further developments observed in ideas, choice of words, structure and presentation.

A Road I Would Like To Take
(Peter's third draft)
(November 1989)

The road I would like to take is one that is carefree and not restricted. I would like to leave school with a definite pass and with no problems <u>arrising</u> around me. After I leave school I would like to travel up north for about six months and discover new people and experience picturesque scenes.* Then for the next six months I would like to return to civilisation and get a part time job. In the new year I would like to return to complete some sort of* tertiary degree, to set myself up for a respectable job that will set me up* for the rest of my life.

Changes

Presentation:
- Word processed
- Three paragraphs

Ideas
- six months' travel up north, not a year
- next six months — part-time job, not a 'steady job', and tertiary degree
- setting up for the rest of his life
- point about marriage moved to next paragraph

Choice of words
- 'restrained' becomes 'restricted'
- 'fascinating sites' becomes 'experience picturesque scenes'
- 'real world' becomes 'civilisation'
- accurate syntax and tense but lacking variety e.g. 'would like'

I do not intend to get married because it would* lead to misunderstandings <u>between my wife and I</u>, which I am very <u>sensative</u> to and would cause stress to be put upon me. The only reason that I would get married is if I found a very wealthy and attractive <u>women</u>.* I could do this because money is my main goal for the future, for if I have money it will take care of all my financial difficulties and I will be able to enjoy myself better*.

Ideas
- main goal now identified: 'money'
- not much development in attitude to women

Choice of words
- 'good-looking' becomes 'attractive'

Structure
- marriage now in a second paragraph

I feel that I would like to take this path because I would like to enjoy the freedom that I have been deprived of in my childhood, and be able to do anything I wish, within certain guidelines. These guidelines would restrict me from coming into conflict with the law, for I have learnt <u>through the years of experience in my life</u>, that whenever I am faced with difficulties I <u>can not</u> handle the pressure and go through some <u>trecherous fazes</u> of anger and depression. Which then leads to trouble, which is not what I want*.

Ideas and structure
- 'guidelines' explained in separate sentence
- 'treacherous phases' explained — 'of anger and depression'
- searching for separate last sentence about what he doesn't want

Choice of words
- 'please' becomes 'wish'
- 'keeping out of trouble' becomes 'restrict me from coming into conflict'

Teacher's response
The sections marked with an asterisk or underlined were discussed in a conference with the teacher. Ways of tightening the expression were suggested and Peter was asked to find the correct spellings. His partner, Ben, was still not happy with Peter's attitude to women, and this was also raised in conference with the teacher.

Perhaps the most striking thing about the third draft is that Peter did not significantly alter his stance on marriage and women. In fact, he reinforced it by adding the statement that 'money is going to be my main goal for the future'. Peter did not shift his position on these matters, not even to the extent of using different, more moderate words. However, there are obvious and substantial changes in this new version of the piece, and the values implicit in the statement about marriage and women had been challenged during the conference between student and teacher.

As for most classroom writing, there was a deadline for Peter to meet and the piece had to remain very much as it is in the third draft. To clarify Peter's attitudes and values required a longer process of thinking and rethinking than was possible within the course of one piece of writing. In the following year, Peter and the same teacher met again in Year 11 English, and so this cultural text continued to unfold as Peter encountered Lady Macbeth and other characters in literature.

What was observed about this student's work to this stage of the development of his piece of writing? What abilities could be described? What was Peter achieving? Answers to these questions stemmed from signs of development observed by the teacher as Peter worked on his piece. As we have seen, the final product was likely to be muddled in thought and full of uncharted feelings. Peter did not have the personal experience to identify his personal goals or explain them in clear detail. What Year 10 student does? The more important focus should rest upon what Peter demonstrated he could do, and what he had achieved, through his work on this piece of writing. The writing activity was essentially exploratory in nature and so the quality of the work on this piece should most appropriately be described in terms of the ways in which Peter showed that he could use writing to explore and develop his thoughts and feelings.

ASSESSING PETER'S ACHIEVEMENT IN ENGLISH

In his work on this activity, from listening to a reading of the poem to writing 'A Road I'd Like To Take', Peter showed that he could:
- respond to text in an appreciative way. His work on the poem, listening to other people's ideas, and responding in his piece of writing, indicated that he recognised the significance of the poem's message to his own life.
- listen to the views of others. This ability was shown by his willingness to ask questions of the poem, listen to other people's ideas, and take note of questions his partner asked about his own writing.
- make decisions and take action. Peter acted on the questions asked of his piece and built in material that addressed them. He was prepared to act on the advice of others.
- write fluently and continuously. Peter's output for the fifteen minutes indicated that he could write fluently, but the topic clearly challenged him. The context and the questions encouraged Peter to think more carefully about what he was saying.
- choose appropriate words to match his ideas and feelings. On the second draft his vocabulary expanded with the use of new words to describe his thoughts. He seemed to be confident enough to use words that he wanted to use, and not to worry about misspellings. He was encouraged to use the right words even if he couldn't spell them, and his second draft showed that he could use words effectively. Overall, he showed a good command of spelling but needed to check the spelling of several words he wanted to use. In this third draft, Peter had made many changes to the words he used, and most of these were improvements on his original choices.
- express personal attitudes and feelings in writing. At this stage, this ability was developing in Peter's work and he needed many more opportunities to reflect on his own views and aspirations. His struggle

to explain his point about guidelines suggests that he was learning to use writing to explore his own values. His decision, during the writing of a third draft, to insert a paragraph on marriage and money was a response to readers' questions. 'Trecherous fazes' was elaborated by the addition of 'of anger and depression'. In making these decisions, Peter showed that he was able and prepared to respond to the needs of his audience.

- write for different purposes. This activity was designed to create opportunities for these Year 10 students to reflect on their own attitudes and aspirations and to convey these to a partner. Peter's second draft suggested that he was able to write in a coherent way for this particular purpose. The activity was designed to extend students' experience of the range of purposes for writing.

- organise ideas logically in writing. The opportunity to hear a listener's questions and to redraft showed that Peter could organise two main points into logical paragraphs. Part of the benefit of hearing the listener's questions may have been to give Peter a better idea of how to organise his piece, by suggesting the reader's interest in guidelines for his life. This could have prompted Peter to use the second paragraph to explain this idea.

In the third draft, it is clear that Peter has achieved improved coherence and logic in the composition of this piece. This results from the insertion of a new paragraph on marriage and money which stemmed from questions asked by his readers, and is evidence of the effectiveness of peer response and teacher feedback during composition in encouraging students to explain their ideas. To do so, to explain ideas clearly for such immediate readers, involves writing new sentences and paragraphs that fill the gaps in the reader's knowledge. The process of achieving a more coherent sequence or flow of information implies attention to logic and structure. As Peter elaborated his ideas by inserting the new paragraph, he implicitly improved the coherence of his piece, if not the values.

- write sentences and paragraphs. Despite the problem of values in his second paragraph, Peter shows that he can use systems of written language to construct meaning. His reorganisation of the second paragraph was particularly significant here. His second draft suggested a clear idea of ways to achieve coherence in writing, and this was obvious in the structure of his third draft.

- rewrite to clarify meaning and diversify language. This ability is implicit in other signs of development listed above. Peter knows what can be achieved by revising his piece. Experience in re-ordering his material in response to a reader's interest has further developed his abilities in the composition processes.

- respond to the needs of the reader. The response from his partner illustrated the particular ideas that were of interest to a reader. Peter's awareness of audience is shown by the many structural and semantic revisions he made.

The pieces also suggested a number of things Peter's language development requires. Like many students at this level of schooling, he needs further experience of composing for a widening range of readers and purposes. By the third draft, he still had not checked his approximated spelling of 'woman', 'phases' and 'treacherous', even when these were pointed out by the teacher, but he was prepared to elaborate his ideas further by inserting a new paragraph about money and women. However, as we have seen, what he wrote in this new paragraph brought problems of a new and different order.

CODA

An interesting coda to this story is that when working with the same teacher in Year 11, Peter began the year by writing a piece called 'Some Stories About Myself'. This piece contained a similar statement about women and money, and he was again challenged about this, by another student and by the teacher. The gist of the feedback is contained in a blunt question from a classmate who had read his piece: 'Why would a rich woman marry you?'

In his final draft, Peter omitted all reference to this. Progress?

ASSESSING WAYS OF WORKING

What *can* be said about the way in which Peter worked, and about the attitudes and values he displayed? As described in the introduction to this section, the development of attitudes and values often forms part of the focus of classroom observation, and evidence of this development can be found most clearly when students work on the various language activities connected by projects such as 'A Road I'd Like To Take'. The wide range of evidence provided by Peter's work on his writing, and his interaction with others in his response group, indicates that he had developed or was developing the ability to:
• ask questions
• experiment with ideas
• solve problems
• work with others
• organise his work processes
• reflect on and evaluate his own work
• imagine and predict new possibilities
• communicate ideas, information and experience to others.

Further, Peter's work on this project can tell us, more or less, that he was:
- curious about other people's experiences and ideas. This was illustrated by his willingness to listen to other people's ideas, and to learn what they thought of his own ideas.
- willing to offer helpful ideas to other people. Peter was keen to read other people's work and was a very enthusiastic respondent during group work, and in whole-class situations.
- willing to accept ideas from other people. He was not keen to go much further with some of the ideas expressed in his writing. Why, for example, was he so concerned about the stress which certain experiences might bring him? However, he certainly worked hard to clarify several important issues raised by his readers.
- willing to explore new ideas. Peter was prepared to adapt and change his piece to meet the ideas he acquired from talking with his partner and his teacher, and to consider alternative ways of expressing his own ideas.

   That he should be drawn out by his partner on the question of marriage rather surprised him — probably because in his first draft the reference to marriage was almost a throwaway line — but he did explain what he meant and continued to do this by making substantial additions to successive drafts. After several talks with his partner and his teacher, he was prepared to moderate his attitude to marriage and women. On the other hand, he did not wish to elaborate some other issues raised by his piece.
- sensitive to others. He listened to what other people said about his work, and he responded positively to their need for help — a sign of development in a person whose school career has been a little troubled.
- willing to work with others. The range of activities included in this project enabled Peter to work effectively with other people, to help others to complete their tasks and to listen to others' ideas and suggestions. There was clear evidence from the many related signs of development described so far that he was able to work in cooperative contexts. He certainly enjoyed working with other people and the project emphasis on talking with others provided him with this opportunity.
- prepared to persevere and persist with tasks. Peter was prepared to revise his writing and in fact completed three drafts before he was happy to include the piece in his folio. He stopped a long way short of explaining some ideas but this might have been more a matter of personal indecision at this stage of his growth than a comment on his persistence.
- prepared to take responsibility for his work. The classroom context and the plan of work established by this project enabled Peter to show that he could work without close supervision, and that he could plan what he would do each day without being constantly prompted to start work. This is a significant development in Peter's attitude; he seemed to enjoy the chance to state his plans and get on with the work.

- willing to reflect on his own work. Peter was willing to revise his piece in the light of other people's ideas and to complete two further drafts before he suggested to the teacher that the piece was finished.

Many such things can be said about the work of individual students when observed in such contexts. The range of evidence generated by drafting and revising writing in collaboration with others is a fertile source of answers to our professional questions.

∎EXTENDING LEARNING

New questions arise from observing students at work on an activity such as A Road I'd Like To Take. Observing the work of individual students like Peter might prompt these kinds of questions:
- What new learning can be built on the signs observed?
- What new signs of learning do I wish to see?
- Which activities are likely to promote this new learning?

In Peter's case, it seemed clear that he needed many more opportunities to write about his own thoughts and feelings, or to express a point of view on various issues — activities which would develop his range of language use as well as providing scope for exploring his own attitudes and values.

Knowing where one activity might lead helps teachers to provide the time and the other resources necessary to make such connections. The questions, the issues and the options that give students new goals for

Development and planning

Signs of development observed in particular contexts can provide the basis of an evaluation of the classroom program with a view to extending learning by planning further activities.

Signs of learning	Appropriate activities
Have students had opportunities to: ■ tell a story to a group? ■ develop awareness of audience?	■ telling stories from personal experience to a group ■ writing stories with a partner ■ listening to other students' stories ■ asking questions to help writers revise stories ■ reading finished stories to another class

Signs of learning	Appropriate activities
▪ create atmosphere in descriptive writing? ▪ develop understanding of figurative language? ▪ use a wider range of descriptive words?	▪ reading highly imaginative poetry ▪ reading poems aloud to the class ▪ writing poems about personal experiences ▪ presenting a dramatic program of original poetry
▪ learn to spell new and difficult words? ▪ find correct spelling?	▪ reading newspaper articles and making a bank of new words ▪ writing articles from different points of view ▪ using dictionaries and thesauruses as resources
▪ use appropriate tense in writing? ▪ write paragraphs in logical sequence? ▪ link ideas and information in writing?	▪ in pairs, writing a report of a dramatic event from the point of view of a participant, a spectator, a journalist ▪ taking turns to write each paragraph ▪ jumbling one of the reports for another pair to put in order
▪ collect information in methodical ways? ▪ identify a problem and suggest solutions? ▪ make inferences from a range of data or information?	▪ group project on a community issue ▪ investigating sources of information ▪ interviewing concerned people ▪ making recommendations for action ▪ developing different ways of reporting conclusions
▪ read silently for an extended period? ▪ read regularly for pleasure? ▪ respond to a story by expressing ideas and feelings? ▪ create new versions of stories?	▪ quiet reading in the library or classroom ▪ providing many different kinds of books ▪ talking about reading in small groups ▪ reading a story to a trusted audience ▪ preparing reading books of students' own stories
▪ negotiate a collaborative project? ▪ make and justify decisions? ▪ carry out an extended plan of work? ▪ review and evaluate own work?	▪ planning a group project (e.g. a new version of a script) ▪ developing an agreed plan of action ▪ recording detailed plans and decisions ▪ presenting ideas in new ways ▪ discussing ways to improve a project
▪ understand and evaluate information presented in different ways? ▪ cope with a variety of information presented on a computer screen? ▪ select relevant information from various texts?	▪ sampling several computer adventure games ▪ gaining access to electronic mail ▪ collecting examples of graphs and statistics used to convey information ▪ recording responses to texts in a logbook ▪ reporting facts, opinions and propaganda
▪ understand that writing conveys meaning? ▪ talk about print in the environment? ▪ develop ideas for writing from experience? ▪ talk about ideas for writing with others?	▪ visiting a shopping centre to look at examples of print ▪ making display cards like those seen there ▪ building a bank of favourite words ▪ providing many picture books ▪ telling and writing own stories ▪ talking together about stories being written

learning can be built into new activities, as shown in the chart 'Development and planning'.

Observing and describing signs of development provides the information that links all these processes: What have the students done? What developments have or have not occurred in their learning? and What do they need to do next? The chart 'Connections in assessing and reporting', included in Chapter 9 (pp. 224–5) illustrates, among other things, these connections between observing, describing and reporting signs of development and achievement, and the planning of activities that help students achieve new goals.

Responsiveness to these signs of development involves efficient and progressive recording in many different classroom contexts; building plans and goals into the design of records kept by students themselves, and using these records for reporting in different ways to students and their parents. What teachers observe and describe, and what students note in their own records, can therefore provide most of the text of record-keeping and reporting, including the substance of talks with students and their parents.

PART 3

RECORDING AND REPORTING DEVELOPMENT

INTRODUCTION

Assessing achievement in English means responding to the evidence, the signs of development, that students demonstrate as they work on and complete classroom activities. The real evidence of achievement is the significant developments observed in students' skills and abilities in making meaning and using language within the context of a wide range of classroom activities.

To compile this wide range of evidence requires the keeping of records that:

- track the learning that occurs in classroom processes, as well as that which is discernable in students' products;
- track the progress of students as they work on projects and activities extending over time;
- record and assess the work of students in independent and cooperative learning situations;
- take into account a broad range of students' work and achievement;
- provide a wide range of evidence for valid, fair reporting — for profiles, summative assessments, records of achievement;
- can be discussed with parents and students themselves; and
- provide evidence for the purposes of assessment for various credentials.

In addition, the formats designed for record-keeping can support and extend teaching: that is, they can help to:

- set goals with students
- organise students' self-assessment
- manage classroom activity
- provide a focus for observation
- identify assessment criteria.

To reiterate, then, assessment that responds to the broad range of students' development and achievement needs to be comprehensive and systematic. Responsive assessment involves observing and describing all of the available evidence of development and achievement.

Accurate, informed reporting is a vital part of responsive assessment. On the occasion of reporting, schools and teachers demonstrate whether or not they can produce valid and fair summaries of achievement. What is said about a student's development and achievement at the end of a term, year or school career carries the priorities of the classroom program. It is therefore essential that summative statements made about students' achievement relate to the goals of the classroom program and to signs of development observed and described during classroom activities. That is:

- What goals have students had opportunities to achieve?

- What signs of development provide evidence that students have achieved these goals?
- How well have they achieved them?

The focus of Part 3 rests on:
- ways of recording evidence of a broad range of development and achievement, and
- ways of creating a dialogue with students and parents that promotes recognition of development and achievement.

We believe that a responsive approach to record-keeping and reporting involves the design of formats that offer scope for:
- making detailed plans of what is to happen on a certain day, and during a week, a term and a year;
- keeping observational records of language learners in action;
- providing opportunities for students' self-assessment;
- consulting with and arranging interviews with parents;
- building profiles of individual development;
- compiling summative reports of individual achievement and development from these records;
- involving students in the gathering of evidence and the formulation of statements to be used in written reports; and
- evaluating teaching programs.

Responsive approaches to assessment mean that for each student there will be a continuing accumulation of evidence of development and achievement. Ways of designing a system of record-keeping that provide this accumulating evidence are described in Chapter 8.

Reporting achievement to students and their parents completes the cycle of communication begun at the outset of classroom activities. Conversations and discussions with students are part of a continuing interaction that promotes language learning as well as communicating the students' progress and development. Classroom conversations between students and parents, and conferences, interviews and discussions between parents and teachers, can be as significant in recognising and celebrating development and achievement as written reports. A responsive approach to reporting development and achievement requires:
- establishing and maintaining an authentic, continuing three-way conversation involving students, teachers and parents;
- basing descriptions of development and achievement on a broad range of evidence; and
- using methods of reporting to recognise the significance of this evidence for language learning.

Chapter 9 describes a cycle of communication in which development and achievement are continuously recognised. For each student, this means a continuing involvement in conversations with teachers and parents in which the significance of learning is recognised and reported.

8 KEEPING RECORDS

Various formats can be designed for recording signs of development and achievement observed in a variety of classroom contexts. In this chapter we illustrate a number of examples of possible formats for recording. These examples suggest ways of recording that can provide accumulating evidence of students' development.

The examples given should be adapted to the contexts and priorities of particular classrooms and schools, and to particular levels of schooling. Formats for recording development need to be flexibly designed: that is, the structure of formats should respond to the nature of the work and to the goals and criteria satisfied when students do this work. Many of these formats would usually be associated with particular programs of work and are not 'stand alone' formats suitable for every occasion. The evidence or content to be recorded — the goals and criteria that form the questions which focus observation — determine the purpose, content, structure and timing of these methods of recording development.

Formats for recording that respond to students' development should therefore be designed to:
- suit the particular activity in which students' development is to be observed;
- reflect the main goals of the activity;
- provide ways of involving students in assessing their own progress; and
- enable recording of information at various points in the activity.

In this way, a system of formats can provide a wide range of evidence of development and achievement.

Not all examples illustrated in this chapter are needed at all times. Rather, we believe, a number of formats are needed that provide space and scope for the continuous recording of signs of development, and that provide the evidence on which reports can be validly based.

The kinds of episodes that can form contexts for observation of work and development have been illustrated in the earlier chapters on talking and listening, reading and writing. Here we offer some examples of formats that teachers can use to record observations of development.

Within each of the following sections we have included some examples of formats that can be used by students to make plans, set goals, describe work in progress and assess their own learning. Record-keeping by students is one of the ways in which the workload involved in making continuous records of work and development can be effectively managed.

The sample formats included in this chapter are presented under the following headings:

1 *Planners and plans* — for planning by teachers and students of goals to be achieved and work to be completed.

2 *Class lists* — for planning daily and weekly activities and recording participation and outcomes.

3 *Observation records* — for teachers to record signs of development observed while students are at work.

4 *Work records* — for teachers and students to record details of work in progress, work completed and goals and outcomes achieved.

5 *Self-assessment records* — for students to evaluate their work and development as illustrated on particular activities and projects, and to assess their overall progress.

6 *Program evaluation records* — for evaluating aspects of the program.

The order in which these formats are presented suggests the likely sequence of planning, recording and reporting. Sometimes, however, this sequence might not be followed, as, for example, when students' plans change during activities. As suggested above, to enable sensitive and flexible responses to students' work and development, a number of formats might be used at the same time. For example, where students are working on a folio of writing, records might be kept on several complementary formats such as:

• a list of writing goals set by each student;
• a class list of writing tasks undertaken by each student;
• a folio log in which students record the progress of drafts of writing;
• the teacher's own anecdotal records of signs of development on particular pieces of writing; and
• the student's record of the range of writings undertaken for the folio.

All of these formats work together by providing related pieces of evidence of students' work and development. Underlying the work that is done and the development observed and recorded are the plans made by teachers and students.

1 PLANNERS AND PLANS

WORK PLANS AND REQUIREMENTS

A practical link between plans, records and reports can be achieved by using work plan formats that offer a range of connected activities. As students work on these plans, they can achieve goals by doing and completing the work, and many signs of development and achievement are generated. Work plans, such as those included in Chapters 3 and 7, state clear goals at the outset of activities, so that students know what is required and what language abilities the classroom program is intended to develop, consolidate or extend. When students complete the tasks and activities outlined in the work plan, they demonstrate what language goals they have or have not achieved.

Criteria for assessing achievement are embedded in the work required, and the goals of the program, encompassing both processes and products, are met by the work done. If students are asked to complete several pieces of writing for different purposes and audiences, completing a folio of pieces can, in the process, satisfy:

- the work requirement of a variety of pieces;
- the goals of drafting and revising to achieve the purpose of each piece; and
- the criterion of versatility in writing abilities.

Many other goals and criteria might also be satisfied by completion of a folio of different kinds of writing; for example:

- goals of exploring and using different kinds of language for different readers;
- criteria of accurate, varied use of language and demonstrated knowledge of genre.

When students are asked to prepare a group presentation of poetry readings, the work requirement — the presentation — will involve the achievement of such goals as:

- finding and selecting appropriate poems;
- exploring the language and feelings in poetry through the rehearsal process;
- sharing ideas and feelings with others;
- listening to others' points of view;
- negotiating a plan of action in a group; and
- communicating ideas and feelings to an audience.

Since the presentation involves students working together, the work requirement can provide evidence of whether or not students can:

- work effectively as members of a group;
- analyse imaginative language used in poetry;
- use speech in ways that bring out thoughts and feelings;
- express a personal response to the ideas and feelings encountered in poetry; and
- read and understand this kind of text.

In this way, teachers' goals, students' goals and assessment criteria are all met, more or less well, by completion of the various activities. The completion of the work requirement and the achievement of goals implicit in working on the task provide evidence of how well students meet criteria that will be used for providing feedback to students and for reporting to parents.

PLANS FOR THE WEEK

There are many possible formats for planning activities for a session, a day, a week and so on. The format shown could form a basis for negotiation with younger students learning to choose from a range of possible activities designed by the teacher to accomplish certain learning goals, and to make contracts with the teacher to complete these activities during the week.

My plans for this week

Things to choose

My plan for the week

Monday	Tuesday

	Wednesday	

Thursday	Friday

SETTING PERSONAL GOALS

Opportunities to set personal learning goals can help students to develop greater commitment to the classroom program, to manage and direct their independent study. Experience has shown that many students find difficulty in setting personal goals. They have not often been asked to take such an active interest in the directions of their work.

Formats for this purpose do not need sophisticated design. Students might talk in groups about questions such as these:
• What are some of the goals that can be achieved in English?
• What goals would you like to achieve?
• What goals do you feel that you have achieved so far in your work in English?

With younger students, this discussion might focus on such questions as:
• What do you want to be able to achieve in English?
• How do you think you will achieve these things?

Discussions based on questions like these help students to become accustomed to being involved in the process of setting goals for the classroom program and for their own work.

Goal-setting sessions can be held at several points in the program, with students returning to the original statements, measuring their own progress, and setting new goals. This allows students to build their knowledge and understanding of desirable goals and to perceive more clearly opportunities for achieving them. Teachers can provide some examples of desirable goals and students can offer others that seem important to them. Special formats can be designed to encourage students to set their own goals in areas of their studies. For example, the format shown opposite provides a number of goals for reading which students can re-express as their own statements.

In this way, goals are negotiated between teachers and students; students' understanding of goals is fostered; and they can monitor their own progress more readily.

RECORDS OF WORK REQUIRED

Various formats can be designed to help students to plan their work and to manage their time effectively. A day planner can provide them with a list of goals to be achieved in the short term, and can thereby supply evidence of the range of work done on particular days and over an extended period. Older students can also assess their use of time by drawing up their own time logs in which they record — almost minute by minute — the details of their activities during any particular day. This provides students with a clear picture of how time was used, and can therefore lead to responsible decision-making about improved time management.

Goals for reading

Goals
Possibilities:

<table>
<tr><td>

Possibilities:
- read and understand a variety of texts
- develop and defend my own views about what I read
- use new words gathered from reading
- listen to other people's ideas about texts
- show a detailed knowledge of a particular text
- draw conclusions from reading several texts dealing with one topic or issue

</td><td>

- produce an overview of an issue from reading several texts
- recognise propaganda
- compare points of view contained in various texts
- develop and use research skills
- show awareness of themes and issues in reading
-
-
-
-
-

</td></tr>
</table>

Rewrite these as your own statements of goals for reading. Use the space below to draft these goals.

My goals   **Date**

We have reproduced overleaf a work requirements record which, in order to meet predetermined or negotiated deadlines, students can use to plan the work to be done over an extended period. This format was designed for older students who are ready to take increased responsibility for planning and completing their work, but can be valuable when used with younger students to encourage the growth of attitudes that enable them to work more independently.

ACTION PLANS

Drawn up by students for work on individual and group tasks and projects, action plans like the one shown overleaf enable students to assess their own progress towards completing tasks and to provide evidence of their achievements. When students work in groups, an action plan can specify the roles of each group member and therefore demonstrate abilities in working with other people. It can also describe the exact nature of the work done by each individual in group situations.

Work requirements record

Work requirements	Description	Due dates
Plans & goals		
Journal/Workbook		
Project • progress • final		
Project • progress • final		
Folios		
Presentation		

Action plan

Action	Roles	Deadline dates

CONTRACTS

Contracts between students and teachers can be negotiated for a variety of purposes: for example, for the use of particular classroom sessions, to work on a particular task such as reading a novel, to specify work to be

Contract

Contract between _____ (student) and _____ (teacher)			
Date	Session time	Activities	Comments

Workshop record

Activities						
Names	Date	Date	Date	Date	Date	Homework

done towards the achievement of certain goals, and to provide a record of work done out of the classroom. The successful fulfillment of contracts provides evidence of a range of abilities in managing time and setting and working towards the achievement of goals, as well as of development in using English. Completion of a contract can provide a basis for reporting on achievement in English and on the development of skills and attitudes.

WORKSHOP RECORDS

The format given shown above provides space for students to plan or log daily activities. Workshops are classroom contexts where students work in various groupings or independently to complete a range of connected activities and tasks, such as drafting and revising writing, working in groups to prepare a dramatised version of an incident from a novel, or independently on a project. Examples of workshop activities are described in Chapters 3 and 7.

In these settings, students set their own pace of work towards the completion of tasks and the meeting of deadlines, and can make decisions about what they do in each of the sessions allotted to the workshop. They are asked to note on the workshop record what they intend to do in each session of the allotted time — for example, over a week — or to write in what they have done at the end of each session. As part of this process, students also record what they will do at home or in other independent study time. When a class works in this way, the teacher can talk with individual students, make incidental notes about students' work and development, and confer with students on aspects of their work such as drafts of writing or the development of reading logs.

In these ways, this format responds to the nature of classroom activities and to the varying needs and interests of students. When completed over time, a workshop record provides an overview of the range of work done by students and can therefore be a valuable record for assessing the abilities of students to work on a range of tasks and to manage their own programs. The workshop record can also be used by teachers to make incidental and informal notes about particular aspects of students' work.

2 CLASS LISTS

A list of all students in a class is one of the simplest yet most flexible systems of keeping a record. There are many possible uses for class lists, and many ways of setting them out to record information about students' work and development. The workshop record shown above is one variety of class list, as are many planning formats, and class lists can be designed to record a variety of activities and evidence.

Grids can be designed to meet special needs. For example, a class list could enable teachers to record, over several weeks, such details of classroom activities as reading choices or the membership of working groups in the class.

Headings relevant to particular activities or to development in modes of language can be devised to transform a simple grid into a very useful record of students' work. The size of the space provided in each of the boxes of which a grid is composed can be increased in order to allow the teacher or students to record detailed information. The following formats illustrate how class lists can be varied in design to record:
• work completed
• attendance and participation.

Work completed
TERM ONE

Students										

Record of participation in class
TERM ONE

Students	1	2	3	4	5	6	7	8	9	10

3 OBSERVATION RECORDS

These records are designed to provide space and scope for making notes on the development of individual students during the course of particular activities. Flexibility of response to development is facilitated by designing a range of formats that can be efficiently used for different purposes. For example, when students are working on responses to texts, the teacher might note that a student has written a particularly imaginative story as a sequel to a novel, or that a student is having difficulty reading a novel.

Name _____

Reading

Writing

Talking and listening

General

BLANK PAGES

For these incidental notes, an open format such as a blank page for each student is necessary. The example given illustrates a filled out version of such a page from a teacher's record book where incidental notes have been made.

NAME
ADRIAN SIBILLA

READING

27/2   Participated in group reading. Took role of narrator. Helped to change text and think up actions.

7/4   Workbook entries — initiating ideas on characters and relationships.

25/7   Very detailed chart on relationships

21/8   Workbook entries on Juli very thorough.

....

WRITING

21/3   Not keen to draft pieces. Hands in writing without drafting

7/4   Workbook / folio indicated lack of drafting and revising.

      Many simple technical problems — mainly spelling e.g. "shore" for "Sure"

16/5   Asked me to read drafts — keen to be more accurate in folio.

23/6   Folio of much improved writings — wide range.

18/7   Very clear and well-organised pieces on work experience
    — informative (report) + instructional (skill)
    — still not attending to details

TEACHERS' JOURNALS

In journals and note-pads, teachers can write freely about any aspect of the life of the classroom and the work of individual students. A journal provides a place for describing what has been happening over a period of time, to write reflectively about the success of a particular activity, or to note the progress of an activity that a teacher has introduced for the first time. In this way, journal entries focus on what is important or on problems that need clarification. A journal can also be used to record anecdotal evidence about students' work, and this accumulating evidence might provide the database from which patterns of development and learning can be recognised.

Here is part of the journal entry written during a session in which a Year 9 class used the workshop record (see p. 201) for the first time.

WORKSHOP RECORD

DIFFERENT KINDS OF WRITING

CLASS 10.2.

NAME	8/5	9/5	10/5	11/5	1?/5	HOMEWORK
Jason ABRAHAM	Swagmen	Free Draft	Draft on Computers	Finish other Drafts	Absent	Presentation Folio
Matthew AUSTIN	Reading	away	Reading	Swagman	Finished unfinished piece	FOLIO
Chris BEHRENBRUCH	rough draft fr bk	draft for books	Final copy	Finish Swagman	Maybe	Presentation Folio anything
Cameron BISHOP	Sw...	Start on folio	Work on...	...	Start on...	Final ger...
Sam BRYANT	Research for pre-lang write	Swagman complete	complete Swagman	Folio start folio homwk read	Folio work	Oddessa File
Andrew CHEASLEY	Swa+b...	...	...	"	Folio	...
Ben DAVIDSON	Drafts & Revising	Swaggies	Swaggies	Final copy	Final copy	Book Final copy Swaggies
John ELSTON	Drafts	Read	Work Book	Folio	Folio	Begg Drafts
Alan GROSS	Workbook	Workbook	Folio	Folio	Folio	Read book
Stephen HILL	Essay and Quest. Swaggies	Swaggie	Free draft on novel	Free draft on NOVEL	Finish all other	1.1 1.2 1.3 1.4 + Read
Simon KEARNEY						
Peter KINNAIRD	Questions Arthur the kick fu Swaggie	Dialogue story	Political Poem Dialogue Story	Political Poem	Dialogue Story	Story on "the nerve"
Chris LYLE	Swagmen	Descriptive Beginning	Poem	Folio	Poem (final)	Read Book Work on Folio
Scott MANLEY	NOVEL	SWAGMAN NOVEL	NOVEL	FOLIO	BONO	WORK OF FOLIO
Guy MENZ	Words	Swaggie Questions	Swaggie Essay	Begin Novel Work	Complete Novel work	Continue Novel work
Shaun OLSEN	Words	Swaggie questions	Writing for a purpose	Swaggie essay 250	Folio	Folio
Brendan PITTARD	Swagmen	Swagmen	True draft - Spit MacPhee	PLCE WKBK START FOLIO	FOLIO	Swagmen Free Spit MacPhee Folio
James PRICE	SWAGMEN	E	Stories in Medi-eval Lang	Folio on NOVEL	Finish all Work Book	Swagmen - Folio Workbook - drafts
James RUDDOCK	SWAGMEN	SWAGMEN	Finish Swag work and begin novel	Complete Novel work	Polish up weakbook	Read book and complete work book
Adrian SIBILLA	Workbook	Workbook	...	...	...	Presentation folio
Travis STEWART	Read	Swagmen Free draft	Read	Folio	Presentation folio	
Chris TOROSSI	Workbook	Workbook	Folio	Folio	Folio	Read book Folio
Simon WOOLLARD	Absent	Absent	Words.	Swaggie questions	swaggie essay	swaggie questions.

Several months later, the class used the workshop record sheet again, and these are the first few lines of what was recorded in the teacher's journal:

TEACHER'S JOURNAL

YEAR 10   15-22 MAY 1989   Journal Summary

ACTIVITY: LETTER TO THE EDITOR OF A NEWSPAPER giving your views on a current issue.

1. Students thought of a list of issues that concerned them. Posed a question about each one. As they were writing these questions, they kept writing one or two issues. Were these the issues that they felt most strongly about?

2. Selected one issue and wrote their views in a paragraph.

3. Formed small group and gave their views. Invited questions and challenges. Then said how they would support their views.

4. Looked at examples of letters to newspapers. Also watched TV current affairs programs and documentaries (e.g. Nobody's Children) in that week.

5. Drafts written and read to groups. Peer conference idea built in to drafting. Groups guided by questions such as:
   • What views would you challenge? evidence?
   • What other evidence could be used? i.e. Have you thought about...?
   • What do you think of ... (opposing argument)?

6. Final draft in letter form – sent them off.

7. Responses of students to peer conferences:
   BD: "Changed sentence structure. Words altered."
   JA: "Took out unnecessary words."
   CB: "Found a good conclusion + introduction – by working with person doing same topic"
   JP: "Got different ideas."
   JL: "Had to deal with problems in my argument."

STUDENTS' JOURNALS AND FOLIOS

Various records of work kept by students can provide a basis for assessing the development of students' thinking and use of language. Journals such as workbooks, diaries, reading and viewing logs can be kept by students. Folios of work on texts, issues and writing can also provide a wide range of signs of development and achievement.

Students can be helped to make use of these records by the design of a format for a table of contents such as that shown on p. 209.

When complete, the table of contents of a workbook, for example, can provide the kind of accessible overview of work valuable for consultations with parents and students, and for the writing of reports. When students are involved in assessing their own progress, they can use the evidence contained in their journals, workbooks and folios to draw conclusions about their progress and to set new goals.

. . . AND JOTTERS

Formats for jottings — such as a note pad for each class — allow quick notes to be made about any aspect of classroom work, and these can sometimes be expanded in a journal when there is time to write more reflectively.

LANGUAGE CHECKPOINTS

At the end of each chapter concerned with development in the modes of language, there are formats for recording observations according to open-ended lists of criteria. Records such as these can provide a bridge between progressive classroom observations and the writing of reports. If copies of this format were used to record signs of development demonstrated by students in a variety of contexts and activities, these records could eventually provide a comprehensive picture of the development of each student's language abilities. As students work on particular activities and projects, new signs of learning might gradually be observed and noted, yielding an accumulating record.

4 WORK RECORDS

Students can play a major role in keeping records of their work in progress. These records can become valuable sources of information for discussion with the teacher about their personal development in English. When involved in the record-keeping process, students develop greater commitment to their work and to its completion, and can more readily identify the goals they need to achieve.

As they help to compile these records, they set goals for their own learning, and recognise the extent to which they have achieved these goals. Sometimes, keeping a record of all the writing they have done over a certain period, the kinds of oral activities in which they have participated, or the books they have been reading, helps students to recognise the patterns and progression in their learning, and then sparks their motivation to learn more.

When work has been completed, students' own records can provide an overview of the range of tasks undertaken and can indicate areas where important goals have been achieved. Criteria for assessing their own progress can be profitably discussed and negotiated with most groups of students.

In these ways, too, students perceive that their record-keeping is of equal status to that of the teacher — a perception that generates responsibility for their learning as well as an understanding of what they are being helped to achieve.

Formats for recording the progress of work can be kept by students as they work towards achieving the goals of projects and activities. Many of these formats provide structures that encourage students to keep learning logs of various kinds. Some examples of these different kinds of logs are shown below.

WRITING RECORDS

These formats can be used by students to record the variety of writing that they have completed and the range of purposes which their writings have achieved. A table of contents for a writing folio is a simple means by which students can keep a record of the range of writings they have completed.

As these records are built up by students, a clear picture of their individual reading and viewing interests and abilities is developed. This record enables them to make brief comments about each text they enter, but longer extended responses might be invited to novels and films read and talked about by the class.

Table of contents

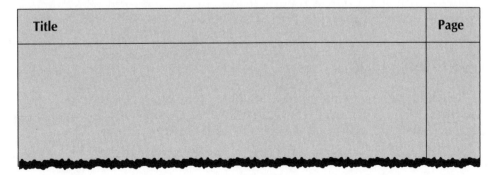

Title	Page

Folio record

Title of piece	Date	Date	Date	Date

Writing record

Name: _____ Year: _____

Started	Title	Finished	Type of writing

PROJECT LOGS

A format of this kind provides a structure for students to record the progress of particular projects. It can be particularly useful in helping students to make progress reports to the teacher and to the class as they work on extended activities such as projects.

WRITING LOGS

Where students are required to draft and revise a range of writings, they can keep a log of the progress of a particular piece through two or three drafts. This kind of format requires careful management as some pieces of writing might not need the number of drafts suggested by the design of the sheet; the design of others might require a longer drafting process.

DIFFERENT KINDS OF WRITING

Kinds of writing I have done

Name: _____ **Year:** _____

Advertisements	_____	Pamphlets	_____
Anecdotes	_____	Pen portraits	_____
Autobiographies	_____	Photo stories	_____
Children's books	_____	Play scripts	_____
Comic strips	_____	Poetry	_____
Commercials	_____	Posters	_____
Confessions	_____	Questionnaires	_____
Crosswords	_____	Questions	_____
Descriptions	_____	Radio scripts	_____
Dialogues	_____	Research reports	_____
Diaries	_____	Reviews	_____
Essays	_____	Riddles	_____
Factual reports	_____	School handbook	_____
Form filling	_____	Short stories	_____
Graffiti	_____	Songs	_____
Greeting cards	_____	Sports reports	_____
Group story writing	_____	Submissions	_____
Jokes	_____	Summaries	_____
Jottings	_____	Telegrams	_____
Letters	_____	Television scripts	_____
Magazines	_____	Word collages	_____
Messages	_____	Word squares	_____
Newspapers	_____	Writing folios	_____
Notes	_____		
Novels	_____		

Project log

Task/Activity	Date started	Completed

GROUP-WORK RECORDS

Where students are asked to work in groups on particular tasks and projects, it can sometimes be difficult to establish exactly how the work is being done and who is doing what. A format can be designed to enable students to keep a record of the variety of tasks being undertaken by members of a group, and also indicate the work roles of each member.

READING AND VIEWING LOGS

On this sheet, students record their own reading and viewing during the year. The records made by students could refer to newspapers, magazines, films and television programs, as well as to books.

LISTENING TO A TALK

This format contains a number of statements that describe aspects of listening abilities. These statements can be drawn from prior discussion with students about the need for attentive listening and how they might demonstrate that ability. Students can suggest several ways in which they might show how well they listen and these suggestions can be encompassed within goals described on the self-assessment sheet.

When you listen to a talk

Things to notice	What did you notice?
1 Was the speaker interesting? 2 Did he or she know the subject? 3 Did the talk have a plan? 4 Did he or she show a sense of humour? 5 Were you interested all the time? 6 Were you disappointed when the speaker finished? 7 Did you learn anything new?	

Group work record

Group member	Jobs
Comments e.g. What would you do differently next time?	

Reading and viewing log

Date	Opinion

5 SELF-ASSESSMENT RECORDS

The range of formats included in this section are offered as examples of opportunities for students to assess their own work and progress. Students can be involved in assessing:
• their own work and development on particular activities and projects;
• their participation in and the effectiveness of small-group work;

The Untouchable Juli
Assessment sheet, Year 11 English

Work requirement	Comments	Date
1 *Reading log* Regular entries, questions, comments, ideas, notes on own experience & other books. June 7		
2 *Character web* Detail, connections, organisation June 5		
3 *Word bank* Task completed, range of words, accurate definitions Due: June 5		
4 *Poetry reading* Choice of poem, interpretation. June 12		
5 *Three pieces of writing* Evidence of drafting and revision, careful reading. Planning & structure, detail. Knowledge of book, response. Due: June 5, 13, 19		
6 *Oral presentation* Choice of passage, clear voice, appropriate interpretation. Due: June 19		
7 *Participation* Completion of tasks, independence in work patterns, evidence of reading novel, contribution to discussion and group activities, punctuality, involvement, attentiveness.		

Comments on whole unit:

- their achievement of personal goals; and
- their development and achievement over time.

Records kept by students of work in progress, described on p. 214, can provide a valuable source of information for students' self-assessment.

The examples of self-assessment formats offered below, assessment sheets designed to accompany the work plans included above, illustrate the meshing of teacher and student responsibility for monitoring progress. Such approaches, conducted in workshop settings, generate a continuing discussion about progress between individual students and the teacher.

The space provided for students' comments is an important aspect of the design of these formats. Giving space for students' comments on record-keeping formats, and involving them in keeping records of their work, is a signal to students of the role they can play in monitoring their own progress. A working example of a format designed to fit a particular classroom context, 'Taking a Trip', is included in Chapter 3.

Students can be involved also in keeping records of the range of their classroom or personal experience in areas of language development. Such records, of which the format shown, Talking check, is an example, can provide significant evidence of the variety of students' use of language. and of the expanding range of language contexts in which they can participate.

Talking check

Activity	Dates
Sharing ideas with others	— — — — — — —
Asking questions	— — — — — — —
Listening to answers to questions	— — — — — — —
Giving directions	— — — — — — —
Remembering simple instructions	— — — — — — —
Retelling main facts, events	— — — — — — —
Expressing opinions	— — — — — — —
Talking about writing	— — — — — — —
Describing situations or events	— — — — — — —
Exploring ideas in groups	— — — — — — —
Solving problems in groups	— — — — — — —
Working on group projects	— — — — — — —
Writing and performing a script	— — — — — — —
Reading aloud	— — — — — — —
Making a radio program	— — — — — — —
Preparing and conducting interviews	— — — — — — —
Speaking on prepared topics	— — — — — — —
Listening to talks	— — — — — — —

PROJECT REPORTS

When students work on extended activities such as projects, they can be involved in evaluating the work done and the outcomes achieved. The format Project Report is an example of a format designed for this purpose — especially when students have worked a members of a project team. They might discuss the project with other members of the team and use this sheet to summarise the main points of their evaluation.

GROUP-WORK RECORDS

The items used in this format were drawn from discussion with a Year 8 class about the purposes of group activities. In this way, students felt that they had discussed and negotiated criteria for cooperative learning and were aware of what group activities were designed to achieve. This focusing discussion helped to direct group work and to generate under-standings of the benefit of working with other people.

EFFECTIVE WORKING

When students have finished major pieces of work, or at the end of semester, they can be invited to review the work they have done. At such a stage, the records kept by students throughout work on the major pieces and built up during the semester can help them to identify the goals they have achieved and to set up new goals for their learning in future studies, projects and activities. Two ways of designing formats that provide opportunities for this review are illustrated below.

6 PROGRAM EVALUATION RECORDS

From time to time, it's important to look at what has been done and to measure this against the agreed objectives for the whole teaching pro-gram. Such an evaluation involves consideration of the range of activities and the effectiveness of particular activities and experiences within each part of the program.

Here we offer three examples of formats designed to help program evaluation. A teaching strategies checklist can indicate the range and balance of experiences involving students; a program overview sheet can provide a basis for reflecting on what students have done and what they need to do next. A format such as Program Check — Oral Communica-tion can further sharpen the focus by directing it to specific parts of the

Project report

1 **Action plan** List the steps in your action plan.

2 **Achievement of goals** List the goals that were achieved.

3 **Problem solving** What problems did you encounter and how did you overcome them?

4 **Evaluation** What did you learn? What would you do differently next time?

Group activity record

Did members of your group:	Your opinion
■ listen to other people's ideas? ■ share ideas with other members? ■ make plans? ■ each have a part to play? ■ all help? ■ think of new ideas to help your task? ■ learn more about the topic or the text? ■ do a number of different things to help? ■ work with different people this time? ■ know what your group was doing? ■ all help to decide what to say or do? ■ finish the task?	

Review

Topic: _____

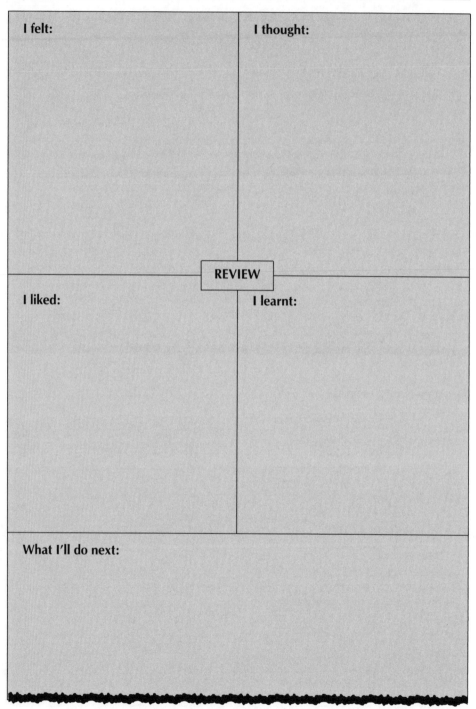

I felt:

I thought:

REVIEW

I liked:

I learnt:

What I'll do next:

Work review

Teacher's comments	Your plans and goals

TEACHING STRATEGIES CHECKLIST

Teaching strategies checklist

Strategy	Activity	Date
Small-group exploratory talk		
Small-group focused talk		
Small-group projects		
Role play		
Drama and dance		
Film and video		
Journals and diaries — personal observations		
Journals and diaries — imaginative		
Writing stories or imaginative pieces		
Making notes		
Writing reports		
Class projects		
Individual research		
Demonstrations		
Displays		
Debates		
Teacher instructions		
Practical investigations		
Excursions		
Talks by students		
Computer simulations		
Word processing		
Analysis of various texts		
Speakers		
Building models		

PROGRAM OVERVIEW
Program overview

Language activities completed by Year ____	Date

PROGRAM CHECK — ORAL COMMUNICATION
Program check: oral communication

Activity	Dates
Sharing ideas with others	
Asking questions	
Listening to answers to questions	
Giving directions	
Remembering simple instructions	
Retelling main facts, events	
Expressing opinions	
Talking about writing	
Describing situations or events	
Exploring ideas in groups	
Solving problems in groups	
Working on group projects	
Writing and performing a script	
Reading poetry and stories aloud	
Making a radio program	
Preparing and conducting interviews	
Speaking on prepared topics	
Listening to talks	

program. Records of students' participation and self-assessment can also supply useful evidence of the effectiveness of activities and programs.

∎CONCLUSION

Our purpose in offering these examples is to suggest a wide range of format designs appropriate for various aspects of assessment in English. When used within the context of a broad range of activities and experiences, these formats provide clerically simple means of keeping track of what students do and what they achieve.

These kinds of records can be used to marshal the wide range of evidence on which to base an assessment of students' learning. Such real evidence of the achievement of competence in language might include:
• folders of writing, including finished work and drafts
• audio and video tapes
• photographs of groups at work
• oral presentations and performances
• workbooks, logbooks and journals.

Development and achievement in English are demonstrated as much by the ways in which students work — the processes and skills — as by the outcomes they produce. As illustrated by the episodes in Chapters 4, 5 and 6, development and achievement in English can also be demonstrated by a very wide range of indicators. This complexity of language development and variety of achievement need to be matched by record-keeping procedures and formats that do justice to students' learning.

A record-keeping system that is comprehensive and systematic responds to:
• the variety of classroom activities that are needed to promote development;
• the nature of students' development and achievement as observed in both process and product;
• the interactive basis of language learning; and
• the gradual and continuous nature of language development.

A system of record-keeping comprising a range of formats such as those described in this chapter continously involves students in a discussion of their progress. The evidence of development and achievement that accumulates through the use of record-keeping systems informs discussions between students, parents and teachers about the significance of learning and provides a valid basis for reporting development and achievement.

9 RECOGNISING DEVELOPMENT AND ACHIEVEMENT

The acknowledgement of development and achievement is integral to responsive assessment. Responsive approaches to assessment mean that, for each student, a continuing, comprehensive and varied range of evidence of development and achievement will accumulate. How can the significance of this evidence about what students have learnt be acknowledged and recognised by students, parents, other teachers, and — at certain points in schooling — communicated to employers or tertiary institutions? For teachers, communication of development and achievement, or 'reporting', involves:

- recognising the nature and extent of learning;
- acknowledging that learning has occurred;
- describing the significance of this evidence in regard to learning; and
- sharing these perceptions in a continuous dialogue with students and parents.

Much of this recognition and acknowledgement can be effectively interwoven with activities and programs and with the progress of individual pieces of work. Given the interdependence, in language learning, between process and product, conversations between student and teacher about development and achievement draw upon the accumulating evidence of learning. In this way, reporting development and achievement can continuously respond to:

- the processes of language learning;
- the needs of students and parents for a broad range of information about progress and achievement;
- the goals set by students themselves; and
- the nature of the work done.

Recognition of development and achievement provides an opportunity for language learning. The processes of communication engaged here involve the connectedness, continuity and purposefulness that characterise conversations between partners in a shared enterprise or joint venture. This interaction, or conversation, is also reflexive, cycling back to plans and goals, through work in progress to outcomes, and onwards to further learning and development, as is shown with reference to five Year 10 students in the chart 'Connections in assessing and reporting'.

Talking with students about their development and achievement is as important an occasion for language learning as any aspect of the classroom program. Opportunities for talking with students about their achievement can be planned — such as when a teacher is talking with a student about a piece of writing, or about the setting and achievement of personal goals for reading. Teachers talking with individual students about their language development can promote further learning by describing achievement. Often incidental, unplanned moments for talking with individual students occur, and these allow teachers and students to share their perceptions of what has been done and achieved. Students will want to know at these times:

- What have I learnt?
- What developments in my work have occurred?
- What have I achieved?

In such conversations, the perceptions of the teacher can help students to recognise the significance of their learning.

A dialogue between students and teachers, sometimes private and confidential in nature, runs through all learning activities and is part of their relationship that develops in the classroom. Talks with parents can occur at various stages of the school year, sustaining a conversation in which the achievement of individual students is continuously discussed. A responsive approach to communication concerning the progress of a student's language learning has the flexibility, interactiveness and sensitivity of conversation, in that it:

- invites and responds to students' and parents' questions about development and achievement: What work has been done or is in progress? What signs of development and achievement have been observed?
- focuses on the accumulating evidence of development and achievement: that is, describes what has been observed;
- creates opportunities for students and parents to recognise significant learning;
- occurs in various contexts and at various stages in classroom activities — whenever opportunities for conversations arise;
- continues throughout a student's schooling; and
- celebrates achievement.

Within this conversation, it is possible to identify several ways of recognising and responding to development and achievement. We suggest that each of these ways has equal status: that is, aspects of development

Connections in assessing and reporting

This chart illustrates the connections, in the work done by individual students, between activities, records, signs of development, achievement, response to parents and the formulation of new goals of development and achievement.

Student	Activity	Records	Signs of learning
JK	Poetry readings	■ Reading log ■ Workbook notes: e.g. ■ Lists of poems ■ Final list	■ Read poems to others ■ Browsed through poetry books ■ Read silently for an extended period ■ Listened to others' readings ■ Memorised poem
AB	Research project	■ Focus questions ■ Workbook notes ■ Project log ■ Drafts ■ Final report	■ Generated important questions ■ Discovered a range of relevant information ■ Gathered information from several sources ■ Organised material to suit audience
JA	Oral presentation	■ Ideas list — planning presentation ■ Decisions about style of presentation ■ Notes and resources	■ Was interested in a special field ■ Planned presentation ■ Made accurate notes ■ Presented information logically ■ Explained unfamiliar terms
LT	Writing folio	■ Ideas list ■ List of possible audiences ■ Drafts ■ Progress log ■ Finished pieces	■ Developed many interesting ideas ■ Listened to responses of peers ■ Revised work by integrating new material ■ Changed words and phrases to suit audience
KY	Group discussion	■ Notes of discussions ■ Questions to explore or decide upon ■ Draft report ■ Final report	■ Was keen to learn other people's ideas and experiences ■ Suggested ideas for the group to consider ■ Asked relevant questions ■ Negotiated a plan of action with others

and achievement can be discussed at any appropriate moment during classroom activities and programs. Any point in this dialogue can be as influential and as responsive as another in promoting development and in acknowledging achievement.

The timing of these discussions will depend upon:

● the progress of activities;

● the incidence of questions asked by individual students;

● the need of teachers to talk with individual students or their parents;

Achievement	Response to parents	New goals
■ Presented an effective sequence of readings ■ Showed a high level of appreciation of poet's use of language	JK presented an effective sequence of poetry readings in which she demonstrated a high level of appreciation of the use of language.	■ to offer encouragement to the contribution of others ■ to draw on her reading to widen her written vocabulary
■ Gathered information from a variety of texts ■ Showed initiative in finding information ■ Completed a challenging project	AB completed a challenging research project in which he showed initiative in gathering information from a variety of sources.	■ to evaluate a wider range of information and opinions ■ to write more logically about information gathered
■ Talked about a topic of personal interest to the class ■ Presented information in ways that promoted audience understanding	JA's oral presentation showed that she can clearly explain new ideas and information to an audience unfamiliar with the topic.	■ to be more open-minded when discussing issues ■ to explain interests to different audiences
■ Compiled a folio of writings for different purposes and audiences ■ Used a wide range of appropriate words ■ Showed awareness of the needs of the reader	LT compiled a folio of varied and interesting writings which illustrated her wide vocabulary and her understanding of the purposes of writing.	■ to use accurate syntax ■ to argue logically towards a decision or action
■ Talked constructively in a small-group discussion ■ Kept written records of group discussions ■ Contributed effectively to the group report	KY participated constructively in a small-group discussion and showed that he can play valuable roles in assisting the work of a group.	■ to find useful information for group tasks ■ to work effectively without close supervision

- opportunities for more organised means of communication, such as parent–teacher interviews; and
- the need to report in writing.

All these occasions, however, draw upon the accumulating evidence of development observed and described from classroom work.

In English, as shown in earlier chapters, the development of skills and abilities can be observed in classroom processes — for example, the progress of projects, exploratory group talk, the preparation of oral presentations — as well as in outcomes such as a finished piece of writing or a student's leading a tutorial. For this reason, development and achievement can be noted and communicated within the progress of classroom activities. When passed on to students on such occasions, this kind of observation can powerfully promote further development. Conversations with students engaged in activities are part of a cycle of communication in which signs of development are observed and described and in which new goals are set. The conversation about development and achievement can continue throughout activities and beyond the outcomes of students' work.

Growth and development in language continues throughout a person's life. Growth in students' language, observed as students work on and complete classroom activities, continues throughout schooling. The continuing conversation about achievement responds to signs of such growth and learning whenever they occur.

■ WAYS OF SHARING RECOGNITION OF DEVELOPMENT AND ACHIEVEMENT

What are the special moments that can occur within the dialogue involving students, teachers and parents, and that constitute a cycle of communication about development and achievement? These moments may be planned or unplanned, but all can be decisive when students recognise their own achievements and new learning and set new goals; and when students, teachers and parents work together to promote further development and achievement. We suggest, therefore, that each of the episodes described below has equal status: that, for example, talking with individual students about the progress of a piece of writing can be as important, and sometimes more important, to their development and achievement as written reports on their writing abilities.

DISCUSSIONS WITH INDIVIDUAL STUDENTS

Any incidental comment from the teacher during classroom activities can be perceived by a student as a comment upon his or her progress or abilities. For example:

- In writing conferences, it is important for the teacher to talk with writers about the strengths of particular pieces. Such talk can help to convince a student that 'I can do this'. This can lead to talk about things that the writer needs to develop, and so new goals for development and achievement are negotiated.
- When a teacher writes in a student's reading log: 'I hadn't thought of it like that', the student knows that he or she can read perceptively, and from this response can gain the confidence to read more complex texts. The comment carries at the same time important status as communication about achievement and an impetus to further development.
- When a small group of students outline their plans for leading a class forum, questions from the teacher such as 'What are you going to talk about?' and 'Have you decided how you will organise the forum?' help the students understand the goals they have achieved and those they need to achieve. After such activities, discussions with members of the audience, and among group members, can help students to arrive at a realistic appraisal of their achievement.

There are various ways of creating and managing the time for teachers to talk with students. The use of work plans and workshop approaches where students enter their plans for several sessions on a workshop record, as described on pp. 201–2 in the previous chapter, enables teachers to confer with individual students — for a few minutes or at length. Where students are engaged in an extended writing task in a workshop setting, there is time to talk with individual students about progress on particular writings and about their development in general. When working with younger students, teachers can establish a 'conference corner' where talks with students are conducted and where drafts of writing and files are stored for easy access during conferences.

Many of the signs of development observed and described with reference to the classroom episodes included in Chapters 4, 5 and 6 can be used as the basis of talks with individual students about their achievement and the need for further development.

CLASSROOM DISCUSSIONS

Discussions with students about goals to be achieved and about records to be kept provide another important mechanism by which evidence of development and achievement can be compiled and recognised. When goals are negotiated with students, they can monitor their own progress and assess their own development and achievement. They also are helped to recognise the significance to their learning of particular pieces of work.

In order to recognise the significance of their work, students need to know the criteria by which their work will be judged. When the goals of a classroom program or piece of work are formulated in a classroom discussion with students, they are also helping to formulate these criteria. The goals of their work include the criteria by which their development and achievement will be judged. Examples of goals and criteria formulated for classroom projects are described in Chapters 4 and 7, and each of the episodes in the chapters on observing and describing development include descriptive statements that can form the basis of classroom discussions about goals and criteria.

Classroom discussions can be useful in monitoring the progress of work. Where students are engaged in a group project, they can report to the class at certain points in the project on the work they have done. These reports might include the goals that they have achieved so far and the goals that they still need to achieve. These reports can indicate evidence of learning that is as significant to students' development and achievement as the product of their group work.

For example, the students who, as described in Chapter 4, interviewed a popular music group, completed many tasks upon which a successful outcome depended, but the completion of these tasks themselves indicated development in particular skills and abilities. Progress reports that describe the completion of incidental tasks such as those involved in the Bon Jovi project can provide important evidence of development and achievement.

TALKING WITH PARENTS

Conferences between parents and teachers are important opportunities for teachers to answer parents' questions:
• What work have the children done?
• How well have they done it?
• What development has been observed?
• How has this work been judged?

By adding to parents' knowledge of the nature of the classroom program and of the participation of their children within it, teachers can create a partnership that works in the children's interests.

If parents know what criteria are being used to judge their children's achievement, they become aware of the real standards of judgement and are therefore better able to support their children in achieving these goals. They can see the relevance of the work done, and can recognise the complexity of the teacher's task in assessing their children's development and achievement. Most importantly, they can appreciate the extent of their children's development. Discussions with parents therefore need to involve a description of the criteria by which their children's work and learning are judged.

Learning what their children have done is an effective way for parents to gain answers to these questions. Material describing the plan of work for the class and the work of individual students can provide a focus of discussions with parents and lead to a realistic, shared appraisal of the student's achievements. Information nights and parent-teacher interviews provide the vehicles for discussion focusing on the goals and evidence of students' work.

SHARING INFORMATION ABOUT DEVELOPMENT AND ACHIEVEMENT

PARENT-TEACHER CONFERENCES

Communication between parents and teachers can be enriched by the creation of opportunities for parents to contribute to talks about their children. To achieve authentic conversation in which information about students' development is shared, talks between parents and teachers can be structured as conferences rather than as interviews, creating opportunities for parents to participate actively in what is said. For example, introductory questions such as: 'How do you think she's going?' or 'Do you have any questions you would like to ask?' establish an active role for parents at the outset. Parents often have information about their children's needs, interests and development that is not known to teachers and this can help teachers to arrive at a more balanced picture of students' development and achievement. When focused on the accumulating evidence of achievement described earlier in this section, this kind of talk shifts the emphasis away from comparison and competition towards a realistic appraisal of individual students' expanding skills and abilities and towards a consideration of their individual needs as learners.

THREE-WAY CONFERENCES

Conferences involving students, teachers and parents can provide a useful context for developing plans of action that involve all parties. The openness of this kind of conference can help students to feel that they have a role in the process of assessing their achievement. Also, by involving them in the laying of plans for further development, such conferences can encourage the active commitment of students to the achievement of important language goals.

An appraisal by students of their own strengths and weaknesses can help teachers to plan new programs and negotiate new goals, and records of this appraisal can help parents to understand the directions of the classroom program and to support students and teachers in achieving these goals. In these ways, students, teachers and parents can work together to support development and promote achievement.

HOME-SCHOOL CONTACT

Where parents find it difficult to come to organised parent-teacher interviews, several other strategies of communication can be employed, such as:

- *Telephone conferences* Parents often initiate telephone contact to discuss their child's achievement. These are opportunities for discussions of students' achievement based upon the evidence accumulating in, for example, folders of writing.
- *Home visits* Parents who do not wish to come to the school can be invited to ask teachers to visit them, bringing samples of students' work and records of work and development.
- *Special invitations* Parents can be invited to come to the school at any time to discuss their children's development. They can make appointments to come to the school at times convenient to them.
- *School visits by parents* When parents come to a conference, the teacher can ask if there is anything they want to ask and teacher and student can quickly locate examples of work relevant to the question. The teacher refers to records on file cards as well. If parents have no questions to ask, teacher and students have plenty to show. In this way, parents see the whole range of work that has been done, in contrast to the fragmentary evidence of work and achievement they might see during a school year. The range of work displayed in these ways indicates how much has been achieved. The involvement of students in setting up the display and in the conferences again promotes self-evaluation of work and achievement.

The kinds of evidence that can be used to provide this focus are as follows.

WORK PLANS

Plans of work negotiated with students which outline goals and activities can be shared with parents. This is another way of helping parents to be aware of what their children are doing and the goals that they are asked to achieve. With this knowledge, parents can play a more supportive and active role in their children's learning.

RECORDS OF STUDENTS' WORK

Parents should have access to the records of their children's work and development. The pages in a record book where such information is recorded should be sighted by parents during a conference with teachers. Of particular significance can be collections of work completed and the expanding range of skills and abilities shown by students.

EXAMPLES OF STUDENTS' WORK

By collecting evidence describing the work of each child in the class teachers can prepare for consultations with parents. Focusing discussion on this evidence is the most effective way of using the time available for the conference. A collection of evidence illustrating a student's work and achievement can also help parents to understand the purposes of classroom activities. Parents sometimes feel that classroom programs do not match the strengths and weaknesses that they see in their child's work. Why, for example, is a child ask to write a poem when it is the child's spelling and grammar that need attention? Why is a child who often reads novels asked to write a report on a social issue for a newspaper? Connections between the needs of the child and the classroom program are not always evident to parents. In conferences with parents, where a collection of samples of students' work and records of development provide the focus for talk, these connections can be explained.

Parents are also likely to appreciate the extent to which the class teacher knows their child, and this can be demonstrated quite clearly by a discussion that centres on the evidence of students' work and development. By sharing this information, the teacher demonstrates knowledge of individual students.

The contents of a folio of writing can demonstrate the range of children's writing and their skills and abilities in responding to texts. From drafts and finished pieces of writing, parents can see how intensively their children work on improving their writings, including their control of the conventions of writing. Workbooks or folders of work kept by students can serve a similar purpose.

DISPLAYS OF STUDENTS' WORK

Displays of students' work, project nights, dramatic and other activities are other ways in which evidence of students' achievement can be shared with parents. With younger students, samples of writing can be chosen by students for display books available to parents at parent–teacher interview or information sessions. These books contain a contribution from every member of the class, and are demonstrations of the work done by the class and the achievement of individual students. In selecting an example of their writing for inclusion in the book, students are evaluating their progress as writers. Such a book can demonstrate the achievement of the class in writing for an expanding range of purposes.

A 'finished work folder' can be made by each child in the class. In this folder or folio, each student stores all finished work across the whole range of curriculum areas, such as:

• finished writing
• project work
• posters
• published books
• complete workbooks.

The folders are stored in the classroom and when parent–teacher sessions are held, the children set up their own tables with their whole folder, as well as with workbooks still in use, and writing folders of work in progress. In this way, students display everything that they have worked on to that time.

ACCUMULATING PROFILES OF DEVELOPMENT AND ACHIEVEMENT

How can an efficient overview of a student's achievement be provided? It is difficult in the context of day-to-day involvement in teaching for teachers to formulate an overview of each student's work and development. But every now and then, at the end of the term, semester or year, for example, it is useful to summarise what, so far, students have shown they can and cannot do.

Examples of profiles of development in talking and listening, reading and writing are described in Chapters 4, 5 and 6. The following profiles are examples of summaries of information about development in the modes of language learning. The circular profile shown opposite is an example of one format that can be used to provide a periodic summary. Different colours can be used to indicate strengths and weaknesses.

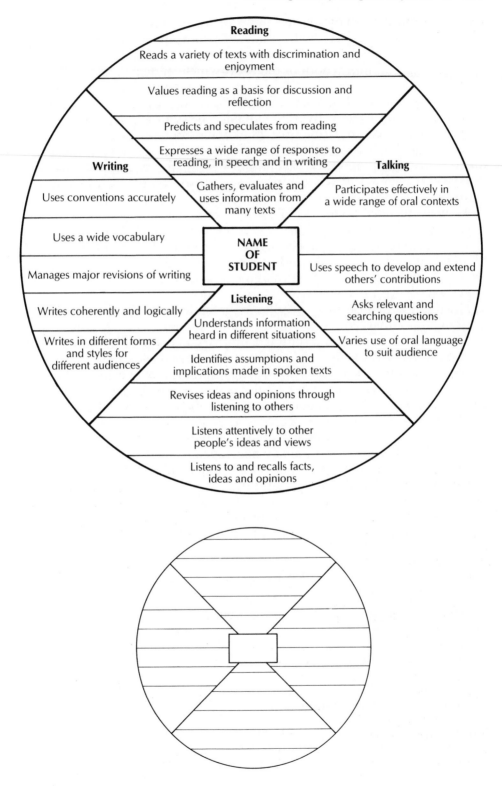

Reading

Reads a variety of texts with discrimination and enjoyment

Values reading as a basis for discussion and reflection

Predicts and speculates from reading

Expresses a wide range of responses to reading, in speech and in writing

Writing

Gathers, evaluates and uses information from many texts

Uses conventions accurately

Talking

Participates effectively in a wide range of oral contexts

NAME OF STUDENT

Uses a wide vocabulary

Uses speech to develop and extend others' contributions

Manages major revisions of writing

Listening

Asks relevant and searching questions

Writes coherently and logically

Understands information heard in different situations

Varies use of oral language to suit audience

Writes in different forms and styles for different audiences

Identifies assumptions and implications made in spoken texts

Revises ideas and opinions through listening to others

Listens attentively to other people's ideas and views

Listens to and recalls facts, ideas and opinions

In this profile, we have chosen a number of statements about language learning that help to describe the kinds of achievements at which English programs are aimed. These statements serve two closely related functions: they are examples both of the goals which students can and need to achieve, and of the criteria by which their achievements can be measured. Another kind of profile is shown below. This profile can be built up from observations and records over an extended period of time, perhaps two or three years. Accumulating profiles like this can be passed on from year to year, and further detail added as development and achievement are noted. Periodic reviews of students' progress, for example in parent-teacher interviews and when written reports are prepared, can provide occasions for updating the profile.

As well, profiles of this kind can be compiled at different points in schooling — for example, Years K–12, Years 5–7, and Years 8–10.

Systems of filing cards can be used to make notes that might contribute to updating the profiles. File cards can be formatted so that information is recorded under aspects of development and achievement that relate directly to the content and structure of profiles.

The criteria used on these profiles are intended as a guide to the kinds of statements that could be made about students' development and achievement at the end of a semester or year. These profiles can be filed with other records of students' work, and reviewed each year.

Since development in English depends upon the provision of successively enriched classroom contexts for language learning, what was said about a student in Year 5 cannot necessarily be assumed to be so in the work of the same student in Years 6 or 7. Language learning — along with personality — expands in range, complexity and purpose, so that these goals need to be continuously developed in successive years.

Summaries of development and achievement like those contained in the profiles described above can form the basis of the agenda for conferences with students and parents. For example, at the end of a term or semester, a partially-completed profile, perhaps a record of development in the previous year, can be given to students so that they might

A language profile, K–12

Name: ———————— Period covered: from ————— to —————

Aspects of language	Comments	Date
Talking and listening ■ effective participation in a range of oral contexts ■ sense of appropriateness of oral language for different audiences and purposes ■ effective listening		

Aspects of language	Comments	Date
Reading ■ demonstrated ability to comprehend and respond to a wide range of print and non-print texts ■ ability to express discriminating responses to different texts, orally and in writing ■ competence in using knowledge and ideas gained from reading for a wide range of purposes		
Writing ■ capacity to communicate meaning effectively in writing ■ knowledge and control of drafting, revision and editing ■ mastery of conventions of written language to support meaning ■ experience in writing for a range of different purposes and audiences ■ capacity to make appropriate choices of tone, style, structure for different purposes and audiences		
Ways of working ■ ability to work independently ■ ability to work in cooperation with others ■ ability to sustain work until pieces of work and extended projects are finished ■ capacity to set learning goals and assess effectiveness of own work		
Special achievements		
General comments		

help the teacher to add to the profile of achievement based on the present year's work. Students can update this information by listing items of work completed over a certain period and, in conference with the teacher, negotiate new entries on the profile. This enables perceptions of progress to be matched and compared in a way that can lead to cooperative, agreed report writing and provide valuable talking points with parents. If desirable, parents and students can be given copies of profiles at the end of a semester or school year.

WRITING REPORTS

A written report that responds to the quality and range of students' work will not come as a surprise to the students concerned. Students who:
• have shared in setting goals;
• are aware of the criteria by which their achievement will be judged;
• have talked with their teacher about their progress;
• know what they have done and how well they have done it; and
• have helped to compile records of their work and development

will know what will be written in their report. They will have been involved from the start in working through whatever is to be reported at the end. The continuous dialogue about development and achievement can be enriched when students are involved in the writing of their own reports. This can be done by asking students to:
• list the activities in which they have participated;
• list the products of these activities;
• summarise the goals that they have achieved during the period of work being reported;
• write statements that they believe are fair judgements of the quality of their work;
• offer these statements as possibilities for reports to be written by the teacher; and
• negotiate with the teacher as to entries and statements to be made on the report format.

It is possible to negotiate the contents of written reports, to a greater or lesser extent, with students of all ages. In itself, matching their perceptions of development and achievement with those of teachers is a valuable experience for students. This is also a valuable language learning activity — listing, summarising, thinking up and writing general statements, interacting with an adult.

To involve students in the keeping of records and the writing of reports is consistent with the active role that they need to play in their language development. Students need to know what is to be said in reports and on what evidence these statements are based. They should also have the opportunity to write statements that they think would be fair summaries of their work and achievement, and ask that these be considered for inclusion in their reports. In this way, written reports, compiled on a negotiated basis, assume the dimensions of a contract: they summarise in an agreed way what has been done and what needs to be done.

To assist these discussions, formats can be designed that invite students to describe the goals that they believe they have achieved and the areas that they think they need to develop. Here are two examples of such formats. The entries students make on these sheets can provide an agenda for consultation with teachers about the contents of reports, and also serve as a database for the teacher at report writing time.

The status of written reports as agreed, fair and accurate summaries stems from the continous conversation about development and achievement built in to the classroom program. The partnership of students and teachers in setting goals, managing activities, keeping records and monitoring achievement can extend, in ways such as these, to the writing of reports.

When addressed to students, for example: 'Leanne, you have been very successful in completing . . .', written reports can reflect the negotiated, contractual characteristics of the continuing conversation between students and their teachers. They become another episode in an authentic conversation rather than a formal message about students from teachers to parents.

Addressing reports to students is also a way of maintaining the confidentiality of this information. While it is customary for teachers to think of reports as the property of students and parents, many reports are written in ways that suggest that they will and therefore ought to be read by others. Reports that summarise students' achievement over a period of time can be considered formative and temporary accounts of what

Your profile

Achievements	Abilities	Interests
Goals		

students have done: they give a picture of students' development to that time. Addressing written reports to students is appropriate to a view of assessment and reporting as a private conversation about development between teachers, students and their parents. A more formal or public report of students' achievement can be prepared for audiences beyond students and their parents.

When addressed to parents, written reports can suggest development in various skills and abilities as observed in a comprehensive range of activities and based upon accumulating evidence. Periodic written reports such as those compiled at the end of the first and second semesters can together provide a clear picture of development over the year. Here is an example of such development:

> C. has completed ten out of the twelve pieces of work required for assessment this semester. The two pieces she missed were whilst she was away, and she has an extension on the autobiography. C. has developed her written skills well. Her writing is fluent and well-structured and her use of vocabulary appropriate. Her strengths are reflected in her literature assignments. She shows a perceptive understanding of the set novels, and a thoughtful response to class discussion.
>
> In her personal and descriptive writing, C. writes in a highly original and sensitive manner. She must endeavour to organise her approach to work and make sure work is submitted on time. A fine effort overall.   (*July*)

> C. has successfully completed the requirements in English for this semester. She has read the prescribed novels for study and has shown a perceptive understanding of the issues which arise from literature. She has submitted all written work for evaluation and has strengthened the structure and fluency of her writing. Included in her writing have been three major literature assignments on both novels and plays; theatre and film reviews; a biography and autobiography; and a folio of writing. She has the ability to write in a variety of modes, and uses language appropriately and with sensitivity. She has been valuable in group work and shared tasks.   (*December*)

By using such phrases as 'must endeavour to' and 'strengthened the structure and fluency', these reports indicate development over time. Each report clearly describes the range of work done and the range of development noted. Details such as 'completed ten out of twelve pieces' and 'submitted all written work' suggest that the reports draw upon extensive accumulating records. Reference to numerous specific tasks and projects suggests the wide range of work completed.

Formats for written reports can be designed to provide a structure for describing the range of work completed and the range of development and achievement recognised. An effective format for reporting development and achievement in English might accommodate descriptions of several related dimensions:
- work completed;
- goals achieved or criteria met in the process of doing that work;

- an overview of students' development and achievement;
- suggestions for further development; and
- comments on attitude.

A combination of these dimensions gives a written report validity and comprehensiveness. By providing space for describing the work required and completed, a report format can allow for statements based on the actual work of individual students. By providing space for writing about a student in different but connected ways, a report format enhances teachers' capacity to respond in reports to the variability of students' development and the range of their work. Statements written in such a format demonstrate that awareness of the individual students' strengths and weaknesses. Overall, such a format can provide a summary of students' development and achievement that has been the focus of much of the talk between teacher and students from the outset.

COMPILING RECORDS OF ACHIEVEMENT

Students can compile records of their achievement that will be valuable for employment and further study. This record might contain:
- copies of school reports
- examples of writing
- tables of contents from writing folios and workbooks
- sample written comments from teachers
- project records
- references from school and work experience
- letters
- certificates and records of participation
- work experience.

The accumulating evidence of classroom work and their own development can provide many records and statements which enable students to illustrate their achievement.

Based on real evidence of development and achievement, a responsive cycle of communication reports, across the Years K–12, a continuing expansion of different aspects of achievement in English, as students learn to use spoken and written language for increasingly complex and sophisticated purposes.

CONCLUSION

Our purpose in this book has been to show how, in a broad range of classroom contexts, students can achieve in English, what it is they can achieve and how that achievement can be assessed. We view the assessment of achievement in English as a responsive process in which students' learning and development are observed and described within the context of classroom action. Assessment that is responsive to the interactive nature of language development will take account of a broad range of evidence, observed in classroom activities and in the work that students complete, and will be based on active collaboration between students and teachers in the setting of goals that provide signposts for learning and for teaching. Assessment of students' achievement responds to the nature of the work done and is based upon a broad range of evidence, including students' self-assessment.

This kind of assessment is valid because it stems from perceptive, continuous observation of students' participation in classroom activities and on the work they have done; and it is fair because it is based on contexts that provide students with opportunities to achieve a broad, varied range of language-learning goals and to feel that they are playing an active role in their learning and in the assessment of their achievement. Responsive assessment values students' learning by describing accurately what they have done, and establishes intimate connections between the goals of classroom work, the nature of classroom contexts and work requirements, the formulation of assessment criteria, feedback to students and their parents, and the planning of opportunities for extending learning. A responsive approach to assessment reflects the richness and variety of students' classroom experience and the continuity and sensitivity of classroom conversations about progress and achievement. In these ways, too, meaningful and accurate information on the strengths and weaknesses of individual students can be continuously provided.

Classrooms where students work on a wide range of connected activities provide the contexts in which teachers can respond to learning, development and achievement. The planning of these classroom contexts promotes the kinds of learning and development on which achievement is based and builds in opportunities to observe and describe what is being or has been achieved, and for teachers to respond to this achievement. Many moments or opportunities for observation of signs of learning and development arise within these contexts: as students work on and complete activities and tasks, their achievements can be described and new contexts can be designed to extend learning.

The contexts we have described represent a range of the kinds of classroom experiences in English that students might meet in their journey through school. These contexts reflect the interactive, social qualities which provide the foundations for language development. They also reflect the wide range of goals and purposes that can help students to become effective, competent makers and users of the English language.

By the nature of their design and operation, these contexts contain features and elements that generate valid and fair assessment: there is a spontaneous, natural dialogue between students and teachers as they work together; there are clear goals, often collaboratively negotiated, and agreed criteria; and there is a very wide range of activities and tasks in which students can demonstrate their abilities across the language modes.

The examples of these contexts described in several chapters in this book take the form of interconnected sets of activities. In this way, they provide activities where students can be talkers, listeners, thinkers, readers and writers to achieve goals important to their development in literacy and language. In these contexts, development in talking, listening, reading and writing can be promoted simultaneously. Development in language is promoted by this interaction between the language modes, between students as they work together, and by the collaboration between students and teacher. These are situations in which oral language is the foundation for growth, and where students work in many different roles, cooperatively at times and independently at others. These contexts generate opportunities for students to achieve significant language learning goals and at the same time to meet a wide range of language learning criteria. These contexts therefore provide an agenda for responsive assessment in that, through activities and tasks, interconnected processes and products, students can show what they can achieve and teachers can describe the achievement they have observed.

As students encounter these experiences, they respond in different ways, and with varying degrees of success in reaching the planned destinations. If they are side-tracked or meet difficult terrain, they can be guided towards new learning and development. In these contexts, the work of students and teachers generates natural, spontaneous feedback appropriate to the nature of language learning and to the variability and complexity of individual development. Observation and description of their progress and development suggests the kinds of guidance they need and the directions that their future work in English should take.

As we have shown, the making of judgements about the performance of individual students can be informed and validated by observation of students' work across many different classroom contexts. An important feature of these contexts is that active participation on the part of students is built into classroom processes. Indeed, learning and development depend largely on the extent to which there is scope in classroom activities for students to play an active role in their learning. This active role naturally extends to the processes of assessment; in these contexts, talk with individual students about their progress is a frequent item on

REFERENCES

Chapter 4, Talking and listening

Education Department of South Australia. *The Connecting Conversation*, Adelaide, 1987, p. 42.

Hogan, Triscia. 'So nervous about noise', in *Australian Journal of Reading*, Vol. 10, No. 2, June 1987, Australian Reading Association, p. 71.

Jagger, Angela & Smith-Burke, Trika. *Observing the Language Learner*. International Reading Association/NCTE, 1985.

Jones, Pat. *Lipservice: the story of talk in schools*. Open University Press, Milton Keynes, 1988, p. 169.

Meiers, Marion. '"It was a really contoured performance, wasn't it?": Oral English in Practice', *Idiom*, Vol. XVIII, No. 1, Summer 1983, Victorian Association for the Teaching of English, p. 5.

Meiers, Marion & McGregor, Robert. *Readings: Experiences and Memories*. McGraw-Hill, Melbourne, 1988, pp. 5–6.

Mowbray, Gwen. *Pro-file: Language Aloud . . . Allowed*, Ontario Ministry of Education, Canada, 1987, p. 12.

Reid, Ian. *Enlarging Literature. An Inclusive Role for Australian Writing*. Bulletin 5, Bicentennial Australian Studies Schools Project, Curriculum Development Centre, Canberra, 1987, p. 4.

Torbe, Mike & Medway, Peter. *The Climate for Learning*. Ward Lock Educational, London, 1981.

Wells, Gordon & Gen Ling Chan. 'From Speech to writing: some evidence on the relationship between oracy and literacy', in *The Writing of Writing*, ed. Andrew Wilkinson. Open University Press, Milton Keynes, 1986, pp. 129–30.

Chapter 5, Reading

Early, Margaret. 'Stages of Growth in Literary Appreciation' in *English Journal* 49, March 1960.

Jagger, Angela & Smith-Burke, Trika. *Observing the Language Learner*. International Reading Association/NCTE, 1985, p. 5.

Harding, D. W. in *Response to Literature* ed. J. Squire, NCTE, Champaign, Illinois, 1968, p.00.

Moffett, James. *Active Voice*. Boynton/Cook Publishers, Upper Montclair, 1981 p. 10.

Morris, A. & Stewart-Dore, N. *Learning to Learn from Text: Effective Reading in the Content Areas*. Addison-Wesley, 1984, pp. 32, 33.

Thomson, Jack. *Understanding Teenagers Reading: Reading Processes and the Teaching of Literature*. Methuen, Sydney, 1987, pp. 360–1.

Watson, Dorothy. 'Watching and Listening to Children Read', in Jagger, Angela & Smith-Burke, Trika, *Observing the Language Learner*, International Reading Association/NCTE, 1985, p. 127.

Chapter 6, Writing

Anson, Chris (ed.) *Writing and response*. National Council of Teachers of English. Urbana, Illinois, 1989.

Christie, Frances (ed.) *Literacy for a Changing World*. Australian Council for Educational Research, Melbourne, 1990.

D'Arcy, Pat. *Making Sense, Shaping Meaning. Writing in the Context of a Capacity-Based Approach to Learning*. Boynton/Cook–Heineman Educational, New Hampshire, 1989, p. 27.

Freedman, Sarah Warshauer. *Response to Student Writing*. NCTE Research Report No. 28, National Council of Teachers of English, Urbana, Illinois, 1987.

Halliday, M. A. K. *An Introduction to Functional Grammar*. Edward Arnold, London, 1985.

Hayes, J. R. & Flower, L. S. 'Identifying the organisation of writing processes' in L. Gregg and E. Steinberg (eds), *Cognitive Processes in Writing: An Interdisciplinary Approach*. Lawrence Erlbaum, Hillsdale, NJ, 1980.

Rodrigues, Dawn & Rodrigues, Raymond J. *Teaching Writing with a Word Processor, Grades 7–13*. ERIC Clearinghouse on Reading and Communication Skills and the National Council of Teachers of English, Urbana, Illinois, 1986.

Snyder, Ilana. 'Writing and Computers', in *English in Australia* 79. The Australian Association for the Teaching of English, March 1987.

Wilkinson, Andrew. *The Quality of Writing*. Open University Press, Milton Keynes, 1986, p. 14.

Chapter 7, Observing students at work

Spear, Karen. *Sharing Writing — Peer Response Groups in English Classes*. Boynton/Cook–Heinemann, Portsmouth, NH, 1988.

Reading List

This reading list identifies many of the books which have influenced our thinking about learning, teaching and assessment. For readers who wish to read more widely, we have also included a range of titles, offering perspectives which match and extend the approaches to English teaching we have described in this book.

1. Books about assessment

Broadfoot, Patricia. *Introducing Profiling. A Practical Manual*. Macmillan Education Ltd, London, 1987.

Cambourne, Brian. *Natural Learning and Literacy Education*. Ashton Scholastic, 1987.

Chater, Pauline. *Marking and Assessment in English*. Methuen, London, 1984.

Daly, Elizabeth (ed.) *Monitoring Children's Language Development*, Australian Reading Association, Melbourne, 1989.

Department of Education and the Arts, Tasmania, Australia. *Pathways of Language Development*, Australian Council for Educational Research, Melbourne, 1987, 1988, 1989, 1990.

Evans, Peter (ed.) *Directions and Misdirections in English Evaluation*. The Canadian Council of Teachers of English, Ottawa, 1985.

Garforth, David & Macintosh, Henry. *Profiling. A User's Manual*. Stanley Thornes (Publishers) Limited, Cheltenham (UK), 1986.

Goodman, Kenneth, Goodman, Yetta & Hood, Wendy J. (eds). *The Whole Language Evaluation Book*. Heinemann, Portsmouth, 1988.

Jagger, Angela & Smith-Burke, Trika. *Observing the Language Learner*. International Reading Association/NCTE, 1985.

Johnston, Brian. *Assessing English*. St Clair Press, Sydney; 2nd edn, Open University Press, Milton Keynes, 1983.

Johnston, Brian & Dowdy, Stephen. *Work Required. Teaching and Assessing in a Negotiated Curriculum*. Martin Educational in association with Robert Andersen and Associates, Melbourne, 1988.

Kemp, Max. *Watching Children Reading and Writing. Observational Records for Children with Special Needs*. Nelson, Melbourne, 1987.

McGaw, B., Eyers, V., Montgomery, J., Nicholls B. & Poole, M. *Assessment in the Victorian Certificate of Education*. Victorian Curriculum and Assessment Board, Melbourne, 1990.

McGregor, Robert & Meiers, Marion. *Evaluating English Curriculum: Some approaches to the evaluation of English programs*. Education Department of Victoria, Melbourne, 1983.

—— *The English Record Book*. Collins Dove, Melbourne, 1989.

—— *Checkpoints. Primary Teacher's Record File*. The English Club, Mt Eliza (Victoria), 1989.

Meiers, Marion & McGregor, Robert. *Assessment in English, Years 7–10*. Education Department of Victoria, Melbourne, 1982.

School Programs Division, Ministry of Education, Victoria. *Literacy Profiles Handbook.* The Education Shop, Ministry of Education, Victoria, 1990.

Stibbs, Andrew. *Assessing Children's Language.* Ward Lock/NATE, London, 1980.

Suggett, Dale. *Guidelines for Descriptive Assessment.* Victorian Institute of Secondary Education, Melbourne, 1985.

Wilkinson, A. M., Barnsley, G., Hanna, P. & Swan, M. *Assessing Language Development.* Oxford University Press, Oxford, 1980.

2. Books about the development of language

Barnes, Douglas, Britton, James & Torbe, Mike. *Language, The Learner and The School.* Penguin Books, Harmondsworth, 1986.

Brown, Hazel & Cambourne, Brian. *Read and Retell.* Methuen, North Ryde (NSW), 1987.

Calkins, Lucy McCormick. *Lessons from a Child: On the Teaching and Learning of Writing.* Heinemann Educational Books, New Hampshire, 1983.

Christie, Frances (ed.) *Writing in School.* Deakin University Press, Geelong, 1989.

D'Arcy, Pat. *Making Sense, Shaping Meaning. Writing in the Context of a Capacity-Based Approach to Learning.* Boynton/Cook–Heinemann Educational, New Hampshire, 1989.

Dixon, John & Stratta, Leslie. *Writing Narrative — and Beyond.* The Canadian Council of Teachers of English, 1986.

Gilbert, Pam, with Kate Rowe. *Gender, Literacy and the Classroom.* Australian Reading Association, Melbourne, 1989.

Graves, Donald. *Writing: Teachers and Children at Work.* Heinemann, Exeter, 1983.

—— *A Researcher Learns to Write.* Heinemann, Exeter, 1984.

Haarste, Jerome C., Burke, Caroline L., & Woodward, Virginia A. *Language Stories and Literacy.* Heinemann, 1984.

Hillocks, George, Jr. *Research on Written Composition, New Directions for Teaching.* ERIC Clearinghouse on Reading and Communication Skills, and the National Conference on Research in English, Illinois, 1986.

Jones, Pat. *Lipservice: the story of talk in schools.* Open University Press, Milton Keynes, 1988.

Kamler, Barbara & Woods, Claire. *Two Pathways to Literacy, AATE Action Research Studies No. 2.* AATE, Adelaide, 1987.

MacLure, Margaret, Phillips, Terry & Wilkinson, Andrew. *Oracy Matters.* Open University Press, Milton Keynes, 1988.

Martin, Nancy *et al. Understanding Children Talking.* Penguin, Harmondsworth, 1976.

Meek, Margaret. *Learning to Read.* The Bodley Head, London, 1982.

—— *Achieving Literacy.* Routledge and Kegan Paul, London, 1983.

—— *How Texts Teach What Readers Learn.* Thimble Press, Bath, 1988.

Morris, A. & Stewart-Dore, N. *Learning to Learn from Text: Effective Reading in the Content Areas.* Addison-Wesley, 1984.

Perera, Katharine. *Children's Writing and Reading*. Blackwell, Oxford, 1984.

Poynton, Cate. *Language and Gender: Making the Difference*. Deakin University, Geelong, 1985.

Reid, Ian. *The Making of Literature*. AATE, Adelaide, 1984.

—— (ed.) *The Place of Genre in Learning: Current Debates*. Typereader Publications no. 1, Centre for Studies in Literary Education, Deakin University, Geelong, 1987.

Scholes, Robert. *Textual Power. Literacy Theory and the Teaching of English*. Yale University Press, New Haven and London, 1985.

Squire, James (ed.) *The Dynamics of Language Learning. Research in Reading and English*. ERIC Clearinghouse on Reading and Communication Skills, and the National Conference on Research in English, Illinois, 1987.

Thomson, Jack. *Understanding Teenagers Reading: Reading Processes and the Teaching of Literature*. Methuen, Sydney, 1987.

Wells, Gordon. *The Meaning Makers. Children Learning Language and Using Language to Learn*. Heinemann Educational Books, Portsmouth, New Hampshire, 1986.

3. Books about activities and strategies for English classrooms

Atwell, Nancie. *In the Middle*. Boynton/Cook, Upper Montclair, New Jersey, 1987.

Brooks, G., Latham, J. & Rex, A. *Developing Oral Skills. A Resource Pack for the Teaching of Oral Communication*. Heinemann Educational Books, London, 1986.

Chandler, Daniel & Marcus, Stephen (eds). *Computers and Literacy*. Open University Press, Milton Keynes, 1985.

Corcoran, Bill & Evans, Emrys (eds). *Readers, Texts, Teachers*. Boynton/Cook–Heinemann Educational, Upper Montclair, New Jersey, 1987.

Dalton, Joan. *Adventures in Thinking. Creative Thinking and Co-operative Talk in Small Groups*. Nelson, Melbourne, 1985.

Education Department of South Australia. *The Connecting Conversation*. Adelaide, 1987.

Flower, Linda. *Problem-Solving Strategies for Writing*. Harcourt Brace Jovanovich, San Diego, 1985.

Fulwiler, Toby (ed.) *The Journal Book*. Boynton/Cook–Heinemann, Portsmouth, NH, 1987.

Hayhoe, Mike & Parker, Stephen. *Words Large as Apples, Teaching Poetry, 11–18*. Cambridge University Press, Cambridge, 1988.

Howe, Alan. *Expanding Horizons. Teaching and Learning Through Whole Class Discussion*. The National Association for the Teaching of English, Sheffield, 1988.

Jackson, David. *Encounters With Books: Teaching Fiction 11–16*. Methuen, London, 1983.

Johnson, Terry D. & Louis, Daphne R. *Literacy Through Literature*. Methuen, Sydney, 1985.

Knapp, Peter & Callaghan, Mike. *Teaching Guide for the Discussion Genre*.

The Disadvantaged School's Program, Metropolitan East Region, NSW, 1989.

McGregor, Robert. *Writing in the Primary School.* Edward Carroll, Melbourne, 1985.

—— *Working Together.* Nelson, Melbourne, 1989.

McGregor, Robert & Meiers, Marion. *English Teaching in Practice.* St Clair Press, Sydney, 1983.

—— *The Newspaper Book.* McGraw-Hill, Melbourne, 1989.

McVitty, Walter (ed.) *Getting it Together. Organising the reading-writing classroom.* Primary English Teaching Association, Sydney, 1986.

Meiers, Marion & McGregor, Robert. *The Writer's File.* Jacaranda Press, Brisbane, 1986.

—— *Writings from the Classroom.* Jacaranda Press, Brisbane, 1986.

—— *Readings: Experiences and Memories.* McGraw-Hill, Melbourne, 1988.

—— *Adventurers, Projects and Workshops in English, Book 1.* Jacaranda Press, Brisbane, 1988.

—— *The Senior Writer's File.* Jacaranda Press, Brisbane, 1989.

—— *Travellers, Projects and Workshops in English, Book 2.* Jacaranda Press, Brisbane, 1989.

—— *Explorers, Projects and Workshops in English, Book 3.* Jacaranda Press, Brisbane, 1990.

—— *English Course Book 1.* Jacaranda Press, Brisbane, 1990.

—— *Texts and Responses.* Longman Cheshire, Melbourne, 1991.

Milner, Joseph O'Beirne & Milner, Lucy Floyd Morcock (eds). *Passages to Literature. Essays on Teaching in Australia, Canada, England, The United States and Wales.* National Council of Teachers of English, Urbana, Illinois, 1989.

Moffett, James. *Active Voice.* Boynton/Cook Publishers, Upper Montclair, 1981.

Moffett, James & Wagner, Betty Jane. *Student-Centered Language Arts and Reading, K–13: A Handbook for Teachers.* Houghton Mifflin, Boston, 1983.

Rainer, Tristine. *The New Diary.* Angus and Robertson, North Ryde, NSW, 1980.

Reid, Jo-Anne, Forrestal, Peter & Cook, Jonathon. *Small Group Learning in the Classroom.* Primary English Teaching Association, Rozelle, NSW/Chalkface Press, Scarborough, WA, 1989.

Scardamalia, Marlene, Bereiter, Carl & Fillion, Bryant. *Writing for Results: A Sourcebook of Consequential Composing Activities.* Ontario Institute for Studies in Education, 1981.

Spear, Karen. *Sharing Writing. Peer Response Groups in English Classes.* Boynton/Cook–Heinemann Educational, Portsmouth, New Hampshire, 1988.

Trelease, Jim. *The Read-Aloud Handbook.* Penguin, Harmondsworth, 1986.

Wilkinson, Andrew. *The Quality of Writing.* Open University Press, Milton Keynes, 1986.

INDEX